15 International One-Act Plays

The foremost one-act plays of the world's leading dramatists—selected for their superb craftsmanship, their dramatic impact, and their lasting contribution to the development of modern dramatic literature.

JOHN GASSNER, Sterling Professor of Playwrighting and Dramatic Literature at the School of Drama of Yale University until his death in 1967, was acclaimed by *Commonweal* as "the greatest authority on the drama living in America" and by *Theatre Arts* as "the American theatre's official anthologist-in-chief." A world-renowned teacher, lecturer, and drama critic, he published more than two dozen books on drama, theatrical art, motion pictures, and comparative literature, including the widely praised three-volume anthology *A Treasury of the Theatre.*

MOLLIE GASSNER, his wife, has continued to further his important contributions to the study and advancement of theatre in America.

MORRIS SWEETKIND, Chairman of the Department of English at The Cheshire Academy, collaborated with Mr. Gassner on two earlier anthologies of drama with critical introductions, *Introducing the Drama* and *Tragedy, History and Romance.*

15 International One-Act Plays

EDITED BY
John and Mollie Gassner

With an Introduction
and Prefaces to the plays by
Morris Sweetkind

PUBLISHED BY POCKET BOOKS NEW YORK

To the memory of John Gassner

POCKET BOOKS, a Simon & Schuster division of GULF & WESTERN CORPORATION
1230 Avenue of the Americas, New York, N.Y. 10020

ISBN: 0-671-49110-5

First Pocket Books printing June, 1969

10   9   8   7   6   5

Trademarks registered in the United States and other countries.

Printed in the U.S.A.

CONTENTS

PREFACE

The idea of getting together a volume of one-act plays arose when, one day, taking our usual walk, my husband told me he'd just given his students an examination to find out what they knew in the fields of drama, art, and music and found that *Don Giovanni, Tristan and Isolde,* and *The Magic Flute* elicited answers which showed him that his reason for giving the test was sound; there was a definite lack of "preparatory" education. When we discussed the matter further, the question arose as to whether it wouldn't be advisable to introduce a volume of broadly representative one-act plays for the upper secondary school level that the undergraduate college student and the general reader would also find helpful.

Over a period of years we'd discuss this, with the feeling that this would be a project to work on after current publishers' obligations had been met. The day finally came when we could turn to this project; contracts were signed, the preliminary work was done, and there was nothing left to do but write the introductions. But Fate had other plans and my husband's life terminated at the height of his career.

The wisdom of my husband's request that the survivor carry on hit me forcefully, but the joy of working on the project was gone. I therefore asked the publishers to release me from the contract, pointing out that the main signee was no longer alive. When I was urged by the editors at Washington Square Press to complete the project, I asked that I be allowed to bring in a collaborator; fortunately I met with no opposition.

I had no difficulty on deciding whom to ask; it seemed only natural that I ask Mr. Morris Sweetkind to write the introductions, as he and my husband had co-edited two other works. Mr. Sweetkind graciously agreed, and after reviewing the list we decided to cut it somewhat but to retain the original idea of giving thumbnail examples of world drama that the reader would find interesting and informative. We also chose plays that could be produced by students—plays that would enhance students' understanding of the medium, since plays should also be seen for maximum gratification. On reexamining the final selection, I find that the representation is precisely what my late husband had in mind.

MOLLIE GASSNER

New Haven, Connecticut
February 15, 1968

INTRODUCTION:
The One-Act Play

In the twenty-five-hundred-year history of drama an interesting phenomenon is the emergence, in recent times, of the one-act play as a separate artistic genre. In the twentieth century we find our leading dramatists, both abroad and in the United States, writing one-act plays that are produced by professionals and amateurs in commercial, community, and experimental theaters as well as in coffeehouses. Modern dramatists, taking advantage of the unity, economy, and swift characterization of the one-act play, are exploring the many facets of this new theatrical art form and are writing short plays that range from the conventional farcical "vaudeville" of Anton Chekhov's *The Proposal* to John Millington Synge's tragedy *Riders to the Sea,* to Samuel Beckett's pantomime *Act without Words I,* to Eugene Ionesco's absurdist *The Bald Soprano*. The present popularity of the one-act play can be explained by its brevity, its shock emotional effect, and its flexibility of treatment by skilled practitioners who are expanding its potentialities.

From a historical viewpoint, although the short play has existed in previous eras, only in this century has it fully matured as a new dramatic genre. The short Noh plays of Japan, highly stylized and appealing to the upper classes, were written in the fourteenth and fifteenth centuries. In Europe and in England cyclical "mystery" plays—really one-acters dealing with religious episodes drawn from the Bible—were performed in the Middle Ages. In the eighteenth century the one-act play was subordinated to the role of a theatrical stopgap and used as a curtain raiser or as an afterpiece. In France and Russia in the nineteenth century it was a "vaudeville," a species of light entertainment, usually farcical or satirical in nature.

An important factor in the development of the one-act play was the establishment in several countries of experimental theaters as a reaction against conventional commercialistic plays. In 1887 André Antoine founded the *Théâtre Libre* in Paris; two years later a group of Germans established the *Freie Bühne* in Berlin with Otto Brahm as the first director; in 1891 Thomas Grein, the English dramatic critic, founded the Independent Theatre; and at the turn of the century the Irish Literary Theatre emerged in Dublin. These "free" theaters produced not only full-length plays but encouraged the performance of naturalistic, symbolic, and unconventional one-act plays in prose and in verse. The Grand Guignol Théâtre, which opened in 1897 in Montmarte, Paris, shocked its audiences for many years by presenting one-act plays of terror and violence. With a more serious intention Max Reinhardt in his *Kleines Theater* (1902) and August Strindberg in his *Intimate Theater* (1907) opened up their stages to the new playwrights experimenting with the freer form of the one-act play.

The success of these European dramatic ventures stimulated the development of the one-act play in America. In the first quarter of the twentieth century the popularity of vaudeville as an entertainment medium offered playwrights the opportunity to write dramatic "sketches," as they were called, which became an obligatory feature of every bill. George Kelly, George S. Kaufman, and even Bernard Shaw wrote such plays for special actors on tour. The growing popularity of the movies and especially the introduction of the "talkies" killed vaudeville.

During this period, another outlet for the one-act play was the rapid spread of "the little theater" movement across the country. Several hundred civic and community theaters established by professionals and amateurs in schools, universities, and churches encouraged the performance of one-acters. Annual tournaments with prizes awarded for the best plays were held in many cities. From 1912 to 1933 Professor George Pierce Baker in his famous "47 Workshop" sharpened the technique of many playwrights, including Eugene O'Neill, in the new medium. The Workshop was first at Harvard and then, after 1925, at Yale.

The profoundest influence, however, came from two theatrical groups, the Washington Square Players and the Provincetown Players. From 1914 to 1918 the Washington Square Players of New York, made up of intellectuals and idealists, presented sixty-one realistic and satiric one-acters and six full-length plays. Although America's involvement in World War I brought a temporary cessation of its activities, it reassembled its forces after the war and evolved into the influential Broadway organization, the Theatre Guild. Some of its members formed the Group Theater, which in the thirties produced many plays of social significance, including Odets' stirring one-acter, *Waiting for Lefty,* as well as Saroyan's touching *The Man with the Heart in the Highlands.* Others joined the Actor's Repertory Company, which performed Irwin Shaw's tragic antiwar fantasy *Bury the Dead.*

Organized informally in 1915, the Provincetown Players was a group of artists and intellectuals whose primary aim was to produce the work of young American playwrights who were experimenting with new dramatic forms, particularly in the one-act medium. In their small wharf theater in Provincetown and later in more ample quarters in New York, they produced such well-known one-act plays as Susan Glaspell's *Trifles* and (with the collaboration of her husband, George Cram Cook) *Suppressed Desires.* Perhaps their greatest contribution to the American theater was their discovery and encouragement of the young Eugene O'Neill. The Provincetown Players first presented his four short plays of the sea— *Ile, The Long Voyage Home, The Moon of the Caribbees,* and *Bound East for Cardiff*—as well as his early longer plays. The economic depression of 1929 caused the dissolution of the company.

After World War II the rising cost of Broadway productions and the conventional dramatic fare of the commercial theater drove the experimenters with new plays to the small makeshift playhouses of cheaper off-Broadway. Here were presented many one-act plays dealing with subjects previously taboo in the conventional theater; homosexuality, drug addiction, and racial violence. Freedom of language and the avant-garde techniques of the Theater of the Absurd offended some theatergoers but stimulated others emotionally and intellectually. The small off-Broadway "playhouses" did, however, give the participating audiences the opportunity to see one-acters by such diverse playwrights as Thornton Wilder, Tennessee Williams, Edward Albee, Eugene Ionesco, and LeRoi Jones. Furthermore, the theatrical ferment of these plays even influenced staid Broadway to put on more experimental plays and even commercial productions of one-act plays. Thus the one-act play became firmly established as an important dramatic genre in the contemporary theater.

What the short story is to prose fiction, the one-acter is to a full-length play, a related but separate genre with its own structure and technique. A good short story is not a condensed novel, nor is a one-act play an abbreviated drama. By developing but one episode, not a series of situations, a one-act play by its brevity creates a singleness of dramatic effect. Because it is performed without a break or read at a single sitting, the one-act play by an economy of means and a unified tone produces a powerful emotional impact. Working on a miniature scale, the playwright must be highly selective in his material and must quickly bring all his dramatic elements—plot, character, setting and dialogue—into sharp focus to express the central meaning of the play, its *theme*.

The opening portion of the one-act play consists of *exposition*, which establishes the tone, gives the setting, and presents the situation in which the main characters are involved. Frequently some *antecedent action* (i.e., an event that occurred before the opening of the play) is also introduced. The situation usually involving conflict is then developed through action and dialogue. The turning point (*climax*) brings a resolution to the conflict and the brief concluding action (*dénouement*) completes the play. Because of its natural limitations of size, the one-act play usually preserves the so-called "classical unities" of time, place, and action.

The nature and intensity of conflict in plays vary considerably, and these variations, in great measure, determine the plot structure. Ferdinand Brunetière's famous "law of the theater" states:

> . . . Drama is the representation of the will of man in conflict with the mysterious powers or natural forces which limit and belittle us; it is one of us thrown living upon the stage, there to struggle against fatality, against social law, against one of his fellow mortals, against himself, if need be, against the ambitions, the interests,

the prejudices, the folly, the malevolence of those who surround him.*

Characters who are motivated by strong desires to attain love, power, popularity, happiness, inner dignity, knowledge, or who are trying to avoid suffering and death inevitably become involved in conflict with others, with the conventions of society, with fate, or with themselves.

The conflict may take the form of a clash of wills and wits, as in Shaw's *The Man of Destiny* (Napoleon versus the Strange Lady). It may be a conflict between two civilizations— pagan and Christian—as in Ibsen's *The Warrior's Barrow,* or it may be man versus the destructiveness of nature, as in Synge's somber *Riders to the Sea.*

Some plays, however, subordinate conflict to emphasize other aspects of drama and thus lay less stress on plot. Maurice Maeterlinck's "static drama" *Interior* creates a mood of humanity's tragic resignation in the acceptance of death. Leonid Andreyev's bitter satire *Love of One's Neighbor* emphasizes theme: society's love of sensation and violence and its commercialization, as W. S. Gilbert's farce *Trial by Jury* attacks the administration of justice. Frank Wedekind's *The Tenor* and Chekhov's *The Proposal* primarily depict character. Giovanni Verga's *Cavalleria Rusticana* and García Lorca's *Love of Don Perlimplín and Belisa in the Garden* present, respectively, Italian and Spanish village folkways.

Despite the limitations of the one-act play in time and scope, competent playwrights have successfully utilized the restricted dramatic medium to produce miniature masterpieces, for example, Chekhov's *Proposal,* Josephina Niggli's folk comedy *Sunday Costs Five Pesos,* Jean Giradoux's philosophical satire *The Apollo of Bellac,* Wilder's modern morality play *The Long Christmas Dinner,* and Synge's *Riders to the Sea.*

MORRIS SWEETKIND

New Haven, Connecticut

---

* Translated by William Archer in his *Playmaking* (New York and Boston: Small, Maynard Company, 1926), p. 23.

The Warrior's Barrow

A Dramatic Poem in One Act

by HENRIK IBSEN

Translated from the Norwegian by ANDERS ORBECK

Henrik Ibsen (1828–1906)

In the half-century from the completion of the drama *Catiline* in 1849 to the publication of *When We Dead Awaken* in 1899, Henrik Ibsen produced a body of work that made him the most influential figure in the modern theater. However, it was only after he had been a playwright for thirty years that the revolutionary impact of his work was felt with a series of social dramas initiated by *A Doll's House* in 1879. His problem plays—*Ghosts, An Enemy of the People, The Wild Duck*—and his psychological character-studies in *Rosmersholm* and in *Hedda Gabler* earned him the title "the father of modern drama." Less popular were the visionary, symbolic plays of his last period: *The Master Builder, Little Eyolf, John Gabriel Borkman,* and *When We Dead Awaken.* Ibsen's biographer Halvdan Koht has stressed the point that Ibsen should be considered primarily as a creative artist, not as a thinker, philosopher, or reformer. For all his life he was a poet who declared, "To be a poet is to *see*." Although his international fame and influence are most dependent on the realistic dramas of social criticism of his middle period, his work as a whole has deep roots in the romantic and nationalistic traditions of Norway. To neglect the first thirty years of Ibsen's dramatic and poetic career is to give us a false perspective of his artistic development.

Ibsen's early life was embittered by poverty and failure. He was born in 1828 in Skien, a provincial seaport in southeastern Norway. When he was eight, his family, because of a financial depression, fell into poverty and suffered social ostracism. The sensitive, introspective youth in the following seven years, after receiving an inadequate education, apprenticed himself as an apothecary's assistant in Grimstad, a small, dull town. Cut off from his family and depressed by the drudgery of his work, he immersed himself in the romantic literature of Germany and Norway and in nationalistic political activities. He wrote impassioned, patriotic poems and begot an illegitimate child, whom he supported for many years. Two years after the failure of the revolutions of 1848, he wrote the first drafts of two verse dramas, *Catiline* and the one-act play *The Warrior's Barrow*. He determined to study medicine at the University of Christiania (Oslo), but failed to pass the entrance examinations. In the fall of 1851 he was appointed theater poet and stage manager at the Bergen theater. Here he proved to be a timid producer directing inexperienced actors. The romantic historical plays that he wrote, with two exceptions—*Lady Inger of Östraat* and *The Feast of Solhaug*—were not successful; and his ambition to become his country's national poet and dramatist was frustrated by the success of his contemporary Björnson. However, the many plays in the classical repertory that he produced in the next six years gave him invaluable experience in the inner workings of the theater.

In 1857 he was appointed the director of the run-down Norwegian Theatre in Christiania and wrote his violent, romantic play *The Vikings of Helgeland*. The following year he married Susannah Thoresen and became the father of a son. But in 1862 disaster again overtook Ibsen in the stormy condemnation and failure of his verse-satire on marriage, *Love's Comedy*, and the bankruptcy of the Norwegian Theatre. For a year he fell into a profound depression and then rallied to write a successful historical drama, *The Pretenders*, which won him a small travel stipend. Saddened by the outcome of the Prussian-Danish war, he left Norway with his family to live in self-exile for the next twenty-seven years. Like James Joyce, another famous expatriate, Ibsen was not simply renouncing his native land but, in his seclusion, evaluating it critically with the perspective of distance. Separated from home and friends, he was free to expose Norway's timidity and provincialism as his creative powers further developed.

Still the poet, Ibsen in Rome wrote two impressive verse plays that established his reputation as an important European dramatist. These were *Brand* (1866), whose tragic hero is an uncompromising idealist, and *Peer Gynt* (1867), whose weak, compromising protagonist in his romantic flight from reality ends his fantastic, reprehensible career as a penitent scapegrace whose only chance of redemption lies in the faithful love of Solveig.

For several years Ibsen worked on a historical epic-drama dealing with the clash of pagan and Christian ideas, *Emperor and Galilean*. In 1873 he completed the ten-act philosophical play which he, but not his critics, considered his masterpiece.

Temporarily abandoning his career as a dramatic poet dealing with historical material, Ibsen wrote two successful prose satires that stirred up considerable controversy. These were *The League of Youth* (1869) and *The Pillars of Society* (1877). That Ibsen's fame was now assured was indicated by the honorary doctor's degree he received from the University of Uppsala.

Two years later with the production of *A Doll's House* the storm broke, and it was intensified in 1881 by its polemical sequel, *Ghosts*. These dramas of the conflict of the individual versus the conventions of society ushered in the new, realistic drama of ideas, which influenced the theater of Bernard Shaw and Arthur Miller.

At the age of sixty-three, ending his long exile, Ibsen returned to his homeland to complete his career as a dramatist. The poet in Ibsen found expression in the symbolic plays of his last period, although these have not been as popular or as influential as his social problem plays.

In 1900 Ibsen suffered a stroke which clouded his mind. And he never completely recovered from this attack.

Although *The Warrior's Barrow*, Ibsen's only one-act play, is the work of his early apprenticeship to the theater, it forecasts his dramatic development in the next thirty years. He had started the play at Grimstad, but completed the first version in May 1850, when it was accepted for production at the Christiania Theatre. It was performed three times during the following autumn.

This crude but effective short play reveals Ibsen's interest in the romantic folklore and history of Norway, which was being rediscovered in his day. The young Ibsen felt it was his mission to interpret Norwegian nationalism in terms of poetic drama. Although the plot is melodramatic, it presents the theme of the conflict of two civilizations—the pagan and Christian—which he was to develop in his more mature play *Emperor and Galilean*.

CHARACTERS

RODERIK,
  an old recluse

BLANKA,
  his foster-daughter

GANDALF,
  a sea-king from Norway

ASGAUT,
  an old Viking

HROLLOUG

JOSTEJN

Several Vikings

HEMMING,
  a young scald in GANDALF's service

*The action takes place on a small island off the coast of
Sicily shortly before the introduction
of Christianity into Norway.*

*An open place surrounded by trees near the shore.
To the left, in the background, the ruins of an old temple.
In the center of the scene, a huge barrow,
upon which is a monument decked with flower wreaths.*

SCENE ONE

At the right of the stage sits RODERIK *writing. To the left* BLANKA *in a half-reclining position.*

BLANKA: Lo! the sky in dying glory
Surges like a sea ablaze,—
It is all so still before me,
Still as in a sylvan maze.
Summer evening's mellow power
Settles around us like a dove,
Hovers like a swan above
Ocean wave and forest flower.
In the orange thicket slumber
Gods and goddesses of yore,
Stone reminders in great number
Of a world that is no more.
Virtue, valor, trust are gone,
Rich in memory alone;
Could there be a more complete
Picture of the South effete?

(Rises)

But my father has related
Stories of a distant land,
Of a life, fresh, unabated,
Neither carved nor wrought by hand!
Here the spirit has forever
Vanished into stone and wave—
There it breathes as free as ever,
Like a warrior strong and brave!
When the evening's crystallizing
Vapors settle on my breast,

7

Lo! I see before me rising
Norway's snow-illumined crest!
Here is life decayed and dying,
Sunk in torpor, still, forlorn—
There go avalanches flying,
Life anew in death is born!
If I had the white swan's coat—

RODERIK (*after a pause writing*): "Then, it is said, will Rag-
    narök have stilled
The wilder powers, brought forth a chastened life;
All-Father, Balder, and the gentle Freya
Will rule again the race of man in peace!"—

(*After having watched her for a moment*)

But, Blanka, now you dream away again;
You stare through space completely lost in thought—
What is it that you seek?
BLANKA (*draws near*): Forgive me, father!
I merely followed for a space the swan,
That sailed on snowy wings across the sea.
RODERIK: And if I had not stopped you in your flight,
My young and pretty little swan! who knows
How far you might have flown away from me,—
Perchance to Thule?
BLANKA: And indeed why not?
To Thule flies the swan in early spring,
If only to return again each fall.

(*Seats herself at his feet*)

Yet I—I am no swan—no, call me rather
A captured falcon, sitting tame and true,
A golden ring about his foot.
RODERIK: Well—and the ring?
BLANKA: The ring? That is my love for you, dear father!
With that you have your youthful falcon bound,
I cannot fly,—not even though I wished to.

(*Rises*)

But when I see the swan sail o'er the wave,
Light as a cloud before the summer wind,
Then I remember all that you have told
Of the heroic life in distant Thule;

Then, as it seems, the bird is like a bark
With dragon head and wings of burnished gold;
I see the youthful hero in the prow,
A copper helmet on his yellow locks,
With eyes of blue, a manly, heaving breast,
His sword held firmly in his mighty hand.
I follow him upon his rapid course,
And all my dreams run riot round his bark,
And frolic sportively like merry dolphins
In fancy's deep and cooling sea!

RODERIK: O you,—
You are an ardent dreamer, my good child—
I almost fear your thoughts too often dwell
Upon the people in the rugged North.

BLANKA: And, father, whose the fault, if it were so?

RODERIK: You mean that I—?

BLANKA: Yes, what else could I mean;
You live yourself but in the memory
Of early days among these mighty Norsemen;
Do not deny that often as you speak
Of warlike forays, combats, fights,
Your cheek begins to flush, your eye to glow;
It seems to me that you grow young again.

RODERIK: Yes, yes, but I have reason so to do;
For I have lived among them in the North,
And every bit that memory calls to mind
Is like a page to me from my own saga.
But you, however, fostered in the South,
Who never saw the silver-tinted mountains,
Who never heard the trumpet's echoing song—
Ah, how could you be moved by what I tell?

BLANKA: Oh, must a human being see and hear
All things but with his outer senses then?
Has not the inner soul, too, eye and ear,
With which it can both see and hearken well?
'Tis true it is with eyes of flesh I see
The richly glowing color of the rose;
But with the spirit's eye I see within
A lovely elf, a fairy butterfly,
Who archly hides behind the crimson leaves,
And singeth of a secret power from heaven
That gave the flower brightness and perfume.

RODERIK: True, true, my child!

BLANKA: I almost do believe
That just because I do not really see,
The whole looms up more beautiful in thought;
That, father, is the way with you at least!
The ancient sagas and heroic lays—
These you remember, speak of with delight,
And scratch in runic script upon your parchment;
But if I ask about your youthful life
In Norway's distant realm, your eyes grow dark,
Your lips are silent, and it seems at times
Your bosom houses gloomy memories.

RODERIK (*rises*): Come, speak no more, good child, about the
          past.
Who is there then whose youthful memories
Are altogether free from self-reproach;
You know, the Norsemen are a savage lot.

BLANKA: But are the warriors of the South less fierce?
Have you forgot that night, now ten years past,
The time the strangers landed on the coast,
And plundered—?

RODERIK (*visibly ill at ease*): Say no more now—let us hence;
The sundown soon will be upon us;—come!

BLANKA (*as they go*): Give me your hand!

     (*Stops*)

                    No, wait!
RODERIK: What is the matter?
BLANKA: I have today for the first time forgot—
RODERIK: And what have you forgot?
BLANKA (*points to the barrow*):   Behold the wreath!
RODERIK: It is—
BLANKA: The withered one of yesterday;
I have forgot today to make the change;
Yet, let me take you to the cabin first,
Then shall I venture out in search of flowers;
The violet never is so sweet and rare
As when the dew has bathed its silver lining;
The budding rose is never quite so fair
As when 'tis plucked in childlike sleep reclining!

     (*They go out at the back to the right.*)

SCENE
TWO

GANDALF *and the Vikings enter from right.*

ASGAUT: Now we shall soon be there.
GANDALF: Point out the place!
ASGAUT: No, wait till we have gone beyond the wood.
There was still standing on the rocky cliff
Against the sea a remnant of the wall—
I daresay it is standing there today.
JOSTEJN: But tell us, king, what can it profit us
To tramp about here on the isle like fools?
HROLLOUG: Yes, tell us what shall—
GANDALF: You shall hold your tongues!
And blindly follow where your king commands!

(To ASGAUT*)*

It seems to me, however, you cleaned house
Too well when you were last here on the isle;
You might have left a little, I should think,
For me and my revenge!
HROLLOUG: You are the king,
And loyalty we pledged you at the thing,
But when we followed you upon the warpath,
It was to win our share of fame and glory.
JOSTEJN: And golden treasures, Hrolloug, golden treasures.
SEVERAL: That, Gandalf, is the law, and heed it well!
GANDALF: I know the law perhaps as well as you;
But is there not since days of old a law
And covenant with us that when a kinsman
Falls slain before the enemy and his corpse
Unburied lies a prey unto the raven,
Blood vengeance must be had?

11

SOME: Yes, so it is!
GANDALF: Then stand you ready with your sword and shield—
You have a king to avenge and I a father!

(Commotion among the Vikings.)

JOSTEJN: A king?
HROLLOUG: A father?
GANDALF: Wait—I shall relate
How all this stands. You know, my father was
A mighty viking. Twelve years gone it is
Since he the last time sallied forth one spring
With Asgaut there and all his old-time warriors.
Two years he roamed about from strand to strand,
Visiting Bratland, Valland, even Blaaland;
At length he went and harried Sicily,
And there heard stories of a wealthy chief,
Who lived upon this island in a castle
With sturdy walls built on a rocky base,
And in it there were costly treasures hid.
At night he took his men and went ashore,
And razed the castle walls with fire and sword.
Himself went foremost like an angry bear,
And in the fury of the fight saw not
How all his warriors fell about him dead;
And when the morning sun rose in the east,
There lay the castle smoldering in ruin.
Asgaut alone survived with one or two—
My father and the hundred others there
Had ridden to Valhalla through the flames.
ASGAUT: I hoisted every sail upon the bark,
And turned the prow straight homeward to the North;
There sought I all in vain for Gandalf king;
The youthful eagle, I was told, had flown
Across the sea to Iceland or the Faroes.
I hastened after him but found no trace—
Yet everywhere I went his name was known;
For though his bark sped cloudlike in the storm,
Yet flew his fame on even swifter wings.
At last this spring I found him, as you know;
It was in Italy; I told him then
What things had happened, how his father died,

And Gandalf swore by all Valhalla's gods
Blood-vengeance he would take with fire and sword.
JOSTEJN: It is an ancient law and should be honored!
But had I been in your place, Gandalf king,
I should have lingered on in Italy—
For there was gold to win.
HROLLOUG: And honor too.
GANDALF: That is your loyalty to your dead king.
JOSTEJN: Come, come now; no offense; I merely meant
The dead could wait perhaps.
ASGAUT (*with suppressed rage*): You paltry race!
JOSTEJN: But now that we are here—
HROLLOUG: Yes, let us raise
Unto the king a worthy monument!
SOME: Yes, yes!
OTHERS: With bloodshed and with fire!
ASGAUT: Now that I like!
GANDALF: And now away to spy around the island;
For even tonight blood-vengeance shall be mine;
If not, I must myself fall.
ASGAUT: So he swore.
GANDALF: I swore it solemnly by all the gods!
And once again I swear it—
HEMMING (*with a harp on his shoulder has during the pre-
          ceding emerged from among the Warriors and cries
          out imploringly*): Swear not, Gandalf!
GANDALF: What troubles you?
HEMMING: Swear not here in this wood!
Here in the South our gods can never hear;
Out on your bark, up North among the hills,
There they still hearken to you, but not here!
ASGAUT: Have you too breathed the poison of the South?
HEMMING: In Italy I heard the pious monks
Tell lovely stories of the holy Christ,
And what they told still lingers in my mind
Through night and day and will no more be gone.
GANDALF: I had you brought with me because in youth
You showed great promise of poetic gifts.
You were to see my bold and warlike deeds,
So that when I, King Gandalf, old and gray,
Sat with my warriors round the oaken table,
The king's young scald might while away

Long winter evenings with heroic lays,
And sing at last a saga of my deeds;
The hero's fame voiced in the poet's song
Outlives the monument upon his grave.
But now, be off, and if you choose go cast
Your harp aside and don the monkish cowl.
Aha! King Gandalf has a mighty scald!

> (*The Vikings go into the forest to the left;* HEMMING
> *follows them.*)

ASGAUT: It is a mouldy time we live in now;
Our faith and customs from the olden days
Are everywhere upon the downward path.
Lucky it is that I am growing old;
My eyes shall never see the North decay.
But you, King Gandalf, you are young and strong;
And wheresoe'er you roam in distant lands,
Remember that it is a royal task
To guard the people and defend the gods!

> (*He follows the rest.*)

GANDALF (*after a pause*): Hm, he has no great confidence in
　　me.
'Tis well he went! Whenever he is near,
It is as if a burden weighed me down.
The grim old viking with his rugged face—
He looks like Asathor, who with his belt
Of strength and Mjölnir stood within the grove,
Carved out in marble, near my father's home.
My father's home! Who knows, alas! how things
Around the ancient landmarks now may look!—
Mountains and fields are doubtless still the same;
The people?—Have they still the same old heart?
No, there is fallen mildew o'er the age,
And it is that which saps the Northern life
And eats away like poison what is best.
Well, I will homeward—save what still is left
To save before it falls to utter ruin.

> (*After a pause during which he looks around*)

How lovely in these Southern groves it is;
My pine groves can not boast such sweet perfume.

(He perceives the mound)

What now? A warrior's grave? No doubt it hides
A countryman from those more stirring days.
A warrior's barrow in the South!—'Tis only just;
It was the South gave us our mortal wound.
How lovely it is here! It brings to mind
One winter night when as a lad I sat
Upon my father's knee before the hearth,
The while he told me stories of the gods,
Of Odin, Balder, and the mighty Thor;
And when I mentioned Freya's grove to him,
He pictured it exactly like this grove—
But when I asked him something more of Freya,
What she herself was like, the old man laughed
And answered as he placed me on my feet,
"A woman will in due time tell you that!"

(Listening)

Hush! Footsteps in the forest! Quiet, Gandalf—
They bring the first fruits of your blood-revenge!

*(He steps aside so that he is half-concealed among the
bushes to the right.)*

SCENE THREE

GANDALF. BLANKA *with oak leaves in her hair and a basket of flowers enters from the left.*

BLANKA *(seated at the left busily weaving a flower wreath):*
    Fountains may murmur in the sunny vales,
Resplendent billows roll beneath the shore;
Nor fountain's murmur, nor the billow's song
Has half the magic of those flowers there,
That stand in clusters round the barrow's edge
And nod at one another lovingly;
They draw me hither during night and day—
And it is here I long to come and dream.
The wreath is done. The hero's monument,
So hard and cold, shall under it be hid.
Yes, it is beautiful!

(Pointing to the mound)

                A vanished life,
Of giant strength, lies moldering in the ground—
And the memorial which should speak to men—
A cold unyielding stone like yonder one!
But then comes art, and with a friendly hand
She gathers flowers from the breast of nature
And hides the ugly, unresponsive stone
With snow-white lilies, sweet forget-me-nots.

(She ascends the barrow, hangs the wreath over the monument, and speaks after a pause.)

Again my dreams go sailing to the North
Like birds of passage o'er the ocean waves;
I feel an urging where I long to go,

And willingly I heed the secret power,
Which has its royal seat within the soul.
I stand in Norway, am a hero's bride,
And from the mountain peak watch eaglelike.
O'er shining waves the vessel heaves in sight.—
Oh, like the gull fly to your fatherland!
I am a Southern child, I cannot wait;
I tear the oaken wreath out of my hair—
Take this, my hero! 'Tis the second message
I greet you with—my yearning was the first.

> (*She throws the wreath.* GANDALF *steps forth and seizes it.*)

What's this? There stands a——

> (*She rubs her eyes and stares amazed at him.*)

                              No, it is no dream.
Who are you, stranger? What is it you see,
Here on the shore?
GANDALF: Step first from off the mound—
Then we can talk at ease.
BLANKA (*comes down*): Well, here I am!

> (*Aside as she looks him over.*)

The chain mail o'er his breast, the copper helmet—
Exactly as my father has related.

> (*Aloud*)

Take off your helmet!
GANDALF: Why?
BLANKA: Well, take it off!

> (*Aside*)

Two sparkling eyes, locks like a field of grain—
Exactly as I saw him in my dream.
GANDALF: Who are you, woman?
BLANKA: I? A poor, poor child!
GANDALF: Yet certainly the fairest on the isle.
BLANKA: The fairest? That indeed is possible.
For here there's no one else.
GANDALF: What—no one else?
BLANKA: Unless my father be—but he is old

And has a silver beard, as long as this;
No, after all I think I win the prize.
GANDALF: You have a merry spirit.
BLANKA: Not always now!
GANDALF: But tell me, pray, how this is possible;
You say you live alone here with your father,
Yet I have heard men say most certainly
The island here is thickly populated?
BLANKA: It was so once, three years ago or more;
But—well, it is a sad and mournful tale—
Yet you shall hear it if you wish.
GANDALF: Yes, certainly!
BLANKA: You see, three years ago——

    (Seats herself)

Come, seat yourself!
GANDALF *(steps back a pace)*: No, sit you down, I'll stand.
BLANKA: Three years ago there came, God knows from
    whence,
A warlike band of robbers to the isle;
They plundered madly as they went about,
And murdered everything they found alive.
A few escaped as best they could by flight
And sought protection in my father's castle,
Which stood upon the cliff right near the sea.
GANDALF: Your father's, did you say?
BLANKA: My father's, yes.
It was a cloudy evening when they burst
Upon the castle gate, tore through the wall,
Rushed in the court, and murdered right and left.
I fled into the darkness terrified,
And sought a place of refuge in the forest.
I saw our home go whirling up in flames,
I heard the clang of shields, the cries of death.
Then everything grew still; for all were dead.
The savage band proceeded to the shore
And sailed away. I sat upon the cliff
The morning after, near the smoldering ruins.
I was the only one whom they had spared.
GANDALF: But you just told me that your father lives.
BLANKA: My foster-father; wait, and you shall hear!
I sat upon the cliff oppressed and sad,

And listened to the awful stillness round;
There issued forth a faint and feeble cry,
As from beneath the rocky cleft beneath my feet;
I listened full of fear, then went below
And found a stranger, pale with loss of blood.
I ventured nearer, frightened as I was,
Bound up his wounds and tended him—
GANDALF: And he?
BLANKA: Told me as he recovered from his wounds,
That he had come aboard a merchantman,
Had reached the island on the very day
The castle was destroyed—took refuge there
And fought the robber band with all his might
Until he fell, faint with the loss of blood,
Into the rocky cleft wherein I found him.
And ever since we two have lived together;
He built for us a cabin in the wood,
I grew to love him more than anyone.
But you must see him—come!
GANDALF: No, wait—not now!
We meet in ample time, I have no doubt.
BLANKA: Well, all right, as you please, but rest assured
He would be glad to greet you 'neath his roof;
For you must know that hospitality
Is found not only in the North.
GANDALF: The North?
You know then——
BLANKA: Whence you come, you mean? O, yes!
My father has so often told of you
That I the moment that I saw you——
GANDALF: Yet you
Were not afraid!
BLANKA: Afraid? And why afraid?
GANDALF: Has he not told you then—of course if not—
BLANKA: Told me that you were fearless heroes? Yes!
But pray, why should that frighten me?
I know you seek your fame on distant shores,
In manly combat with all doughty warriors;
But I have neither sword nor coat of mail,
Then why should I fear—
GANDALF: No, of course, of course!
But still, those strangers who destroyed the castle?

BLANKA: And what of them?
GANDALF: Only—has not your father
Told you from whence they came?
BLANKA: Never! How could he!
Strangers they were alike to him and us.
But if you wish I'll ask him right away.
GANDALF (*quickly*): No, let it be.
BLANKA: Ah, now I understand!
You wish to know where you can seek them now,
And take blood-vengeance, as you call it.
GANDALF: Ah,
Blood-vengeance! Thanks! The word I had forgot;
You bring me back—
BLANKA: But do you know, it is
An ugly practice.
GANDALF (*going toward the background*): Farewell!
BLANKA: O, you are going?
GANDALF: We meet in time.

   (*Stops*)

                    Tell me this one thing more:
What warrior is it rests beneath the mound?
BLANKA: I do not know.
GANDALF: You do not know, and still
You scatter flowers on the hero's grave.
BLANKA: My father led me here one morning early
And pointed out to me the fresh-made mound,
Which I had never seen upon the strand.
He bade me say my morning prayers out here,
And in my supplications to remember
Those who had harried us with sword and fire.
GANDALF: And you?
BLANKA: Each morning from that day to this
I sent a prayer to heaven for their salvation;
And every evening flowers afresh I wove
Into a garland for the grave.
GANDALF: Yes, strange!
How can you pray thus for your enemy?
BLANKA: My faith commands me.
GANDALF (*vehemently*):   Such a faith is craven;
It is the faith which saps the hero's strength;

'Twas therefore that the great, heroic life
Died feebly in the South!

BLANKA: But now suppose
My craven faith, as you see fit to call it,
Could be transplanted to your virgin soil—
I know full well, there would spring forth a mass
Of flowers so luxuriant as to hide
The naked mountain.

GANDALF: Let the mountain stand
In nakedness until the end of time!

BLANKA: O! Take me with you!

GANDALF: What do you mean?
I sail for home—

BLANKA: Well, I shall sail with you;
For I have often traveled in my dreams
To far-off Norway, where you live mid snow
And ice and somber woods of towering pines.
There should come mirth and laughter in the hall,
If I could have my say, I promise you;
For I am merry; have you any scald?

GANDALF: I had one, but the sultry Southern air
Has loosened all the strings upon his harp—
They sing no longer—

BLANKA: Good! Then shall I be
Your scald.

GANDALF: And you?—You could go with us there,
And leave your father and your home?

BLANKA (*laughing*):   Aha!
You think I meant it seriously?

GANDALF: Was it
Only a jest?

BLANKA: Alas! a foolish dream
I often used to dream before we met—
Which often I no doubt shall dream again,
When you——

  (*Suddenly breaking off*)

    You stare so fixedly.

GANDALF: Do I?

BLANKA: Why, yes! What are you thinking of?

GANDALF: I? Nothing!

BLANKA: Nothing?

GANDALF: That is, I scarcely know myself;
And yet I do—and you shall hear it now:
I thought of you and how you would transplant
Your flowers in the North, when suddenly
My own faith came as if by chance to mind.
One word therein I never understood
Before; now have you taught me what it means.
BLANKA: And what is what?
GANDALF: Valfader, it is said,
Receives but half the warriors slain in battle;
The other half to Freya goes by right.
That I could never fully comprehend;
But—now I understand—I am myself
A fallen warrior, and to Freya goes
The better part of me.
BLANKA (*amazed*):   What does this mean?
GANDALF: Well, in a word, then know—
BLANKA (*quickly*):   No, say it not!
I dare not tarry longer here tonight—
My father waits, and I must go; farewell!
GANDALF: O, you are going?
BLANKA (*takes the wreath of oak leaves which he has let fall
           and throws it around his helmet*): You can keep it
           now.
Lo, what I hitherto bestowed on you
In dreams, I grant you now awake.
GANDALF: Farewell!

   (*He goes quickly out to the right.*)

SCENE
FOUR

BLANKA (*alone*): He is gone! Ah, perfect stillness
      Rules upon the barren strand.
      Perfect stillness, gravelike stillness
      Rules my heart with heavy hand.

      Came he then to vanish only
      Through the mist, a ray of light?
      Soon he flies, a seagull lonely,
      Far away into the night!
      What is left me of this lover?
      But a flower in the dark:
      In my loneliness to hover
      Like a petrel round his bark!

(The war trumpet of the Vikings is heard from the left.)

Ah! What was that? A trumpet from the wood!

SCENE FIVE

BLANKA. GANDALF *from the right.*

GANDALF (*aside*): It is too late!
BLANKA: O, there he is again!
What do you want?
GANDALF: Quick—quick, away from here!
BLANKA: What do you mean?
GANDALF: Away! There's danger here!
BLANKA: What danger?
GANDALF: Death!
BLANKA: I do not understand you.
GANDALF: I thought to hide it from you—hence I went
To call my people to the ship again
And sail away; you never should have known—
The trumpet warns me that it is too late—
That they are coming.
BLANKA: Who are coming?
GANDALF: Then know—
The strangers who once harried on the isle
Were Vikings like myself.
BLANKA: From Norway?
GANDALF: Yes.
My father, who was chief among them, fell—
Hence must he be avenged.
BLANKA: Avenged?
GANDALF: Such is
The custom.
BLANKA: Ah, I see now!
GANDALF: Here they come!
Stand close behind me!
BLANKA: Man of blood—away!

SCENE SIX

The Preceding, ASGAUT, HEMMING *and the Vikings, who lead* RODERIK *between them.*

ASGAUT *(to* GANDALF*)*: A meager find, yet something, to be sure.

BLANKA: My father!

(She throws herself in his arms.)

RODERIK: Blanka! O, my child!

JOSTEJN: A woman!

He will have company.

ASGAUT: Yes, straight to Hell!

BLANKA: O father, wherefore have you never told me—

RODERIK: Hush! Hush! my child!

(Points to GANDALF*)*

Is this your chieftain?

ASGAUT: Yes.

(To GANDALF*)*

This man can tell you how your father died;
For he was in the thick of it, he says,
The only one to get away alive.

GANDALF: Hush! I will nothing hear.

ASGAUT: Good; let us then

Begin the task.

BLANKA: O God! what will they do?

GANDALF *(in an undertone)*: I cannot, Asgaut!

ASGAUT *(likewise)*: Is our king afraid?

Has woman's flattering tongue beguiled his mind?

GANDALF: No matter—I have said——

25

ASGAUT: Bethink yourself—
Your standing with your warriors is at stake.
Your word you pledged Valhalla's mighty gods,
And if you fail a dastard you'll be judged.
Do not forget our faith is insecure—
And wavering; one blow can strike its root,
And if the blow comes from the king above,
It will have had a mortal wound.

GANDALF: Ah me!
That was a most unhappy oath I swore.

ASGAUT *(to the Vikings)*: Now ready, warriors!

GANDALF: Will you murder him,
An old, defenseless man?

ASGAUT: Down with them both!

BLANKA: O God!

HROLLOUG: The woman is too fair! Let her
Return with us.

JOSTEJN *(laughing)*: Yes, as a warrior maid.

GANDALF: Stand back!

RODERIK: O spare—O spare at least my child!
The slayer of your chieftain I will bring you,
If you will only spare her.

GANDALF *(quickly)*:   Bring him here,
And she is free. What say you?

THE VIKINGS: She is free!

BLANKA *(to RODERIK)*: You promise that?

ASGAUT: Then fetch him!

RODERIK: Here he stands!

SOME: Ha, that old man!

GANDALF: O woe!

BLANKA: No, no, you shall not—

RODERIK: Struck by this hand the viking found his death,
Now rests he peacefully in yonder mound!

GANDALF: My father's barrow!

RODERIK: He was strong and brave;
Wherefore I laid him here in viking style.

GANDALF: Since he is buried, then——

ASGAUT: Though he be buried,
The fallen king cries for revenge—strike, strike!

BLANKA: He is deceiving you!

    (To GANDALF*)*

Do you not see
It is alone his daughter he would save?
Yet, how should your kind understand a soul
That sacrifices all—
GANDALF: I do not understand?
You do not think I can?

(To the Vikings)

He shall not die!

ASGAUT: How so?
BLANKA: O father! he is good like you.
ASGAUT: You mean to break your oath?
GANDALF: No, I shall keep it!
JOSTEJN: Then what have you in mind?
HROLLOUG: Explain!
GANDALF: I swore
To take revenge or else to die myself.
Well, he is free—I to Valhalla go.
BLANKA *(to* RODERIK*)*: What does he mean?
ASGAUT: Your honor you would save?
GANDALF: Go—hold a ship in readiness for me,
With hoisted sail, the pyre light in the prow;
In ancient fashion I shall go aboard!
Behold, the evening breeze blows from the strand—
On crimson wings I sail into Valhalla!

*(*JOSTEJN *goes out to the right.)*

ASGAUT: Ah, 'tis the woman who has cast her spell on you!
BLANKA: No, you must live!
GANDALF: I live? No, to the gods
I must be true, I cannot break with them.
BLANKA: Your oath is bloody, Balder hates it.
GANDALF: Yes,
But Balder lives no longer with us now!
BLANKA: For you he lives; your soul is gentleness.
GANDALF: Yes, to my ruin! It became my task
As king to keep intact our great ideal—
But I lack strength enough! Come, Asgaut, you
Shall take the kingly scepter from my hand;
You are a warrior of the truest steel;
On me the Southern plague has been at work.

But if I cannot for my people live,
I now can die for them.
ASGAUT: Well said, King Gandalf!
BLANKA: Then need no more be said! Die like a hero,
Faithful and true unto the very end!
But now that we must part forever—know
That when you die yourself to keep your oath
You are then likewise marking me for death!
GANDALF: What! You for death?
BLANKA: My life was like a flower,
Transplanted in an unfamiliar soil,
Which therefore slumbered in its prison folds:
Then came a sunbeam from the distant home—
Oh, that was you, my Gandalf! Opened then
The flower its calyx. In another hour,
Alas! the sunbeam paled—the flower died!
GANDALF: Oh, have I understood you right? You could?
Then is my promise thrice unfortunate!
BLANKA: But we shall meet again!
GANDALF: Oh, nevermore!
You go to heaven and the holy Christ,
I to Valhalla; silent I shall take
My place among the rest—but near the door;
Valhalla's merriment is not for me.
JOSTEJN (*returns with a banner in his hand*): See, now the
          bark is ready, as you bade.
ASGAUT: Oh, what a glorious end! Many a man
Will envy you, indeed.
GANDALF (*to* BLANKA): Farewell!
BLANKA: Farewell!
Farewell for life and for eternity!
RODERIK (*struggling with himself*): Wait! Wait!

          (*Prostrates himself before* BLANKA.)

                    Mercy, I cry! Forgive, forgive me!
BLANKA: O God!
GANDALF: What means he?
RODERIK: All will I confess:
My whole life here with you has been deceit!
BLANKA: Ah, terror has unhinged his mind!
RODERIK: No, no!

(To GANDALF *after he has risen)*

You are released forever from your vow;
Your father's shadow needs no blood revenge!
GANDALF: Ah, then explain!
BLANKA: Oh, speak!
RODERIK: Here stands King Rörek!
SOME: The fallen king?
BLANKA: O heavens!
GANDALF *(in doubt)*:   You—my father?
RODERIK: See, Asgaut! Do you still recall the scratch
You gave me on our earliest viking trip,
The time we fought about the booty?

(He uncovers his arm and shows it to ASGAUT.*)*

ASGAUT: Yes,
By Thor, it is King Rörek!
GANDALF *(throws himself in his arms)*: Father! Father!
A second time now have you given me life.
My humble thanks!
RODERIK *(downcast; to* BLANKA*)*: And you now—what will
      you
Grant the old robber?
BLANKA: Love as hitherto!
I am your daughter! Has not three years' care
Wiped off each spot of blood upon your shield?
ASGAUT: Yet now explain—how comes it that you live!
GANDALF: She saved his life.
RODERIK: Yes, like a friendly elf
She healed my wounds and cared for me,
And all the while she told me of the faith
These quiet people in the South believe,
Until my rugged heart itself was moved.
And day by day I kept the truth from her;
I did not dare to tell her—
GANDALF: But the mound there?
RODERIK: I laid therein my armor and my sword,
It seemed to me the grim old savage viking
Was buried then and there. Each day my child
Sent up a prayer for him beside the mound.
ASGAUT: Farewell!
GANDALF: Where do you go?

ASGAUT:　　　　　　　　　　　　Northward again!
I now see clearly that my time is past—
So likewise is the viking life. I go
To Iceland; there the plague has not yet come.

　(To BLANKA*)*

You, woman, take my place beside the king!
For Thor is gone—and Mjölnir out of gear;
Through you now Balder rules—Farewell!

　(He goes.)

GANDALF: Yes, Balder ruleth now, through you, my Blanka!
I see the meaning of my viking life!
'Twas not alone desire for fame and wealth
That drove me hence from my forefathers' home;
No, that which called me was a secret longing,
A quiet yearning after Balder. See,
Now is the longing stilled, now go we home;
There will I live in peace among my people.

　(To the Vikings)

And will you follow?
ALL:　　　　　　　We will follow you!
GANDALF: And you, my Blanka?
BLANKA:　　　　　　　　　I? I too am born
A Northern child; for on your mountain sides
The choicest flowers of my heart took root.
To you it was I journeyed in my dreams,
From you it was that I received my love.
RODERIK: And now away!
GANDALF:　　　　　　But you?
BLANKA:　　　　　　　　　　He comes with us!
RODERIK: I shall remain.

　(He points to the mound.)

　　　　　　　　　My barrow waits for me.
BLANKA: And should I leave you here alone?
HEMMING:　　　　　　　　　No, no!
Be not afraid! For I shall close his eyes
And sing to him a saga from the mound;
My last song it will be.

(Moved as he seizes GANDALF'S *hand)*

Farewell, my king!
Now have you found a better scald than I.

RODERIK *(with firmness)*: It must be so, my Gandalf; you are
     king,
And you have sacred duties to discharge.

(He puts their hands together.)

You are the children of the coming dawn—
Go yonder where the royal throne awaits you;
I am the last one of the by-gone age.
My throne—it is the barrow—grant me that!

*(*GANDALF *and* BLANKA *throw themselves silently into his
    arms.* RODERIK *ascends the burial mound.* HEMMING
    with his harp seats himself at his feet.)*

GANDALF *(with resolution)*: And now to Norway!
HROLLOUG: Home!
ALL: To Norway! Home!
BLANKA *(fired as she seizes the banner from* JOSTEJN'S *hand)*:
     Yes, now away! Our course shall northward run
O'er ocean billow on through storm and sun.
Soon fades the daylight o'er the glacier's peak,
   Soon is the Viking life a memory bleak!
Already sits the hero on his mound;
The time is past when he could sail around
With sword and battlecry from strand to strand.
Thor's hammer will no longer rule the land,
The North will be itself a giant grave.
But bear in mind the pledge All-Father gave:
When moss and flowers shall the barrow hide,
To Idavold the hero's ghost shall ride—
Then Norway, too, shall from the grave be brought
To chastened deeds within the realm of thought!

CURTAIN

Trial by Jury

A Dramatic Cantata in One Act

by WILLIAM SCHWENCK GILBERT

William Schwenck Gilbert (1836–1911)

In 1875 when Richard D'Oyly Carte, the English theatrical manager, produced the one-act "dramatic cantata" *Trial by Jury* as an afterpiece to Offenbach's *La Périchole,* the unforgettable collaboration of Gilbert and Sullivan won its first popular success. For twenty years the satirical lyrics of the librettist combined with the charming music of the composer dominated the comic-opera stage in England and America. The resounding success of *H.M.S. Pinafore* (1878), *The Pirates of Penzance* (1880), and *Patience* (1881) encouraged their manager to build the Savoy Theatre for the special production of the operas. This theater, the first public building in England to be lighted entirely by electricity, saw the premiere of *Iolanthe* on November 25, 1882, followed by *Princess Ida* (1885), *The Mikado* (1887), *Ruddigore* (1888), and several other successes. Down to our own day, continual revivals of these urbane and witty masterpieces attest to their popularity as dramatic and musical entertainment.

Despite the great financial success and fame that these comic operas brought to Gilbert, his lifelong ambition was to be a dramatist, not a librettist. During his long theatrical career of more than forty years, he wrote blank-verse plays dealing with fantasy and magical transformations, sentimental melodramas in prose, and serious problem plays. Bernard Shaw, after doggedly writing five unsuccessful novels, was finally convinced that he was not a novelist. In the same manner, after the failure of *Bramtinghame Hall* (1888) as a serious melodrama, Gilbert declared, "This is my sixth consecutive failure in that class of work, and I simply bow to what I take to be the verdict of the press and the public."

William Schwenck Gilbert was born in London, November 18, 1836. When only two years old, he was kidnapped by brigands in Naples, where his parents were vacationing.

In his youth he revealed a considerable talent for both drawing and writing. In 1857 he was graduated from London
University and later, while a clerk in the Education Department of the Civil Service, studied law. After being admitted
to the bar in 1863 and practicing law listlessly for several
years, he became a journalist and contributed stories and
verse to various periodicals. In 1869 he established his fame
as a humorous versifier by publishing *Bab Ballads, Much
Sound and Little Sense* with his own illustrations. He then
turned his hand to writing theatrical burlesques, operettas,
and blank-verse fairy plays.

His collaboration with Arthur Sullivan began with the unsuccessful production of *Thespis, or the Gods Grown Old*, a
"grotesque opera in two acts," at the Gaiety Theatre, De-
cember 23, 1871. Four years later the renewed partnership
resulted in the successful *Trial by Jury*. During the next
twenty-four years—until a disagreement broke up the famous
partnership—Gilbert and Sullivan produced in rapid succession their delightful operettas.

Gilbert met a tragic death on May 29, 1911. He was
drowned in a lake on his estate while trying to save the life
of a guest.

The plot of *Trial by Jury*, a breach-of-promise suit, is
based on a humorous sketch he had written for *Fun*, a comic
periodical, in the issue of April 11, 1868. His four years as
an unsuccessful barrister stood him in good stead in his
satire on courts and lawyers, a theme which he used in
several of his operettas. Unlike his later operas, *Trial by Jury*
has no spoken dialogue. The cantata reveals his amazing skill
in comic versification. He takes full advantage of the absurd
conflict between the fickle, cynical defendant and the sentimental plaintiff by having the sly judge marry the coy
Angelina.

CHARACTERS

The Learned Judge

Counsel for the Plaintiff

The Defendant

Foreman of the Jury

Usher

The Plaintiff

Bridesmaids, Gentlemen of the Jury, etc.

Scene—A Court of Justice. BARRISTERS,
ATTORNEYS, and JURYMEN *discovered*
with USHER.

Chorus

Hark, the hour of ten is sounding!
Hearts with anxious fears are bounding;
Hall of Justice crowds surrounding,
     Breathing hope and fear—
For to-day in this arena,
Summoned by a stern subpoena,
Edwin, sued by Angelina,
     Shortly will appear.

(The USHER *marshals the* JURY *into Jury-box.)*

Solo, USHER:

Now, Jurymen, hear my advice—
All kinds of vulgar prejudice
     I pray you set aside:
With stern judicial frame of mind,
From bias free of every kind,
     This trial must be tried.

Chorus

From bias free of every kind
This trial must be tried.

(During Choruses, USHER *says, fortissimo, "Silence in*
Court!")

USHER:
Oh, listen to the plaintiff's case:
Observe the features of her face—
    The broken-hearted bride.
Condole with her distress of mind—
From bias free of every kind
    This trial must be tried!

Chorus
From bias free, etc.

USHER:
And when amid the plaintiff's shrieks,
The ruffianly defendant speaks,
    Upon the other side;
What *he* may say you needn't mind—
From bias free of every kind
    This trial must be tried.

Chorus
From bias free, etc.

(Enter DEFENDANT.*)*

Recit., DEFENDANT:
Is this the Court of the Exchequer?

ALL:
It is!

DEFENDANT *(aside)*:
Be firm, my moral pecker,
Your evil star's in the ascendant!

ALL:
Who are you?

DEFENDANT:
I'm the Defendant!

Chorus of JURYMEN *(shaking their fists)*
Monster, dread our damages!

We're the jury,
Dread our fury!

DEFENDANT:

Hear me, hear me, if you please,
 These are very strange proceedings
For, permit me to remark,
 On the merits of my pleadings,
You're at present in the dark.

(DEFENDANT *beckons to* JURYMEN—*they leave the box,
and gather round him as they sing the following.*)

Ha! ha! ha!
That's a very true remark—
On the merits of your pleadings,
We're entirely in the dark!
Ha! ha!—ha! ha!

Song, DEFENDANT:

When first my old, old love I knew,
 My bosom swelled with joy;
My riches at her feet I threw—
 I was a love-sick boy!
No terms seemed extravagant
 Upon her to employ—
I used to mope, and sigh, and pant,
 Just like a love-sick boy!

But joy incessant palls the sense;
 And love, unchanged, will cloy,
And she became a bore intense
 Unto her love-sick boy!
With fitful glimmer burnt my flame
 And I grew cold and coy,
At last, one morning, I became
 Another's love-sick boy!

Chorus of JURYMEN (*advancing stealthily*)

Oh, I was like that when a lad;
A shocking young scamp of a rover!

I behaved like a regular cad;
But that sort of thing is all over.
I'm now a respectable chap
And shine with a virtue resplendent,
And therefore I haven't a scrap
Of sympathy with the defendant!
   He shall treat us with awe,
    If there isn't a flaw,
Singing so merrily—Trial-la-law!
Trial-la-law—Trial-la-law!
Singing so merrily—Trial-la-law!

Recit., USHER:
Silence in Court, and all attention lend.
Behold your Judge! In due submission bend!

(Enter JUDGE *on Bench.)*

   Chorus
  All hail, great Judge!
   To your bright rays
  We never grudge
   Ecstatic praise.
    All hail!
  May each decree
   As statute rank,
  And never be
   Reversed in banc.
    All hail!

Recit., JUDGE:
For these kind words accept my thanks, I pray!
A Breach of Promise we've to try to-day:
But firstly, if the time you'll not begrudge,
I'll tell you how I came to be a judge.

ALL:
He'll tell us how he came to be a judge!

JUDGE:
Let me speak.

ALL:
Let him speak.

JUDGE:
Let me speak.

ALL:
Let him speak. Hush! hush!! hush!!!
(*fortissimo*) He'll tell us how he came to be a judge!

Song, JUDGE:
When I, good friends, was called to the bar,
   I'd an appetite fresh and hearty,
But I was, as many young barristers are,
   An impecunious party:
I'd a swallow-tail coat of a beautiful blue—
   A brief which I bought of a booby—
A couple of shirts and a collar or two,
   And a ring that looked like a ruby!

Chorus
A couple of shirts, etc.

JUDGE:
In Westminster Hall I danced a dance,
   Like a semi-despondent fury;
For I thought I should never hit on a chance
   Of addressing a British jury—
But I soon got tired of third-class journeys,
   And dinners of bread and water;
So I fell in love with a rich attorney's
   Elderly, ugly daughter.

Chorus
So he fell in love, etc.

JUDGE:
The rich attorney he jumped with joy,
   And replied to my fond professions:
"You shall reap the reward of your pluck, my boy,
   At the Bailey and Middlesex Sessions.

You'll soon get used to her looks," said he,
    "And a very nice girl you'll find her!
She may very well pass for forty-three
    In the dusk, with a light behind her!"

Chorus
"She may very well," etc.

JUDGE:

The rich attorney was good as his word:
    The briefs came trooping gaily,
And every day my voice was heard
    At the Sessions or Ancient Bailey.
All thieves who could my fees afford
    Relied on my orations,
And many a burglar I've restored
    To his friends and his relations.

Chorus
And many a burglar, etc.

JUDGE:

At length I became as rich as the Gurneys—
    An incubus then I thought her,
So I threw over that rich attorney's
    Elderly, ugly daughter.
The rich attorney my character high
    Tried vainly to disparage—
And now, if you please, I'm ready to try
    This breach of promise of marriage!

Chorus
And now, if you please, etc.

JUDGE:
For now I am a Judge!

ALL:
And a good Judge too!

JUDGE:
Yes, now I am a Judge!

ALL:
And a good Judge too!

JUDGE:
Though all my law is fudge,
Yet I'll never, never budge,
But I'll live and die a Judge!

ALL:
And a good Judge too!

JUDGE (*pianissimo*):
It was managed by a job!

ALL:
And a good job too!

JUDGE:
It was managed by a job!

ALL:
And a good job too!

JUDGE:
It is patent to the mob,
That my being made a nob
Was effected by a job.

ALL:
And a good job too!

(*Enter* COUNSEL *for* PLAINTIFF.)

Recit., COUNSEL:
Swear thou the Jury!

USHER:
Kneel, Jurymen, oh! kneel!

(*All the* JURY *kneel in the Jury-box, and so are hidden
from audience.*)

USHER:
Oh, will you swear by yonder skies,
Whatever question may arise
'Twixt rich and poor—'twixt low and high,
That you will well and truly try?

JURY (*raising their hands, which alone are visible*):
To all of this we make reply,
By the dull slate of yonder sky:
That we will well and truly try.

(*All rise with the last note, both hands in air.*)

Recit., USHER:
This blind devotion is indeed a crusher!
Pardon the tear-drop of the simple Usher!

(*He weeps.*)

Recit., COUNSEL:
Call the plaintiff!

Recit., USHER:
Oh, Angelina! Angelina!! Come thou into Court.

(*Enter the* BRIDESMAIDS, *each bearing two palm branches, their arms crossed on their bosoms, and rose-wreaths on their arms*)

Chorus of BRIDESMAIDS
Comes the broken flower—
    Comes the cheated maid—
Though the tempest lower,
    Rain and cloud will fade!
Take, O maid, these posies:
    Though thy beauty rare
Shame the blushing roses,
    They are passing fair!
        Wear the flowers till they fade:
        Happy be thy life, O maid!

(The JUDGE, *having taken a great fancy to* FIRST BRIDES-
MAID, *sends her a note by* USHER, *which she reads,
kisses rapturously, and places in her bosom.)*

Solo, ANGELINA:
O'er the season vernal
    Time may cast a shade;
Sunshine, if eternal,
    Makes the roses fade!
Time may do his duty;
    Let the thief alone—
Winter hath a beauty
    That is all his own.
        Fairest days are sun and shade:
        I am no unhappy maid!

(By this time the JUDGE *has transferred his admiration to*
ANGELINA.)*

Chorus of BRIDESMAIDS
Comes the broken flower, etc.

(During Chorus ANGELINA *collects wreaths of roses from*
BRIDESMAIDS *and gives them to the* JURY, *who put
them on, and wear them during the rest of the piece.)*

JUDGE *(to* ASSOCIATE*):*
Oh, never, never, never, since I joined the human race,
Saw I so exquisitely fair a face.

THE JURY *(shaking their forefingers at* JUDGE*):*
Ah, sly dog! Ah, sly dog!

JUDGE *(to* JURY*):*
How say you, is she not designed for capture?

FOREMAN *(after consulting with the* JURY*):*
We've but one word, my lord, and that is—Rapture!

PLAINTIFF *(curtseying):*
Your kindness, gentlemen, quite overpowers!

THE JURY:
We love you fondly, and would make you ours!

THE BRIDESMAIDS (*shaking their forefingers at* JURY):
Ah, sly dogs! Ah, sly dogs!

Recit., COUNSEL *for* PLAINTIFF:
May it please you, my lud!
Gentlemen of the Jury!

Aria
With a sense of deep emotion,
  I approach this painful case;
For I never had a notion
  That a man could be so base,
Or deceive a girl confiding,
Vows, *etcetera,* deriding.

ALL:
He deceived a girl confiding,
Vows, *etcetera,* deriding.

(PLAINTIFF *falls sobbing on* COUNSEL'S *breast, and remains there.*)

COUNSEL:
See my interesting client,
  Victim of a heartless wile!
See the traitor all defiant
  Wears a supercilious smile!
Sweetly smiled my client on him,
Coyly woo'd and gently won him!

ALL:
Sweetly smiled, etc.

COUNSEL:
Swiftly fled each honeyed hour
  Spent with this unmanly male!
Camberwell became a bower,
  Peckham an Arcadian Vale,

Breathing concentrated otto!—
An existence *à la* Watteau.

ALL:
Bless us, concentrated otto! etc.

COUNSEL (*coming down with* PLAINTIFF, *who is still sobbing on his breast*):
Picture, then, my client naming
And insisting on the day:
Picture him excuses framing—
Going from her far away;
Doubly criminal to do so,
For the maid had bought her *trousseau!*

ALL:
Doubly criminal, etc.

COUNSEL (*to* PLAINTIFF, *who weeps*):
Cheer up, my pretty—oh, cheer up!

JURY:
Cheer up, cheer up, we love you!

(COUNSEL *leads* PLAINTIFF *fondly into Witness-box; he takes a tender leave of her, and resumes his place in Court.*)

(PLAINTIFF *reels, as if about to faint.*)

JUDGE:
That she is reeling
Is plain to me!

FOREMAN:
If faint you're feeling,
Recline on me!

(*She falls sobbing on to the* FOREMAN's *breast.*)

PLAINTIFF *(feebly)*:
I shall recover
If left alone.

ALL *(shaking their fists at* DEFENDANT*)*:
Oh, perjured lover,
Atone! atone!

FOREMAN:
Just like a father
I wish to be.   *(Kissing her.)*

JUDGE *(approaching her)*:
Or, if you'd rather,
Recline on me!

(She staggers on to bench, sits down by the JUDGE, *and
falls sobbing on his breast.)*

COUNSEL:
Oh! fetch some water
From far Cologne!

ALL:
For this sad slaughter
Atone! atone!

JURY *(shaking fists at* DEFENDANT*)*:
Monster, monster, dread our fury—
There's the Judge, and we're the Jury!

Song, DEFENDANT:
Oh, gentlemen, listen, I pray,
   Though I own that my heart has been ranging,
Of nature the laws I obey,
   For nature is constantly changing.
The moon in her phases is found,
   The time and the wind and the weather,
The months in succession come round,
   And you don't find two Mondays together.
      Consider the moral, I pray,
         Nor bring a young fellow to sorrow,

Who loves this young lady to-day,
And loves that young lady to-morrow.

BRIDESMAIDS (*rushing forward, and kneeling to* JURY):
Consider the moral, etc.

You cannot eat breakfast all day,
Nor is it the act of a sinner,
When breakfast is taken away,
To turn your attention to dinner;
And it's not in the range of belief,
That you could hold him as a glutton,
Who, when he is tired of beef,
Determines to tackle the mutton.
But this I am ready to say,
If it will appease their sorrow,
I'll marry one lady to-day,
And I'll marry the other to-morrow.

BRIDESMAIDS (*rushing forward as before*):
But this he is ready to say, etc.

Recit., JUDGE:
That seems a reasonable proposition,
To which I think your client may agree.

ALL:
Oh, Judge discerning!

COUNSEL:
But, I submit, my lord, with all submission,
To marry two at once is Burglaree!

(*Referring to law book*)

In the reign of James the Second,
It was generally reckoned
As a very serious crime
To marry two wives at one time.

(*Hands book up to* JUDGE, *who reads it*)

ALL:
Oh, man of learning!

Quartette
JUDGE:
A nice dilemma we have here,
    That calls for all our wit:

COUNSEL:
And at this stage it don't appear
    That we can settle it.

DEFENDANT:
If I to wed the girl am loth
    A breach 'twill surely be!

PLAINTIFF:
And if he goes and marries both
    It counts as Burglaree!

ALL:
A nice dilemma, etc.

Duet, PLAINTIFF *and* DEFENDANT:
PLAINTIFF (*embracing* DEFENDANT *rapturously*):
I love him—I love him—with fervour unceasing,
    I worship and madly adore;
My blind adoration is always increasing,
    My loss I shall ever deplore.
Oh, see what a blessing—what love and caressing
    I've lost, and remember it, pray,
When you I'm addressing are busy assessing
    The damages Edwin must pay.

DEFENDANT (*repelling her furiously*):
I smoke like a furnace—I'm always in liquor,
    A ruffian—a bully—a sot.
I'm sure I should thrash her—perhaps I should kick her,
    I am such a very bad lot!
I'm not prepossessing, as you may be guessing,
    She couldn't endure me a day!

Recall my professing when you are assessing
    The damages Edwin must pay!

(She clings to him passionately; he drags her round stage, and flings her to the ground.)

JURY:
We would be fairly acting,
But this is most distracting!

Recit., JUDGE:
The question, gentlemen, is one of liquor;
    You ask for guidance—this is my reply:
If he, when tipsy, would assault and kick her,
    Let's make him tipsy, gentlemen, and try!

COUNSEL:
With all respect
I do object!

ALL:
With all respect
We do object!

DEFENDANT:
I don't object!

ALL:
We do object!

JUDGE *(tossing his books and papers about)*:
All the legal furies seize you!
No proposal seems to please you;
I can't stop up here all day,
I must shortly go away.
Barristers, and you, attorneys,
Set out on your homeward journeys;
Put your briefs upon the shelf,
I will marry her myself!

(He comes down from Bench to floor of Court. He embraces Angelina.)

Finale

PLAINTIFF:
Oh, joy unbounded!
With wealth surrounded,
The knell is sounded
        Of grief and woe.

COUNSEL:
With love devoted
On you he's doated:
To castle moated
        Away they go!

DEFENDANT:
I wonder whether
They'll live together
In marriage tether
        In manner true?

USHER:
It seems to me, sir,
Of such as she, sir,
A judge is he, sir,
        A good judge too.

Chorus
It seems to me, sir, etc.

JUDGE:
Oh, yes, I am a Judge.

ALL:
And a good Judge too!

JUDGE:
Oh, yes, I am a Judge.

ALL:
And a good Judge too!

JUDGE:
Though homeward as you trudge,

You declare my law is fudge,
Yet of beauty I'm a judge.

ALL:
And a good judge too!

(JUDGE *and* PLAINTIFF *dance back on to the Bench—the* BRIDESMAIDS *take the eight garlands of roses from behind the* JUDGE's *desk (where one end of them is fastened) and draw them across floor of Court, so that they radiate from the desk. Two plaster Cupids in bar wigs descend from flies. Red fire.*)

CURTAIN

Cavalleria Rusticana

by GIOVANNI VERGA

Translated from the Italian
by ALEX SZOGYI

Giovanni Verga (1840–1922)

Giovanni Verga was born in Catania, Sicily, in 1840. In his boyhood, after gaining an intimate knowledge of the peasant speech and folkways of the Sicilians, he was determined to become a novelist. Accepting the literary conventions of his day when romanticism was dominant, he wrote three historical novels and a melodramatic one of contemporary life before he was twenty-five. Anxious to be in contact with a more sophisticated society, he spent five years in Florence, where he wrote a popular novella, *Story of a Linnet*. In 1870 he moved to Milan, where he lived for fifteen years, but took intermittent trips back to Sicily. He published two novels in 1873, *Eva* and *Royal Tigress*, criticizing the cruelty and luxury of fashionable society.

With the publication of a short story called *Nedda* in 1874, Verga became one of the founders of the new school of Italian realism called *verismo*. This literary movement, influenced by the French naturalists Flaubert, Zola, and de Maupassant, was a revolt against the sentimental romanticism of the period. Verga's true genius was now revealed in a series of realistic short stories and novels depicting the conflicts and tragedies in the life of Sicilian peasants and fisherfolk. With artistic simplicity and objectivity he portrayed the religious faith, the poverty, the primitive codes, and the violence of his Sicilian countrymen. His combination of realism and regionalism tempered by compassion and understanding gave him an assured position in Italian literature.

Having found his true bent, he embarked on an ambitious literary project, the writing of a series of five novels called *The Defeated*. However, he completed only two of them, *I Malavoglia*, published in 1881, and *Maestro Don Gesualdo*, published in 1888. While he was working on these novels, he also wrote two collections of short stories dealing with Sicilian life, *Novelle rusticane* and *Vagabondaggio*.

In 1883 Verga rewrote one of his short stories, *Cavalleria rusticana,* as a one-act play. It was produced in the following year with the famous actress Eleonora Duse playing the role of Santuzza. The play was a great success and is credited with inaugurating the reign of realism in the Italian theater. Two minor librettists adapted the play for Mascagni's popular opera, which was first performed in 1890.

Verga wrote little of importance in the last period of his life. He died in Rome, January 27, 1922.

In nine terse scenes of realistic dialogue Verga has written a stark tragedy of jealousy and vengeance enacted, ironically, against the background of an Easter service. While the placid life of the Sicilian peasantry goes on—carting hay, buying eggs, and drinking wine—powerful passions are simmering. Santuzza, crazed with grief at being abandoned during her pregnancy by Turiddu, her lover, pleads with him to give up his affair with Lola, Master Alfio's wife. Turiddu, the local Don Juan, a reckless, happy-go-lucky youth who prizes his independence, scorns her entreaties. Master Alfio, the quiet coachman, in a dramatic confrontation with Turiddu, challenges him to a death combat to avenge his wife's infidelity. The play concludes with the inevitable catastrophe, the death of Turiddu.

CHARACTERS

TURIDDU MACCA

MASTER ALFIO DI LICODIANO

LOLA,
  his wife

SANTUZZA

MAMMA NUNZIA,
  TURIDDU's mother

UNCLE BRASI,
  a groom

CAMILLA,
  his wife

AUNT FILOMENA

PIPPUZZA

A small village square, irregularly shaped. Backstage left, a tree-lined avenue, which leads to the small village church, and the wall of an orchard, which marks the end of the little square. At right, a path between two hedges of prickly pears, which winds off into the distance. Front stage right, MAMMA NUNZIA's tavern with a branch hanging from the entrance. A little bench with eggs, bread, and greens on it, on display; and on the other side of the entrance, a settee leaning up against the wall. The tavern borders on a narrow street leading into the interior of the village. On the other corner, the barracks of the carabinieri, two floors, with their emblem over the door. Further off in the same direction, UNCLE BRASI's stables with an ample overhanging gable in front. At front stage left, a terrace with a pergola . . . then a narrow street. Finally, AUNT FILOMENA's little house.

SCENE ONE

UNCLE BRASI *crosses the stage from the left. On his head is a bundle of hay, which he puts down under the gable . . .* CAMILLA *is on the terrace folding her washing. There are women along the street making their way to church. A peasant sits under the gable, his chin in his hands; he is humming. Church bells*

59

announce Mass. AUNT FILOMENA comes out of MAMMA NUNZIA's tavern carrying things under her apron.

CAMILLA: Been to market, Aunt Filomena?

AUNT FILOMENA: God forgive us, it's Easter!

(She goes into the house.)

CAMILLA *(to SANTUZZA, who arrives all excited, entering from the first path on the left; her face hidden in her cape)*: Well, Santuzza, going off to confession?

(SANTUZZA lifts her head in CAMILLA's direction and goes off without answering.)

UNCLE BRASI *(to CAMILLA, from the stable door)*: Go back in the house and mind your own business, big mouth! *(CAMILLA goes back in. To a carabiniere, who is leaning over the terrace of the barracks)* She's always provoking me, devil of a wife! *(To the peasant under the gable)* Come over here, Peppi.

(Leads him into the stable.)

SANTUZZA *(at the entrance to the tavern)*: Mamma Nunzia!

MAMMA NUNZIA *(leaning out)*: Oh, it's you! . . . What do you want?

(The carabiniere goes back inside.)

SANTUZZA: Don't be afraid. I'm going right away. Only tell me if your son Turiddu's here.

MAMMA NUNZIA: You've come all the way here to look for my son Turiddu? . . . He's not here.

SANTUZZA: Oh, Lord in Heaven!

MAMMA NUNZIA: You know I don't want to have anything to do with your affairs!

SANTUZZA *(thrusting aside her cape)*: Oh, Mamma Nunzia, don't you see what a state I'm in? Treat me as Jesus did Maria Maddalena. Tell me where your son Turiddu is, for the love of Jesus!

MAMMA NUNZIA: He went to Francofonte for the wine.

(AUNT FILOMENA leans out the doorway to her little house; her hands are on her stomach.)

SANTUZZA: No! Last night he was still here. He was seen at two o'clock in the morning.

MAMMA NUNZIA: What are you telling me? . . . he didn't come home last night. . . . Come inside.

SANTUZZA: No, Mamma Nunzia. I cannot enter your house.

UNCLE BRASI (*from the gable*): Oh, Aunt Filomena, today, this blessed Easter day, when mothers-in-law and daughters-in-law make peace, shall we kiss and make up, too?

AUNT FILOMENA: Quiet, you old infidel!

(She goes back into the house.)

MAMMA NUNZIA (*to* SANTUZZA): Well, speak up! What has happened to my son Turiddu?

SANTUZZA: Don't speak so loud, Mamma Nunzia!

PIPPUZZA (*from the little street backstage right, with a basket over her arm*): Want any eggs, Mamma Nunzia?

MAMMA NUNZIA: At three for two soldi, you can content yourself. Look, I have lots of them.

PIPPUZZA: Then I'll content myself by eating them up with the children, and so I'll have a contented Easter. (*About to go*)

UNCLE BRASI: So you haven't yet been to confession, Mamma Nunzia?

MAMMA NUNZIA: All right, because today is Easter, one soldo for each! I'll have a dozen; but add another one for good luck, as a present. Put them together with the others, over there . . . without breaking them; watch out! And here's the money. A fistful of copper coins for you, take a look!

UNCLE BRASI: Listen, listen, Pippuzza; let's do a little business, you and me, too. Come over here to my house.

(He takes her into the little street at the left.)

MAMMA NUNZIA (*to* SANTUZZA): Well, speak up! What do you know about my son Turiddu?

SANTUZZA: I know nothing.

MAMMA NUNZIA: Where was he last night, that he didn't come home?

SANTUZZA (*bursting into tears; her face under her cape*): Oh, Mamma Nunzia! There's a nail stuck right into my heart!

MAMMA NUNZIA: Then you know where Turiddu was?

ALFIO (*from the first little street at the right; a flask in hand*):

Do you still have some of the good stuff for six soldi, Mamma Nunzia?

MAMMA NUNZIA: I'll go and see. Turiddu was supposed to bring some back today from Francofonte.

ALFIO: Your son Turiddu is still here. I saw him this morning. Doesn't he wear the red cap of the bersagliere?

(CAMILLA *leans again over the terrace.*)

SANTUZZA (*taking the flask from* ALFIO's *hands and giving it to* MAMMA NUNZIA): Meanwhile, go and see if there's any left.

(MAMMA NUNZIA *goes back into the tavern.*)

ALFIO: Of course you're at home here, now, eh, Santuzza.

CAMILLA: You've come to celebrate Easter with your wife Lola, Alfio?

ALFIO: Yes, at least the main events.

AUNT FILOMENA (*from the doorway, her cape on her arm; to* CAMILLA): Aren't you coming to Mass?

UNCLE BRASI (*running up from the left*): She's coming! She's coming! Master Alfio, would you take a trip over to Militello?

ALFIO: Tomorrow, yes, Uncle Brasi. Today I've come to celebrate Easter at home.

AUNT FILOMENA: "At Carnival time, go off where you will. But at Christmas and Easter, stay home and be still."

CAMILLA (*to* ALFIO): And your wife, who only sees you at Christmas and Easter, what does she say?

ALFIO: I don't know what she says. It's my trade, Camilla. My trade is to be a coachman and always to travel from here to there.

MAMMA NUNZIA (*returning with the flask full to the brim, and she leaves her cape folded up on the stool with the greens*): It's better than the others, Master Alfio; you'll tell me so when you've drunk it down. It'll do you a world of good. Eighteen soldi.

AUNT FILOMENA: What you say is not right, Alfio: you who have a young wife.

ALFIO: My wife knows I wear my cap the way I like to. (*Hitting his breast pocket*) And I know what's good for my wife, as well as for everybody else. (*Two carabinieri in uniform come out of the barracks and go off by the road to the church.)* I keep my business to myself, without any need of those who wear feathers in their caps. And everybody in these parts knows it, thank the Lord!

(The church bells announce Mass a second time.)

AUNT FILOMENA *(crossing herself)*: Rue the day!

(She locks the entrance door with a key, puts her cape around her shoulders, and sets out for the church.)

CAMILLA: I'm coming, too, Aunt Filomena. I'm coming, too.

(She leaves the terrace.)

AUNT FILOMENA *(to MASTER ALFIO)*: You'd best go and tell your wife it's time for Mass, you infidel!

ALFIO: I'm off to see to the animals. I'll let her know. Have no doubts, I'm a Christian, too, you know.

MAMMA NUNZIA *(to ALFIO)*: Eighteen soldi.

ALFIO: I'm coming, coming, you old bore. Let me count the change.

CAMILLA *(from the first little street to the left, with her cape over her head, goes and gives the key to her husband)*: Here's the key, anyway. And don't you get ready to come as usual when the church services are about over.

(She goes toward the church with AUNT FILOMENA. UNCLE BRASI goes back into the stable. Others, a few at a time, cross the small square to go to church.)

ALFIO *(to MAMMA NUNZIA)*: Here you are, eighteen! Live and be well. *(Goes off in the direction from which he came.)*

MAMMA NUNZIA: Just where did you see my son Turiddu, Alfio?

SANTUZZA *(quietly, snatching at her dress)*: Don't tell him anything, for the love of heaven!

ALFIO *(turning back)*: I saw him around my place, at dawn, just as I was getting back. He was running like he was in a big hurry, and he didn't notice me. Do you want me to send him to you if I run into him?

MAMMA NUNZIA: No, no. *(MASTER ALFIO goes off. To SANTUZZA)* Why did you motion me to keep quiet? *(SANTUZZA doesn't answer and bends her head.)*

MAMMA NUNZIA: Ah! . . . What are you thinking about?

SANTUZZA (*hiding her face in her apron and bursting into tears*): Oh, Mamma Nunzia!

MAMMA NUNZIA (*stupefied*): Lola? . . . Alfio's wife?

SANTUZZA: What shall I do now that Turiddu has abandoned me? . . .

MAMMA NUNZIA: Oh, my poor girl! What have you just told me! . . . It can't be; you're mistaken. Master Alfio is also mistaken! . . . There are so many who wear the red cap of the bersagliere. . . .

SANTUZZA: No, Master Alfio was not mistaken. It was he, Turiddu!

MAMMA NUNZIA: How do you know?

SANTUZZA: I know . . . Master Turiddu, before he became a soldier . . . used to talk to Lola.

MAMMA NUNZIA: Well! But then when he returned, he found her married to Master Alfio di Licodiano, and he resigned himself.

SANTUZZA: But she didn't. She didn't resign herself.

MAMMA NUNZIA: How do you know about that?

SANTUZZA: I know she showed herself every time she saw him pass in front of my door, and she stole him away from me with her eyes, the little heathen! And she'd even try to start up a conversation with him! "Master Turiddu, what are you doing in this neighborhood? Didn't you know it was the will of God? Now let me be; I belong to my husband." As if it were the will of God to tempt him! He began to sing under my window to spite the one who had married another. It's so true that old love is never forgotten. But I, when I heard him sing, like a good Christian, it seemed like my heart had jumped right out of my chest; I was out of my mind, I was! How could I say no when he begged me: "Open up, Santuzza, if it's true that you care for me!" How could I? Then I said to him: "Listen, Master Turiddu, swear to me before God first!" He swore. Later, when she got wind of it, such an evil woman, she became mortally jealous; and she got it into her head to steal him from me. She turned Turiddu right around. (*With a gesture*) He denies it because he's sorry for me; but he has no more love for me! . . . Now that I'm in this state . . . when my brothers find out about it, they'll kill me with their very own hands! A lot I care. If Turiddu didn't care for this other one, I would die happy. Last night he came to tell me: "Farewell, I have work to do." With such a good face! Lord! How is it possible to harbor the treachery of Judas in your heart with such a face? Later, a neighbor who came over to do some spinning told me she had seen Master Turiddu here in the neighborhood, in front of Lola's place.

MAMMA NUNZIA (*crossing herself*): Oh, daughter of God, why do you tell me all this on this holy day! . . .

SANTUZZA: Oh, oh, what a day it's been for me today, Mamma Nunzia!

MAMMA NUNZIA: Listen, you must go and throw yourself at the foot of the crucifix.

SANTUZZA: No, I can't go to church, Mamma Nunzia.

MAMMA NUNZIA (*folding her cape and placing it on her head*): All the more reason for me not to miss the sacred services.

SANTUZZA: You go there, and I'll keep an eye on the store. . . . Have no fear, I'm not a thief as well!

MAMMA NUNZIA: But what will you do?

SANTUZZA: I don't know. I'll wait here (*pointing at the bench beside the entrance*) like a poor beggar woman.

MAMMA NUNZIA: Here? In my house?

SANTUZZA: Don't worry, I won't go inside. Don't drive me from your door. Mamma Nunzia, do as the merciful Lord would do; go and pray in church. Let me stay here, I beg of you! Let me talk with him this one last time, for the love of your dead souls!

MAMMA NUNZIA (*goes off to the church, grumbling*): Oh, Lord, think of us!

UNCLE BRASI (*running out of the stable*): Wait, wait, Mamma Nunzia. We shopkeepers who keep open should arrive the last. (MAMMA NUNZIA *has gone off.* UNCLE BRASI *says to* SANTUZZA) Oh, so you're not even going today to the Easter services, Santa? Do you want us to recite the blessed rosary together?

SANTUZZA: Let me be.

UNCLE BRASI: Eh! . . . I won't eat you, you devil! . . . As if you didn't know that? . . .

SANTUZZA: Let me be.

PIPPUZZA (*from the first path on the left, out of breath*): Do we have time to get to the services, Uncle Brasi?

UNCLE BRASI: If you run, you'll get there. (PIPPUZZA *goes off.*

UNCLE BRASI *to* SANTUZZA) See, I'm like the bell ringer who calls the people to church, and then he stays outside himself. (*Looking toward the path at rear right*) Ah! That's perhaps why she wanted to be left alone! . . . Here comes the foolish fellow. . . . I'll be on my way as well. . . .

(*He goes toward the church.*)

SCENE
TWO

TURIDDU MACCA, *in haste, from the rear
right path and* SANTUZZA, *who jumps to
her feet on seeing him.*

TURIDDU: Ah, Santuzza! . . . what are you doing here?

SANTUZZA: I was waiting for you.

TURIDDU: Where is my mother?

SANTUZZA: She's gone to church.

TURIDDU: Then you go on ahead, too: I'll look after things
here.

SANTUZZA: No, I'm not going to church.

TURIDDU: On Easter day?

SANTUZZA: You know I can't go there.

TURIDDU: Then what do you want to do?

SANTUZZA: I want to talk to you.

TURIDDU: Here? In the middle of the street?

SANTUZZA: It doesn't matter where.

TURIDDU: Everybody can see us!

SANTUZZA: It doesn't matter.

TURIDDU: What's the matter with you?

SANTUZZA: Tell me where you came from.

TURIDDU: Oh, oh! What do you mean by that?

SANTUZZA: Where were you last night?

TURIDDU: Oh! Must I say where I was?

SANTUZZA: Why do you get angry when I ask you where you
were? Can't you tell me?

TURIDDU: I was at Francofonte, if you must know.

SANTUZZA: That's not true. Last night, at two in the morning,
you were still here.

TURIDDU: So I was where I damn please.

SANTUZZA (*letting her cape fall from her shoulders*): Oh, Mas-

67

ter Turiddu, why do you treat me like this? Won't you look me in the face? Won't you see you're killing me?

TURIDDU: It's your fault. I don't know what's got into you. You're shaming me in front of everyone. You're spying on me as if I were still a little boy, as if I didn't have a right to do what I want.

SANTUZZA: No, I didn't go asking. They told me here, just now, that they saw you at dawn at Lola's door.

TURIDDU: Who said so?

SANTUZZA: Master Alfio himself, her husband.

TURIDDU: Him! So, this is the great love you have for me? It makes you go and put a bee in Alfio's bonnet, and I risk getting killed!

SANTUZZA (*falling on her knees, her hands clasped*): Oh, Turiddu, how can you say that?

TURIDDU: Get up. Don't play games with me! Get up, or I'll go away.

SANTUZZA (*getting up slowly*): Oh, so now you're going away? Now that you've left me like our Lady of the Sorrows.

TURIDDU: What do you want me to do if you don't believe my words anymore? What others tell you, however, that, yes, that you believe! It's none of it true, I tell you again. Alfio was mistaken. I had things to get done. Look, you've got it into your head about this Lola business, just when her husband's around! You see how silly you are?

SANTUZZA: Her husband arrived only this morning.

TURIDDU: Oh, oh, you know that, too? Bravo! You're really spying on me in every way, aren't you? There's nowhere I can turn anymore!

SANTUZZA: Yes, Turiddu, you can slaughter me with your own hands, like a sacrificial lamb, or, if you wish, I can lick your hands like a lapdog.

TURIDDU: So?

SANTUZZA: But not Lola, no, you hear! That one would damn my soul.

TURIDDU: Leave Lola out of this. She has her own home.

SANTUZZA: So why doesn't she leave *me* alone? Why does she want to steal you from me, when I have nobody else?

TURIDDU: Mind you don't make a mistake!

SANTUZZA: No, I'm not making any mistake! Didn't you run after her even before you went into the army?

TURIDDU: Water under the bridge! Now Lola is married and has her own home.

SANTUZZA: So what? Didn't you still want her, even though she's married? And hasn't she stolen you from me out of jealousy? And don't I feel this fire for you inside of me here, for you who betray me?

TURIDDU: Keep quiet.

SANTUZZA: No, I can't keep quiet, with this mad fury in my heart! Now what will I do if you abandon me?

TURIDDU: I'm not abandoning you, if you don't keep pushing my back to the wall. But I told you: I want to be able to do what I want to do, when I want to do it. Till now, thank God, I've had no collar around *my* neck.

SANTUZZA: What do you mean by that?

TURIDDU: I mean that you're a mad woman, with your unreasonable jealousy.

SANTUZZA: What fault is it of mine? You see what's happened to me? Lola is better than me, I know! With her neck and hands loaded with gold! Her husband doesn't let her go without, and he sets her up like some Madonna on an altar, the old reprobate!

TURIDDU: Leave her alone!

SANTUZZA: Now you're defending her?

TURIDDU: I'm not. It's of no concern to me if her husband keeps her like a Madonna on an altar. What does concern me is not passing for a man who can't come and go as he pleases. That I cannot take!

SCENE
THREE

LOLA *comes in from the first path at the right.* TURIDDU *and* SANTUZZA.

LOLA: Oh, Master Turiddu! Did you see my husband go into church?

TURIDDU: I don't know, Missus Lola. I just got there.

LOLA: He said to me: "I'm going to the blacksmith because the bay horse has a shoe missing, and I'll join you right away in church." Are you listening to the Easter services from out here, making a little conversation?

TURIDDU: Santa here was saying to me . . .

SANTUZZA: I was telling him today was a great day, and the Lord up above sees everything!

LOLA: And you're not going to church?

SANTUZZA: Those go to church who have clear consciences, Signora Lola.

LOLA: I thank the Lord and kiss the earth. *(She stoops down to touch the ground with the tips of her fingers, which she then brings to her lips.)*

SANTUZZA: Be grateful, Lola, that things go like that for you. It is said sometimes about some people: "He who places his feet upon the ground is not worthy of placing his lips upon it."

TURIDDU: Let us be going, Lola, we have no business here.

LOLA: Don't disturb yourself, Master Turiddu, my feet know the way. I don't wish to trouble.

TURIDDU: But I've told you, we have no business here!

SANTUZZA *(pulling him by the coat)*: No, we still have things to talk over.

LOLA: Live and be well, Master Turiddu! You stay and settle your affairs and I'll go settle mine.

(She goes off toward the church.)

70

SCENE FOUR

TURIDDU *and* SANTUZZA.

TURIDDU (*furious*): So! You see what you've done?

SANTUZZA: Yes, I see!

TURIDDU: Did you do it on purpose then?

SANTUZZA: Yes, I did it on purpose!

TURIDDU: Oh! Blood of Judas!

SANTUZZA: Kill me.

TURIDDU: You did it on purpose! You did it on purpose!

SANTUZZA: Kill me. I don't care anymore, go on!

TURIDDU: No, I don't want even to kill you! (*About to go.*)

SANTUZZA: You're leaving me?

TURIDDU: Yes, that's what you deserve.

(*The church bell rings at the elevation of the Host.*)

SANTUZZA: Don't leave me, Turiddu! Do you hear that bell ringing?

TURIDDU: I won't be led by the nose, you understand?

SANTUZZA: You can walk on me with your feet on my face. But not her, no!

TURIDDU: Let's get it over with! I'll get out and have done with this scene!

SANTUZZA: Where are you running?

TURIDDU: Where I want to: I'm going to Mass.

SANTUZZA: No, you're going off to show Lola that you've dropped me for her, that you don't care anything for me!

TURIDDU: You're crazy!

SANTUZZA: Don't go there, Turiddu! Don't go to church to commit a sin today! Don't add insult to injury in front of this woman.

TURIDDU: But it's you! You're insulting me by showing ev-

71

erybody that I'm not free to take a step, that you've got me tied to your apron strings like some kid! . . .

SANTUZZA: What do you care what she says, if you don't want me to die of despair? . . .

TURIDDU: You're out of your mind!

SANTUZZA: Yes, it's true; I'm out of my mind! Don't leave me with this madness in my head!

TURIDDU (*tearing himself away*): Let's get this over with, I tell you! Go to hell!

SANTUZZA: Turiddu! By that God who now is descending into the consecrated Host, don't leave me for that Lola! (TURIDDU *goes off.*) Ah! I curse you on this Easter day!

SCENE
FIVE

> MASTER ALFIO *in haste from the path at rear right, and* SANTUZZA *at stage center.*

SANTUZZA: Oh, heaven has sent you, Master Alfio!

ALFIO: How far have they gotten with Mass, Santa?

SANTUZZA: You're getting there late. But your wife is there in your place with Turiddu Macca.

ALFIO: What do you mean by that?

SANTUZZA: I say that your wife goes around laden with gold, like some Madonna on the altar. She does you honor, Master Alfio!

ALFIO: Oh, what does that matter to you?

SANTUZZA: It matters to me because while you run the world over to earn your bread and to buy presents for your wife, she adorns the house in another way!

ALFIO: What did you say, Miss Santa?

SANTUZZA: I said that while you're out and around, rain and shine, to earn your living, your wife Lola adorns your house in an evil fashion!

ALFIO: In God's name, Santa, you've gone and gotten drunk rather early this Easter morning. I'll make you puke!

SANTUZZA: I'm not drunk, Alfio, and I'm talking sense.

ALFIO: Listen! If it's the truth that you told me, then I'm grateful, and I kiss your hands, as if you were my mother now returned from the graveyard, Miss Santuzza! But if you lie, by the soul of my dead family, I swear I'll not leave you eyes to cry with, you and all your infamous family!

SANTUZZA: I cannot cry, Master Alfio. And these eyes didn't weep even when they saw Turiddu Macca, who has deprived me of my honor, go off to Signora Lola, your wife!

ALFIO (*turning suddenly deathly calm*): If this be so, well then, good, I thank you, my dear.

SANTUZZA: Don't thank me, no, I am wicked!

ALFIO: You're not wicked, Miss Santa. The wicked ones are those who have plunged this knife into our hearts, yours and mine. And if both their hearts were really to be split in two with a knife poisoned with garlic, that would be as nothing at all! Now, if you see my wife looking for me, tell her I'm going to the house to get a gift for her neighbor Turiddu.

(*He goes off by the first path on the right.*)

(*People begin returning from the church and disperse right and left. TURIDDU MACCA, LOLA, CAMILLA, MAMMA NUNZIA, AUNT FILOMENA come forward, not paying any attention to SANTUZZA, who remains near the path at rear right, wrapped in her cape. Only UNCLE BRASI, who comes last, notices her.*)

UNCLE BRASI; Oh, Miss Santa, are you going to church when nobody's there anymore!

SANTUZZA: I'm in mortal sin, Uncle Brasi!

(*She goes toward the church.*)

SCENE
SIX

> UNCLE BRASI *goes back for a moment into the stable.* CAMILLA *goes to her house.* AUNT FILOMENA *puts her key into the lock.* MAMMA NUNZIA *enters the tavern to take off her cape.*

TURIDDU (*to* LOLA, *who is going off to her house*): Lola, why are you going like this, without a word!

LOLA: I'm going home because my husband's on my mind. I didn't see him in church.

TURIDDU: Don't think of that. He'll be along to the square. Now we must drink a drop of wine, all of us here, friends and neighbors, to our health, and to celebrate Easter. Come over here, Camilla! And you, too, Aunt Filomena!

AUNT FILOMENA: I'm coming, I'm coming.

> (*She goes into the house to leave her cape and returns right away.*)

LOLA: Thank you, brother Turiddu, but I'm not thirsty.

TURIDDU: Don't insult me this way! Are you trying to tell me you're angry with me? . . .

LOLA: For what reason would I be angry with you? . . .

TURIDDU: This I will say: what possible reason would you have to be angry with me, who have done you no ill? . . . And then on Easter day, if we had done each other any harm, it would have to be washed away. Now let's call for Master Alfio, your husband, and have him drink with us as well.

UNCLE BRASI (*coming closer*): Such joy and happiness!

CAMILLA: When such joy occurs, we'll always find you! (*Folds her cape and puts it over her arm.*)

TURIDDU (*calling inside the tavern*): Oh, Mother! Do you still have some of the good stuff?

MAMMA NUNZIA (*appears, grumbling*): Yes, the good stuff you were supposed to bring today from Francofonte! . . .

TURIDDU: Now, now, today is Easter! Don't you go making a long face at me, you too! I'll explain later. You see our friends waiting?

AUNT FILOMENA: Oh, Mamma Nunzia, on what you sell today, you won't profit much!

TURIDDU: I'm paying, I'm paying with my own money!

(MAMMA NUNZIA *goes back in.*)

UNCLE BRASI: Them spends it as has it!

LOLA: Who knows what you did when you were courting the ladies down there in those places while you were a soldier! We can see you've had some practice!

TURIDDU: What ladies! What ladies! My heart was always right here, in this town.

CAMILLA: You can tell that to the dead!

TURIDDU: My word, Camilla! Everybody knows the bersaglieri are like honey to the womenfolk . . . with their feathers. "Hey, tall, dark, and handsome over there!" Eyes stare at you from all sides. . . . But I was not one of those about whom they say "Out of sight, out of mind."

LOLA: Oh, men! Who believes them?

TURIDDU: Say women, rather! At first they swear a thousand oaths and then, when a poor devil goes off far away, leaving his heart behind him, and even his head, when he cannot eat or sleep anymore, thinking of only one thing, all of a sudden the news comes out like a gunshot: "You know what? The girl is getting married!" It's like some terrible stroke!

AUNT FILOMENA: Marriages and cardinals are made in heaven.

LOLA: You believe that? You believe they think always of one thing when they're away, surrounded by all the other women? With not even a look for them? Are you ready to see that all of a sudden they console their little hearts peacefully with the first girl who comes their way?

TURIDDU: I'm sorry, I'm sorry . . .

MAMMA NUNZIA (*returning with a jug and a glass*): It's all that's left. It's his fault!

CAMILLA: Joy and happiness!

UNCLE BRASI: Now, let's have a drink on that, as you said.

TURIDDU: I said it and I meant it. You, Mother, don't you want any?

MAMMA NUNZIA: No, I don't.

(She goes back into the house, grumbling.)

TURIDDU: She's angry about something . . . the old dear! They don't care to remember what they did when they were young! Your health, Lola! You, Camilla! Drink up, Uncle Brasi. No more bad feelings!

SCENE
SEVEN

ALFIO: Greetings one and all.

TURIDDU: Come here, Master Alfio, there's a drop of wine
for you to drink with us, to our health, one and all. (*Filling
his glass.*)

ALFIO (*rejecting the glass with the back of his hand*): Thank
you so much, friend Turiddu. I do not wish any of your
wine; it makes me sick.

TURIDDU: As you wish. (*Flinging the wine to the ground and
placing the glass on the little table. They remain staring into
each other's eyes for a moment.*)

UNCLE BRASI (*makes believe someone is calling him from the
stable*): I'm coming, I'm coming.

TURIDDU: Can I do some little thing for you, Master Alfio?

ALFIO: Nothing, my friend. What I have on my mind you
know about.

TURIDDU: Then I am here at your service.

(UNCLE BRASI *from under his gable signals his wife to
go into the house.* CAMILLA *goes in.*)

LOLA: What does this mean?

ALFIO (*without heeding his wife and thrusting her aside with
his arm*): If you wish to come out here for a moment, we
can discuss this matter freely.

TURIDDU: Wait for me at the last house in the street. I must
go inside for a moment to get what's necessary, and then
I'm all yours.

(*They embrace and kiss.* TURIDDU *bites* ALFIO's *ear
lightly.*)

78

ALFIO: You've done the right thing, brother Turiddu! That means you have good intentions. That's what is known as the word of an honorable man.

LOLA: Oh, Holy Mother of God! Where are you going, Alfio?

ALFIO: Right nearby. What business is it of yours? It'd be better for you if I never came back.

AUNT FILOMENA (*going off, stammering*): Jesus, Mary, and Joseph!

TURIDDU (*calling* ALFIO *aside*): Listen, Alfio, as God's in heaven, I know I'm in the wrong, and I'd let myself be slaughtered by you without a word. But I have a debt of conscience to Miss Santa. I've pushed her over the edge. So, as God exists, I'll kill you like a dog so as not to leave that poor girl alone in the streets.

ALFIO: Very well. Have it your way.

(*He goes off by the little path at rear right.*)

SCENE
EIGHT

TURIDDU *and* LOLA.

LOLA: Oh, Turiddu! I'm in such a state. You too are leaving me?

TURIDDU: I have nothing more to do with you. Now it's all over between us. Didn't you see us both embrace to the death, your husband and me? Oh, Mother!

MAMMA NUNZIA *(appearing)*: What is it now?

TURIDDU: I've got something to get done, Mother. I can't avoid it. Give me the key to the gate so I can go out by the orchard and get there faster. And you, Mother, embrace me as you did when I left to become a soldier and you believed I would never return, for today is Easter.

MAMMA NUNZIA: What are you saying?

TURIDDU: I am saying, it's just the wine talking; I've had a drop too much and I'm going to take a little walk to clear my mind. In any case . . . be good to Santa, she has no one in the world; think of her, Mother.

(He goes into the house.)

SCENE
NINE

> MAMMA NUNZIA *astonished.* LOLA
> *in great agitation,* CAMILLA, *peeping
> around the corner,* AUNT FILOMENA *at
> the doorway,* UNCLE BRASI *near the
> gable.*

MAMMA NUNZIA: What does it all mean?

UNCLE BRASI *(approaching solicitously)*: Lola, return to the house; go home!

LOLA *(terribly upset)*: Why must I go home?

UNCLE BRASI: It's not good for you to be found right here at this moment, in the square! If you want somebody to take you home . . . You, Camilla, stay here with Mamma Nunzia, in case.

AUNT FILOMENA *(approaching)*: Jesus, Mary, and Joseph! Jesus, Mary, and Joseph!

MAMMA NUNZIA: Now where has my son gone?

CAMILLA *(right up to her husband's ear)*: What's happened?

UNCLE BRASI *(in a low voice)*: Didn't you see him, silly, when he bit into his ear? That means I kill you or you kill me.

CAMILLA: Oh, Holy Mother of God!

MAMMA NUNZIA *(more and more dismayed)*: But where has my son Turiddu gone? What does all this mean?

LOLA: It means that evil has come upon us this Easter day, Mamma Nunzia! And the wine we have drunk together will turn into venom!

PIPPUZZA *(running from the rear, yelling)*: They've killed brother Turiddu! They've killed Turiddu!

81

(They all run toward the rear, bawling, MAMMA NUNZIA with her hands in her hair, beside herself. Two carabinieri cross the stage, running.)

CURTAIN

Motherlove

A Play in One Act

by AUGUST STRINDBERG

Translated from the Swedish
by ARVID PAULSON

August Strindberg (1849–1912)

Next to Ibsen, the greatest influence on modern drama has come from the prolific Swedish writer August Strindberg. The author of eight autobiographical novels, volumes of essays, poems, and more than sixty plays, Strindberg has been characterized by Shaw as "the only genuinely Shakespearean modern dramatist." Eugene O'Neill, who was greatly influenced by the Swedish genius, declared, "Strindberg still remains among the most modern of moderns, the greatest interpreter in the theater of the characteristic spiritual conflicts which constitute the drama—the blood—of our lives today." Strindberg's influence is evident in the plays of Sean O'Casey, Eugene O'Neill, Edward Albee, Tennessee Williams, Eugene Ionesco, and Harold Pinter.

Living in a continual state of nervous tension and indulging in ruthless introspection, Strindberg found release for his inner conflicts by writing plays—romantic, realistic, naturalistic, expressionistic, and symbolic—that sounded the full gamut of dramatic creativity. He was the fourth child of a Stockholm barmaid, who married his father only a few months before his birth. Shamed by his lowly birth, the sensitive child was further embittered by a poverty-stricken, unhappy childhood, the early death of his mother, and an irregular education. His three tempestuous marriages—all ending in divorce—caused him to develop a violent antifeminism, which found artistic expression in his reiterated theme of the duel of the sexes. With profound psychological insight, he analyzed the nature of love—sexual and sacred—revealing the tragic consequences of the domination of woman over man. Two of his most popular plays that deal with this "battle of the sexes" are *The Father* (1887) and the powerful one-act drama *Miss Julie* (1888). The cunning Laura and the neurotic Miss Julie, the protagonists of these plays, have become prototypes of the destructive female often found in naturalistic drama.

During a stay in Paris, Strindberg was very much impressed by the short one-act plays performed at André Antoine's Théâtre Libre. Founded in 1887, this Free Theater encouraged the production of concise, realistic and naturalistic plays by contemporary dramatists. Avant-garde French playwrights were strong advocates of concentrated one-act plays, *quarts d'heures,* fifteen-minute playlets. Under this influence, Strindberg in 1889 wrote *The Stronger* and two other one-act plays.

His attempt to establish an intimate theater in Copenhagen, similar to Antoine's in Paris, was doomed to failure. He opened his Scandinavian Experimental Theatre on March 9, 1889 with a production of *The Stronger* (with his wife Siri playing Mrs. X) and two other plays. The triple bill lasted only three performances. Since then, however, this taut dramatic monologue has been successfully performed in many countries by competent actresses who consider it a challenge to their histrionic talents.

Strindberg was the most subjective of the great dramatists. Like *The Father,* his tightly constructed *Motherlove,* stemming from the marital discord of his own life, deals with his obsessive fear of matriarchal dominance in family life. In *The Father* the cunning wife, Laura, destroys her husband, the Captain; in *Motherlove* the parasitic mother ruins the life of her daughter by her selfish possessiveness. This nineteenth-century attack on "Momism" is a bitter psychological study of a mother-daughter relationship. Considering herself "a tenderhearted mother" who is protecting her child, she frustrates her daughter's friendships, acting career, and love affairs. When the sensitive daughter learns from her half-sister Lisen the appalling truth that her mother is an ex-prostitute, that her Aunt Augusta is a procuress, and that she herself is an illegitimate child, the disillusioned Hélène loses her faith in life. Unlike modern rebels, she accepts her bitter heritage and remains in parental bondage. The play is cleverly framed by the daughter's refusal to join the card game in the opening scene and by her acceptance at the end.

CHARACTERS

The Mother,
  once a prostitute; 42 years old

Hélène,
  her daughter, an actress; 20 years of age

Lisen,
  aged 18

Aunt Augusta,
  a dresser in a theatre

> *The action takes place in a fisherman's cottage at a seaside resort.*

A glassed-in veranda in the rear. Beyond, a view of a cove in the skerries.

THE MOTHER *and* AUNT AUGUSTA *each sit smoking a cigar, while sipping stout and playing cards.* HÉLÈNE *is seated by the window. Her eyes are fixed on the scene outside.*

THE MOTHER: Come here and join us now, Hélène! We need a third.

HÉLÈNE: Do I have to play cards on a beautiful day like this?

AUNT AUGUSTA *(sarcastically)*: Always trying to please her mother!

THE MOTHER: You shouldn't sit there on the veranda! You'll get burned in the sun!

HÉLÈNE: I'm not getting burned. . . .

THE MOTHER: Well—but it's drafty there! *(To* AUNT AUGUSTA.*)* It's your turn to shuffle—here you are! *(She hands her the deck of cards.)*

HÉLÈNE: May I go for a swim with the girls today?

THE MOTHER: Not without your mother! You know that!

HÉLÈNE: Yes—but the girls know how to swim, and you don't, Mother. . . .

THE MOTHER: It is not a question of who can swim or who can't! You know perfectly well I don't allow you to go out without your mother, Hélène!

HÉLÈNE: I know it only too well! Haven't I heard it from the time I first was able to understand what you were saying? . . .

AUNT AUGUSTA: That shows you have a loving mother,

87

Hélène, always looking out for what is best for her child, doesn't it? It certainly does!

THE MOTHER (*offers her hand to* AUNT AUGUSTA): Thanks! Thank you for those words, Augusta! Whatever I may have been in other ways, well . . . I have certainly been a good, tender mother. . . . I can truthfully say that!

HÉLÈNE: Well—then I suppose it's no use asking you to let me go and play a game of tennis?

AUNT AUGUSTA: You have no right to be impertinent to your mother, young lady! If you don't want to give even that much joy to your dear ones by joining them in their innocent little pleasures, it's nothing short of audacity to ask to be allowed to amuse yourself in other people's company! That's what I think!

HÉLÈNE: Yes—yes—yes! I know every word of that by heart! I've heard it before!

THE MOTHER: Are you being impudent and nasty again? Why don't you do something useful? Don't sit there doing nothing! You are a big girl!

HÉLÈNE: If I am a big girl, then why do you treat me like a child?

THE MOTHER: Because you *act* like a child!

HÉLÈNE: Why reproach me for that? Isn't that just what you want me to be? Isn't it?

THE MOTHER: Tell me, Hélène—I seem to notice that you have become quite worldly-wise of late. . . . Whom have you been keeping company with recently?

HÉLÈNE: With you two, among others!

THE MOTHER: Are you keeping something from your mother?

HÉLÈNE: It's about time I did, I think—isn't it?

AUNT AUGUSTA: Have you no shame, you little brat, talking back to your own mother?

THE MOTHER: Why don't we do something worth while instead of arguing? Why don't you study your part, for instance, and then let me hear you read it?

HÉLÈNE: Our director has told us we mustn't read for anyone—he's afraid we'll learn our rôles the wrong way.

THE MOTHER: That's the thanks I get for trying to help you! No matter what I do, it's wrong, of course, and stupid!

HÉLÈNE: Then why do you want to help? And why should I be blamed for your stupid errors?

AUNT AUGUSTA: You mean to say, you are rebuking your

mother for having no education? I have never heard anything so outrageous! Never!

HÉLÈNE (*to* AUNT AUGUSTA): You tell me I mean to do that!
I don't mean that at all, and am not doing it! But when
Mother wants to teach me to read my part the wrong way,
then I must speak out, or I would find myself without an
engagement—and then we would be left penniless!

THE MOTHER: Now we find out that you are *supporting* us!
But do you know what we have to thank your Aunt Augusta for? Do you know that it was she who took care of us
and looked after us when your disreputable father abandoned us both? It was she who supported us! That's why
you owe her a debt that you can never repay! Do you
know that? Do you?

(HÉLÈNE *is silent.*)

THE MOTHER: Do you know that? Answer me!

HÉLÈNE: I am not going to answer you!

THE MOTHER (*in a loud, angry voice*): Can't you answer?

AUNT AUGUSTA: Calm yourself, Amélie! The neighbors can
hear us, and they'll start gossiping! Now calm yourself!

THE MOTHER (*to* HÉLÈNE): Now put your clothes on and
we'll all go for a walk. . . .

HÉLÈNE: I don't want to go for a walk just now!

THE MOTHER: This is the third day in a row you refuse to
take a walk with your mother! (*She seems to be weighing
something in her mind.*) Can it be possible? . . . Go outside on the veranda, Hélène, while I have a talk with Aunt
Augusta. . . .

(HÉLÈNE *withdraws to the veranda.*)

THE MOTHER: Do you think it could be possible? . . .

AUNT AUGUSTA: What could be possible?

THE MOTHER: That she has heard something?

AUNT AUGUSTA: It doesn't seem possible!

THE MOTHER: Anything is possible! Not that I believe that
anyone could be so cruel as to tell the child to her face!
I once had a nephew who never found out that his father
had committed suicide until he was thirty-six years old. . . .
Yes—there is something behind Hélène's changed behav-
ior. . . . Eight days ago I had already noticed that she
was ill at ease when we were together—when we went out

walking! She only wanted to go where we wouldn't meet anyone; and, when we did meet anybody, she looked away —she was nervous—I couldn't get a word out of her— and she wanted to go straight home! Yes, there—there *is*— something, I am sure!

AUNT AUGUSTA: You mean to say—or could I have misunderstood you?—you mean to say she is ashamed to be seen with you—to be seen with her own mother?

THE MOTHER: That's exactly what I mean!

AUNT AUGUSTA: No—that's going just a little too far! Really!

THE MOTHER: Oh, but the very worst is . . . Can you imagine? When we went on that boat trip, and some of her acquaintances came over to us, she didn't even introduce me to them!

AUNT AUGUSTA: Do you know what I think? She has met someone who has come here during the last eight days! That's what I think. . . . Let's go down to the post office and find out who the latest summer arrivals are!

THE MOTHER: You are right! That's what we'll do! *(She calls out toward the veranda.)* Hélène! We are going down to the post office for a few minutes—look after the house while we are gone! . . .

HÉLÈNE: Yes, Mother! . . .

THE MOTHER *(to* AUNT AUGUSTA): It's exactly as if I had dreamt all this before. . . .

AUNT AUGUSTA: Well—dreams have a way of coming true sometimes. . . . I know! . . . But never the pretty dreams!

(They go out, left. HÉLÈNE, *alone, waves to someone outside.* LISEN *comes in. She is dressed for tennis, all in white, and wears a white hat.)*

LISEN: Have they gone out?

HÉLÈNE: Yes, just for a few minutes.

LISEN: Well, what did your mother say?

HÉLÈNE: I didn't dare ask her! She has such a quick temper! . . .

LISEN: Poor Hélène! Aren't you coming along to the picnic? I had so much looked forward to having you! . . . If you only knew how very much I like you! *(She embraces and kisses her.)*

HÉLÈNE: And if you only knew how glad I am to have met you—and to be asked to your home! It has meant so much to me! I have never been out among cultured people before. . . . Can you imagine how I must feel—having been brought up in a hovel, with stale, musty air, and with shady people of uncertain livelihood moving about me, whispering, nagging, arguing, quarreling—where I never received a kind word, much less a caress—and where I was watched as if I had been a criminal, a convict? Oh! I am talking about my own mother—and it hurts me so frightfully, so frightfully! . . . You will have nothing but contempt for me now! . . .

LISEN: Nobody can help what their parents are, and . . .

HÉLÈNE: No—but one has to suffer for what they are! There is a saying that we could live with our parents to the end of our days and never really know what kind of human beings they are. I don't doubt there is some truth in that. . . . Yet—even if we found out the worst, we would not believe it.

LISEN (*warily*): You have not been hearing any gossip, have you?

HÉLÈNE: Yes—I have. When I was down at the bathhouse the other day, I heard, through the partition, a couple making remarks about Mother. Do you know what they said?

LISEN: I wouldn't pay any attention to it. . . .

HÉLÈNE: I heard them say that she had been a loose woman! I didn't want to believe it—I still don't believe it—yet I can't help feeling that it is true. Everything points to it— and I feel ashamed, mortified! Ashamed to show myself in her company. Everybody seems to be staring at us— I seem to feel the men ogling us! It's frightful! But can it really be true? Do you think it can be true? Tell me!

LISEN: People tell so many lies—but I haven't heard anything. . . .

HÉLÈNE: Yes—you *have* heard something—you *do* know! You just don't want to say anything. And I feel grateful to you for that. Just the same, I couldn't be more unhappy —whether you tell me or not!

LISEN: Hélène dear, you must forget what you heard! And come over to our place today. . . . There you will meet people you will like. My father came home this morning, and he is anxious to meet you. I must tell you that I have written to him about you in my letters—and I think Cousin Gerhard has done so, too. . . .

HÉLÈNE: You have a father, yes. . . . I had a father, too, when I was young, very young. . . .

LISEN: What became of him?

HÉLÈNE: He left us, Mother says, because he was a good-for-nothing!

LISEN: You can't be so sure of that. . . . However, there is another thing I wanted to tell you. If you'll come with us today, you'll meet the director of the Grand Theatre. . . . You can never tell what it may lead to—perhaps he will engage you. . . .

HÉLÈNE: Really?

LISEN: Yes, that's right! He is already interested in you! You see, Gerhard and I have been talking to him about you—and you know how sometimes just a little thing like that can decide someone's fate. A personal approach, the right word at the right time . . . So you simply can't say no, unless you want to stand in your own way!

HÉLÈNE: Lisen, my dearest! You ask if I would like to! You know only too well I would like to come. But I never go anywhere without Mother.

LISEN: Why? Can you give me *one* good reason?

HÉLÈNE: I don't know. . . . She drummed it into me when I was a child, and it still sticks. . . .

LISEN: Has she made you promise her that?

HÉLÈNE: No—she didn't need to. . . . She simply said, *"This* is what you must say!" And I have followed her advice ever since. . . .

LISEN: Do you feel you would be doing her an injustice if you were away from her for a few hours?

HÉLÈNE: I don't think she would miss me especially. . . . When I am at home, she has always something to remark about. . . . Just the same, it would hurt me to go anywhere, if she were not invited. . . .

LISEN: Have you ever thought of bringing her to see us?

HÉLÈNE: No—that hadn't occurred to me. No.

LISEN: Have you ever thought about the day when you might get married?

HÉLÈNE: I am never going to marry!

LISEN: Has your mother taught you to say that, too?

HÉLÈNE: She may have. Yes, she has always warned me against men.

LISEN: Married men also?

HÉLÈNE: I suppose so.

LISEN: Listen to me, Hélène! It's about time you become emancipated!

HÉLÈNE: Indeed not! That's the one thing I don't want to be— emancipated!

LISEN: Oh, no, I don't mean it the way you mean it! I mean —you need to set yourself free—to stop being dependent on others. You are grown up! And you don't want to ruin your life, do you?

HÉLÈNE: I don't think I can ever learn to be independent. . . . Do you realize that I have been riveted to my mother from the time I was born? Never have I dared to think a thought that was not hers—never could I express a desire that she didn't have! I am aware that it stands in my way, that it is an obstacle . . . but there is nothing I can do about it!

LISEN: But some day—when you no longer have your mother with you—you will be standing quite alone—and you will be helpless for the rest of your life!

HÉLÈNE: I'll have to take that chance. . . .

LISEN: You have no acquaintances of your own—no friends! And none of us can live a solitary life. . . . You must try to find some way out of it! Have you never been in love?

HÉLÈNE: I don't know. I have never dared to think of such things—and Mother doesn't allow young men even to look at me! How about you? Do you ever think about love?

LISEN: Well—if someone should take a liking to me . . . and if I should like him . . .

HÉLÈNE: Then I suppose you will marry your cousin Gerhard.

LISEN: No, I could never marry him! He is not in love with me. . . .

HÉLÈNE *(surprised, quizzically)*: No?

LISEN: No! He is in love with you!

HÉLÈNE *(unbelieving)*: With me?

LISEN: Yes! And one reason for my coming here is this: he wants to ask if he may call on you. . . .

HÉLÈNE: Here? Oh, no—that would never do! You don't think I would want to step between you two, do you? And you don't imagine I could possibly take your place in his

affections—you, who are so beautiful and charming? . . .
(She takes LISEN's *hands in hers.)* What a beautiful hand
you have! And such a dainty wrist! I looked at your feet,
Lisen dear, the last time we went swimming. . . .

(LISEN *sits down.* HÉLÈNE *kneels at her feet.)*

What a sweet little foot—not a bruised nail! And such well-
shaped toes—as lovely and pink as a baby's . . . (HÉLÈNE
kisses LISEN's *foot.)* You are truly a thoroughbred—and so
much finer and nobler than I!

LISEN: You must stop this now, and don't talk such nonsense! *(She rises.)* If you only knew. . . . But I . . .

HÉLÈNE: And I am sure you are just as good as you are
beautiful. . . . We—who only see your kind from a distance—with your fair, delicate faces, free from the rav-
ages of poverty and need, and untouched by the ugly
scars that envy marks us with. . . .

LISEN: Stop it, Hélène! One would almost think that you had
taken a romantic fancy to me!

HÉLÈNE: That's just it! I have! I've been told that I look a
little like you—as a blue anemone resembles a white one—
and that's why I see in you my better self: What I would
like to be, yet never *can* be. . . . You crossed my path
like a shining light—white as an angel—during these last
days of summer. . . . Now autumn is here, and the day
after tomorrow we go back to the city. . . . And then
we'll never see each other again. . . . You will never be
able to lift me up out of my drab surroundings—while I
might drag you down; and that is something I would not
want to do! I want to put you on a pinnacle—away up
high, and so far away that I can't see your shortcomings!
And so, Lisen, my first and only friend—goodbye. . . .

LISEN: Oh, no—I have heard enough! —Hélène! Do you
know whom I am?

(HÉLÈNE *is puzzled.)*

Very well—I am your sister!

HÉLÈNE: You—my sister? . . . What are you saying?

LISEN: You and I have the same father!

HÉLÈNE: You are my sister! My little sister! . . . But then
who is my father? I assume he is a naval commander,
since that's what your father is. . . . How stupid I am!

But he is married now—he must be, of course, since . . . Is he good to you? He was not so good to Mother, you know. . . .

LISEN: How do you know? —But aren't you glad that you have found a little sister now? One who doesn't cry all the time? . . .

HÉLÈNE: Of course I am—I am so happy I don't know what to say! . . .

(They embrace.)

But I can't be as glad as I would like to be, for I don't know what will happen now! What will Mother say? And what will happen when we meet my father?

LISEN: Let me take care of your mother! She can't have gone very far, I imagine. . . . But be sure to keep in the background until you are needed. . . . Now, my little one, come and give me a kiss first!

(They kiss each other.)

HÉLÈNE: My sister! How strange that word sounds—as strange as the word "father"—since I have not used it before. . . .

LISEN: Let's not chatter aimlessly now. Let's stick to the matter at hand. Do you believe that your mother would refuse to let you go, if you were invited to see us? Your sister and your father?

HÉLÈNE: Without Mother, you mean? Oh, she hates your— she hates my father—hates him indescribably!

LISEN: But suppose she had no cause to hate him? If you only knew how full of lies and delusions the world is! And of errors, mistakes and misapprehensions! My father once told me about a fellow cadet of his when he first went into the navy. . . . A gold watch disappeared from the cabin of one of the officers, and the young cadet was suspected of being the thief, God only knows why. . . . His comrades soon shunned him, and this embittered him so, changed him to such a degree, that it became impossible to have anything to do with him. He was constantly getting into fistfights, and he was finally forced to leave the service. Two years later the thief was apprehended—he was a boatswain. But what restitution could possibly be made to the innocent young man, since he had never been anything but a suspect? Yet the suspicion hung over him for the rest of his life, even though his innocence had been established. A malicious nickname given the youngster, he never lost either! The whole evil thing had grown up like a house, his bad reputation was built up and expanded—and when they tried to tear down the false foundation, the building remained, dangling in the air like the castle in *A Thousand and One Nights*. . . . So you see what can happen in this world! But even stranger things can happen! Take the case of the instrument-maker in the city of Arboga, for instance! He was branded an arsonist because someone had set fire to his place of business! . . . Or the case of a certain Andersson. This man was disgraced by being given the nickname of Andersson the Thief, because he had been the *victim* of a notorious theft!

HÉLÈNE: What you mean to say is that my father is not the kind of man I *think* he is?

LISEN: That's exactly what I mean.

HÉLÈNE: That's how I have seen him sometimes in my dreams—after having lost the remembrance of him. . . . Isn't he quite tall—and hasn't he a dark beard—and large blue eyes—a sailor's eyes?

LISEN: Yes—he is not unlike that!

HÉLÈNE: And . . . wait. . . . Now I remember. . . . You see this watch? You see this tiny compass attached to the chain? Where North is, the dial has an eye engraved on it. . . . Who gave it to me? Do you know?

LISEN: My father gave it to you. I was with him when he bought it.

HÉLÈNE: Then it is he I have seen so many times in the theatre, when I've been playing. . . . He would always sit in a box to the right of the stage and keep his opera glasses fixed on me. . . . I didn't dare mention it to Mother—she was always trying to keep me sheltered. . . . One time he threw a bouquet of flowers across the footlights—but Mother promptly burned them. . . . Could that have been he, do you think?

LISEN: Yes, that was he. . . . And, believe me, he has kept an eye on you all these years—as closely as he watches his compass needle. . . .

HÉLÈNE: And now you tell me I am going to meet him—

that he would like to see me? This is almost like a fairy tale. . . .

LISEN: But now it's no longer a fairy tale! I hear your mother coming—she is here. . . . You stay out of sight—let me come under fire first! . . .

HÉLÈNE: I feel as if something terrible were going to happen! I can feel it! Why can't there be peace and goodwill among human beings? Oh, if this were only over with! If only Mother would try to be good! . . . I'll say a prayer to God, asking Him to make her good. . . . But I wonder whether He can—or perhaps He does not wish to. I don't know. . . .

LISEN: He both can and will—if you will only have faith . . . a little faith in luck, at least—and in yourself—in your own ability. . . .

HÉLÈNE: Ability? To do what? To be inconsiderate and insincere? I can't do that, I can't! And we won't enjoy our happiness if it is bought with the tears of others—not for very long. . . .

LISEN: Quick—hurry up—go outside!

HÉLÈNE: I don't understand how you can think this will end happily.

LISEN: Ssh!

(HÉLÈNE *withdraws to the veranda.* THE MOTHER *enters.*)

LISEN: My dear Mrs. . . .

THE MOTHER: Miss, if you please . . .

LISEN: Your daughter . . .

THE MOTHER: Yes, I have a daughter—even though I am not married. . . . I am not the only one—and I am not ashamed of it. . . . What is it you want?

LISEN: I really came to ask permission for Hélène to come to a picnic that some of the summer guests have arranged.

THE MOTHER: Hasn't Hélène told you her answer?

LISEN: Yes, she answered quite correctly that I should see you. . . .

THE MOTHER: That's not a frank answer. (*Goes to the veranda door and calls to* HÉLÈNE.) Hélène! My child! Would you like to accept an invitation without your mother being asked?

HÉLÈNE (*enters*): Yes, if you have no objection. . . .

THE MOTHER: If I have no objection! Why should I make

a decision for you—a big girl like you? You must tell this young lady yourself what you want to do. If you would like to see your mother sit shamefully alone at home, while you are out having a good time . . . if you would like to have the guests at the picnic ask you where your mother is—so that you won't have to say, "Mother was not invited because of this and that and so forth and so on.". . . Make your own decision now!

LISEN: Madam, let us not quibble over words. I know what Hélène would like to do in this case. And I also know your habit of making her say what you want her to say. If you really care as much for your daughter as you say you do, you would do everything that was for her own good—even if you thought it humiliating for you.

THE MOTHER: Listen to me, my child! I know who you are and what your name is—even if I haven't had the honor of being introduced to you! I just wonder if you—at your age —can teach me anything, at my age. . . .

LISEN: Who knows? For the past six years—since my mother died—I have spent my time trying to bring up my younger brothers and sisters. . . . And I have found that there are some people who can never learn anything from life, no matter how old they may be.

THE MOTHER: Just what are you trying to tell me, young lady?

LISEN: What I want to tell you is this! Your daughter has an opportunity to come out among people—and, perhaps, either to advance her career and gain recognition, or to become engaged to and marry a young man of a good, respectable family. . . .

THE MOTHER: All that sounds fine, but where do I come in?

LISEN: We are not discussing you now—we are discussing your daughter! Can't you, for one moment, think of her without thinking about yourself?

THE MOTHER: Let me tell you something, miss! When I think about myself, I am also thinking about my daughter, for she has learned to love her mother. . . .

LISEN: I don't believe a word you say! She has clung to you merely because you kept her apart from everybody—and because she has to have somebody to cling to after you tore her away from her father. . . .

THE MOTHER: What's that you say?

LISEN: I am saying that you took her away from her father, after he refused to marry you! Refused to marry you because you had been unfaithful to him! You refused to let him see his own child—and you took revenge for your crime on both her and her father!

THE MOTHER: Hélène! Don't believe a word she says! Oh, to think that I would have to live to see this happen—to have a stranger come into my home and disgrace me before my own child!

HÉLÈNE (*steps forward; to* LISEN): You mustn't say anything bad about my mother! . . .

LISEN: I can't help it—I simply can't! I have to defend my father! . . . But I can tell that this conversation is nearing its end. . . . I merely wish to give you a piece of advice before leaving. Get rid of that bawdy woman, that procuress, who lives in this house under the name of Aunt Augusta! That is, if you don't want to destroy your daughter's reputation completely! That is point number one! Then get together all your receipts for money given you by my father for Hélène's upbringing and education—for you will soon be asked to account for every penny! That's point number two! And now I shall give you an extra piece of advice. Stop disgracing your daughter with your company on the streets—and above all, at the theatre . . . or she will soon have every door to advancement shut to her! And then you would be just as quick to sell her charms as you in the past have been eager to buy back your lost reputation at the expense of her future!

(THE MOTHER *collapses.*)

HÉLÈNE (*to* LISEN): Leave this house! You—for whom nothing is sacred—not even motherhood!

LISEN: Sacred—yes! . . . As sacred as the boys are when they spit out their prayers! That's holiness, too!

HÉLÈNE: It looks to me now as though your only reason for coming here was to tear down, not to mend. . . .

LISEN: Yes—I came here to see my father given restitution—my father who was as innocent as the man accused of arson, you remember. . . . I also came here to raise you up—after you had been made the victim of a woman who can only be rehabilitated if she withdraws to some place where no one will molest her, and where she won't bother others. That is why I came here. And now it is done—so, goodbye!

THE MOTHER: Don't go yet, miss! I have something I want to say to you first! You didn't come here just to speak about . . . what you just said. . . . You came to ask Hélène to your home, didn't you?

LISEN: I did, yes. We wanted her to meet the director of the Grand Theatre . . . he is interested in Hélène.

THE MOTHER: You really mean it? The director himself! And you didn't say one word about that! Why, certainly . . . certainly Hélène will come! Yes, alone—without me!

(HÉLÈNE *makes a confused gesture of disapproval.*)

LISEN: Well, now—now I see—that you are human, after all. Hélène, your mother is giving you permission to come! Do you hear?

HÉLÈNE: But I don't care to go now. . . .

THE MOTHER: What nonsense is this?

HÉLÈNE: No! I won't fit in there! I won't feel at home among people who have contempt for my mother!

THE MOTHER: Stop acting silly! Do you want to stand in your own way and ruin your career? Put your clothes on and get dressed right away, so that you are presentable. . . .

HÉLÈNE: No—I am not going! I can't leave you alone, Mother—now that I know everything. I can never be happy again. . . . I can never have any faith in anything. . . .

LISEN (*to* THE MOTHER): Now you are reaping the fruits of what you have sown. . . . If ever a man should come along and marry your daughter, you will be sitting alone in your old age and have time to regret your indiscretions! Goodbye! (*She goes over to* HÉLÈNE *and kisses her on the forehead.*) Goodbye, my sister!

HÉLÈNE: Goodbye!

LISEN: Look me in the eye and let me see a gleam of hope!

HÉLÈNE: I can't. And I can't thank you for your good intentions, either. You have done me more harm than you think. . . . I was slumbering in the sunshine on a wooded hillside, and you woke me with a snakebite.

LISEN: Go back to sleep, and I'll come and wake you with

a song and with flowers. . . . Goodnight now! And sleep well! *(She leaves.)*

THE MOTHER: An angel of light dressed in white, ha! Why, she is a regular demon! A regular demon! That's what she is! And you! What a fool you are! What kind of silly nonsense is this? You don't have to be so sensitive when people behave so brutally!

HÉLÈNE: But when I think of all that you have told me! So much that is untrue! And making me tell lies about my father all these years. . . .

THE MOTHER: Ah! What's the good of worrying about the snows of yesteryear?

HÉLÈNE: And then . . . there is Aunt Augusta. . . .

THE MOTHER: Keep quiet! Aunt Augusta is a thoroughly fine woman, and you owe her a great deal. . . .

HÉLÈNE: That isn't true, either! . . . You know that it was my father who paid for my education!

THE MOTHER: Yes—but I had to live, too, didn't I? You are so petty, so small-minded. And vindictive, too. Can't you overlook an innocent little lie? Ah, there is Aunt Augusta! Come now, let's enjoy ourselves as best we can—in our own small way.

AUNT AUGUSTA *(enters gustily)*: Why, yes—it was really he! You see, I wasn't so very wrong, after all, was I?

THE MOTHER: Yes—but let's not bother about that worthless creature anymore. . . .

HÉLÈNE: Don't call him that, Mother! You know it isn't true!

AUNT AUGUSTA: What isn't true?

HÉLÈNE: Come on and let us play a game of cards! I can't pull down the walls it has taken you two so many years to build up! Let's play! *(She seats herself at the card table and starts shuffling the cards.)*

THE MOTHER: Well . . . I am glad to see you are being a sensible girl at last!

CURTAIN

The Proposal

A Jest in One Act

by ANTON CHEKHOV

Translated from the Russian
by CONSTANCE GARNETT

Anton Chekhov (1860–1904)

Physician and humanitarian, Anton Chekhov became Russia's greatest short-story writer and playwright. He was born in Taganrog, and was the son of an impoverished grocer. Chekhov had an unhappy childhood that was relieved only by his attending the local theater and writing dramatic skits to entertain his family and relatives.

After graduation from the local high school in 1879, he entered Moscow University as a medical student. In the next five years, while working for his medical degree, he wrote several hundred humorous stories and articles for newspapers and magazines to support himself and his family. In 1884 he received his medical degree, and from his twenty-fifth to his thirty-first year he wrote eleven one-act plays, eight of which were light comedies like *The Proposal*.

For a century before Chekhov's time, one-act "vaudevilles" had entertained Russian audiences. At first these dramatic "jokes" consisted of adaptations of French farces in verse or prose. For the most part, they were situation comedies with stock "humour" characters dominated by one passion, such as anger, jealousy, or fear. Chekhov modified the traditional genre by creating believable characters, writing sparkling dialogue, and substituting satirical, humorous situations for the customary slapstick. Vladimir Nemirovich-Danchenko, one of the founders of the famous Moscow Art Theater, shrewdly explained the success of Chekhov's one-act comedies: "The charm of these 'jokes' of his is due not only to their comic situations but also to the fact that their characters are living people and not stage vaudeville figures and that their dialogue is full of humour and characteristic dramatic surprises."*

---

* Quoted by David Magarshack in his *Chekhov the Dramatist* (New York: Hill & Wang, 1960), p. 54.

Different as these eight stylized comedies are from the full-length plays of his maturity—*The Sea Gull, Uncle Vanya, The Three Sisters,* and *The Cherry Orchard*—they reveal the gaiety and the compassionate understanding of a true humorist. The popularity of these miniature masterpieces has remained undiminished from their first performances to our own time.

In *The Proposal* Chekhov reveals his artistic ingenuity by constructing his comedy in a frame pattern that cleverly suggests the theme. The play opens with Tchubukov's courteous greeting of Lomov, and the father's joyful acceptance of the proposal of the nervous suitor. It ends with Tchubukov's attempt to establish the amenities of polite society by calling for champagne to celebrate the nuptials. In between these polite gestures, comic confusion reigns as a series of violent quarrels erupt to reveal the true characters of the hypocritical father, the snobbish daughter, and the proud hypochondriac. The dispute over the ownership of the Volovyi meadows quickly shifts to an argument concerning their dogs and degenerates into family recriminations and the exchange of personal insults. The Molièresque satire on bourgeois possessiveness and stubborn self-esteem takes an ironic turn when Natalya Stepanova discovers to her dismay that her pride has driven her suitor away. The play reaches its climax with the supposed death of the overexcited Lomov, and ends with the hasty betrothal of the quarreling lovers.

The central conflict of the farce consists of a clever balancing between the forces of attraction and repulsion. Both Natalya and Lomov have a strong desire to get married, but are separated by their angry stubbornness. As the curtain comes down, we realize that we have witnessed only the first quarrel of a lifelong argument between the tempestuous couple.

Chekhov wrote *The Proposal* in November, 1888, six months after his successful "vaudeville" *The Bear.* Although he wrote it "specially for the provincial stage," it was successfully performed in Moscow and in St. Petersburg. In fact, it became so famous that in September, 1889, it was performed for the Czar at his summer residence.

CHARACTERS

STEPAN STEPANOVITCH TCHUBUKOV,
   a landowner

NATALYA STEPANOVNA,
   his daughter, aged 25

IVAN VASSILYEVITCH LOMOV,
   a neighbor of TCHUBUKOV's, a healthy, well nourished, but
   hypochondriacal landowner

> *Drawing room in* TCHUBUKOV's *house.*
> TCHUBUKOV *and* LOMOV; *the latter en-*
> *ters wearing evening dress and white*
> *gloves.*

TCHUBUKOV (*going to meet him*): My darling, whom do I see? Ivan Vassilyevitch! Delighted! (*Shakes hands*) Well, this is a surprise, dearie. . . . How are you?

LOMOV: I thank you. And pray, how are you?

TCHUBUKOV: We are getting on all right, thanks to your prayers, my angel, and all the rest of it. Please sit down. . . . It's too bad, you know, to forget your neighbors, darling. But, my dear, why this ceremoniousness? A swallowtail, gloves, and all the rest of it! Are you going visiting, my precious?

LOMOV: No, I have only come to see you, honored Stepan Stepanovitch.

TCHUBUKOV: Then why the swallowtail, my charmer? As though you were paying calls on New Year's Day!

LOMOV: You see, this is how it is. (*Takes his arm*) I have come, honored Stepan Stepanovitch, to trouble you with a request. I have more than once had the honor of asking for your assistance, and you have always, so to speak— but pardon me, I am agitated. I will have a drink of water, honored Stepan Stepanovitch. (*Drinks water*)

TCHUBUKOV (*aside*): Come to ask for money! I am not going to give it to him. (*To him*) What is it, my beauty?

LOMOV: You see, Honor Stepanovitch—I beg your pardon, Stepan Honoritch. . . . I am dreadfully agitated, as you see. In short, no one but you can assist me, though, of course, I have done nothing to deserve it, and . . . and have no right to reckon upon your assistance. . . .

TCHUBUKOV: Oh, don't spin it out, dearie. Come to the point. Well?

LOMOV: Immediately—in a moment. The fact is that I have come to ask for the hand of your daughter, Natalya Stepanovna.

TCHUBUKOV (*joyfully*): You precious darling! Ivan Vassilyevitch, say it again! I can't believe my ears.

LOMOV: I have the honor to ask——

TCHUBUKOV (*interrupting*): My darling! I am delighted, and all the rest of it. Yes, indeed, and all that sort of thing. (*Embraces and kisses him*) I have been hoping for it for ages. It has always been my wish. (*Sheds a tear*) And I have always loved you, my angel, as though you were my own son. God give you both love and good counsel, and all the rest of it. I have always wished for it. . . . Why am I standing here like a post? I am stupefied with joy, absolutely stupefied! Oh, from the bottom of my heart. . . . I'll go and call Natasha, and that sort of thing.

LOMOV (*touched*): Honored Stepan Stepanovitch, what do you think? May I hope that she will accept me?

TCHUBUKOV: A beauty like you, and she not accept you! I'll be bound she is as lovesick as a cat, and all the rest of it. . . . In a minute. (*Goes out*)

LOMOV: I am cold—I am trembling all over, as though I were in for an examination. The great thing is to make up one's mind. If one thinks about it too long, hesitates, discusses it, waits for one's ideal or for real love, one will never get married. . . . Brr! I am cold. Natalya Stepanovna is an excellent manager, not bad looking, educated—what more do I want? But I am beginning to have noises in my head. I am so upset. (*Sips water*) And get married I must. To begin with, I am thirty-five—a critical age, so to speak. And secondly, I need a regular, well-ordered life. . . . I have valvular disease of the heart, continual palpitations. I am hasty, and am very easily upset. . . . Now, for instance, my lips are quivering and my right eyelid is twitching. . . . But my worst trouble is with sleep. No sooner have I got into bed and just begun to drop asleep, than I have a shooting pain in my left side and a stabbing at my shoulder and my head. . . . I leap up like a madman. I walk about a little and lie down again, but no sooner do I drop off than there's the shooting pain in my side again. And the same thing twenty times over! . . .

(Enter NATALYA STEPANOVNA*)*

NATALYA: Well, so it's you! Why, and Papa said a purchaser had come for the goods! How do you do, Ivan Vassilyevitch?

LOMOV: How do you do, honored Natalya Stepanovna!

NATALYA: Excuse my apron and negligee. We are shelling peas for drying. How is it you have not been to see us for so long? Sit down. *(They sit down)* Will you have some lunch?

LOMOV: No, thank you, I have already lunched.

NATALYA: Won't you smoke? Here are the matches. . . . It's a magnificent day, but yesterday it rained so hard that the men did no work at all. How many haycocks have you got out? Only fancy, I have been too eager and had the whole meadow mown, and now I am sorry—I am afraid the hay will rot. It would have been better to wait. But what's this? I do believe you have got on your dress coat! That's something new. Are you going to a ball, or what? And, by the way, you are looking nice. . . . Why are you such a swell, really?

LOMOV *(in agitation)*: You see, honored Natalya Stepanovna. . . . The fact is that I have made up my mind to ask you to listen to me. . . . Of course, you will be surprised, and even angry, but I . . . It's horribly cold!

NATALYA: What is it? *(A pause)* Well?

LOMOV: I will try to be brief. You are aware, honored Natalya Stepanovna, that from my earliest childhood I had the honor of knowing your family. My late aunt and her husband, from whom, as you know, I inherited the estate, always entertained a profound respect for your Papa and your late Mamma. The family of the Lomovs and the family of the Tchubukovs have always been on the most friendly and, one may say, intimate terms. Moreover, as you are aware, my land is in close proximity to yours. If you remember, my Volovyi meadows are bounded by your birch copse.

NATALYA: Excuse my interrupting you. You say "*my* Volovyi meadows." . . . But are they yours?

LOMOV: Yes, mine.

NATALYA: Well, what next! The Volovyi meadows are ours, not yours!

LOMOV: No, they are mine, honored Natalya Stepanovna.

NATALYA: That's news to me. How do they come to be yours?

LOMOV: How do they come to be mine? I am speaking of the Volovyi meadows that run like a wedge between your birch copse and the Charred Swamp.

NATALYA: Quite so. Those are ours.

LOMOV: No, you are mistaken, honored Natalya Stepanovna, they are mine.

NATALYA: Think what you are saying, Ivan Vassilyevitch! Have they been yours long?

LOMOV: What do you mean by "long"? As long as I can remember they have always been ours.

NATALYA: Well, there you must excuse me.

LOMOV: There is documentary evidence for it, honored Natalya Stepanovna. The Volovyi meadows were once a matter of dispute, that is true, but now everyone knows that they are mine. And there can be no dispute about it. Kindly consider . . . my aunt's grandmother gave over those meadows to the peasants of your father's grandfather for their use, rent free, for an indefinite period, in return for their firing her bricks. The peasants of your father's grandfather enjoyed the use of the meadows, rent free, for some forty years, and grew used to looking upon them as their own; afterwards, when the settlement came about after the emancipation . . .

NATALYA: It is not at all as you say! Both my grandfather and my great-grandfather considered their land reached to the Charred Swamp—so the Volovyi meadows were ours. I can't understand what there is to argue about. It's really annoying!

LOMOV: I will show you documents, Natalya Stepanovna.

NATALYA: No, you are simply joking, or trying to tease me. . . . A nice sort of surprise! We have owned the land nearly three hundred years, and all of a sudden we are told that the land is not ours! Forgive me, Ivan Vassilyevitch, but I positively cannot believe my ears. . . . I don't care about the meadows. They are not more than fifteen acres, and they are only worth some three hundred rubles, but I am revolted by injustice. You may say what you like, but I cannot endure injustice!

LOMOV: Listen to me, I implore you. The peasants of your father's grandfather, as I had already the honor to inform you, made bricks for my aunt's grandmother. My aunt's grandmother, wishing to do something for them . . .

NATALYA: Grandfather, grandmother, aunt. . . . I don't understand a word of it. The meadows are ours, and that's all about it.

LOMOV: They are mine.

NATALYA: They are ours. If you go on arguing for two days, if you put on fifteen dress coats, they are still ours, ours, ours! . . . I don't want what's yours, but I don't want to lose what's mine. . . . You can take that as you please!

LOMOV: I do not care about the meadows, Natalya Stepanovna, but it is a matter of principle. If you like, I will make you a present of them.

NATALYA: I might make you a present of them, they are mine. All this is very queer, Ivan Vassilyevitch, to say the least of it. Hitherto we have looked upon you as a good neighbor—a friend. Last year we lent you our threshing machine, and through that we couldn't finish our threshing till November; and you treat us as if we were gypsies! Make me a present of my own land! Excuse me, but that is not neighborly. To my thinking it is positively impertinent, if you care to know. . . .

LOMOV: According to you I am a usurper, then? I've never snatched other people's land, madam, and I will allow no one to accuse me of such a thing. . . . *(Goes rapidly to the decanter and drinks water)* The Volovyi meadows are mine!

NATALYA: It's not true: they are ours!

LOMOV: They are mine!

NATALYA: That's not true. I'll prove it. I'll send our mowers to cut the hay there today!

LOMOV: What?

NATALYA: My laborers will be there today.

LOMOV: I'll kick them out.

NATALYA: Don't you dare!

LOMOV *(clutches at his heart)*: The Volovyi meadows are mine! Do you understand? Mine!

NATALYA: Don't shout, please. You can shout and choke with rage when you are at home, if you like; but here I beg you to keep within bounds.

LOMOV: If it were not for these terrible, agonizing palpitations, madam—if it were not for the throbbing in my temples, I should speak to you very differently. *(Shouts)* The Volovyi meadows are mine!

NATALYA: Ours!

LOMOV: Mine!

NATALYA: Ours!

LOMOV: Mine!

(Enter TCHUBUKOV.)

TCHUBUKOV: What is it? What are you shouting about?

NATALYA: Papa, explain to this gentleman, please: to whom do the Volovyi meadows belong—to him or to us?

TCHUBUKOV *(to* LOMOV): My chicken, the meadows are ours.

LOMOV: But upon my word, Stepan Stepanovitch, how did they come to be yours? Do you, at least, be reasonable. My aunt's grandmother gave over the meadows for temporary gratuitous use to your grandfather's peasants. The peasants made use of the land for forty years and got used to regarding it as their own; but when the settlement came . . .

TCHUBUKOV: Allow me, my precious. . . . You forget that the peasants did not pay your grandmother rent and all the rest of it, just because the ownership of the land was in dispute, and so on. . . . And now every dog knows that they are ours. You can't have seen the map.

LOMOV: I will prove to you that they are mine.

TCHUBUKOV: You never will, my pet.

LOMOV: Yes, I will.

TCHUBUKOV: Why are you shouting, my love? You will prove nothing at all by shouting. I don't desire what is yours, and don't intend to give up what is mine. Why ever should I? If it comes to that, my dear, if you intend to wrangle over the meadows, I would rather give them to the peasants than to you, that I would!

LOMOV: I don't understand it. What right have you to give away another man's property?

TCHUBUKOV: Allow me to decide for myself whether I have the right or no. I may say, young man, I am not accustomed to being spoken to in that tone, and all the rest of it. I am twice as old as you are, young man, and I beg you to speak to me without getting excited, and all the rest of it.

LOMOV: Why, you simply take me for a fool and are laughing at me! You call my land yours, and then you expect me to be cool about it and to speak to you properly! That's not the way good neighbors behave, Stepan Stepanovitch. You are not a neighbor, but a usurper!

TCHUBUKOV: What? What did you say?

NATALYA: Papa, send the men at once to mow the meadows.

TCHUBUKOV (to LOMOV): What did you say, sir?

NATALYA: The Volovyi meadows are ours, and I won't give them up. I won't! I won't!

LOMOV: We will see about that. I'll prove to you in court that they are mine.

TCHUBUKOV: In court? You can take it into court, sir, and all the rest of it! You can! I know you—you are only waiting for a chance to go to law, and so on. . . . A pettifogging character! All your family were fond of litigation —all of them!

LOMOV: I beg you not to insult my family. The Lomovs have all been honest men, and not one of them has ever been on his trial for embezzling money like your uncle!

TCHUBUKOV: Well, you Lomovs have all been mad!

NATALYA: Every one of them—every one of them!

TCHUBUKOV: Your grandfather was a dipsomaniac, and your youngest aunt, Nastasya Mihailovna, ran away with an architect, and so on.

LOMOV: And your mother was a hunchback. (Clutches at his heart.) The shooting pain in my side! . . . The blood has rushed to my head. . . . Holy Saints! . . . Water!

TCHUBUKOV: And your father was a gambler and a glutton!

NATALYA: And there was no one like your aunt for talking scandal!

LOMOV: My left leg has all gone numb. . . . And you are an intriguer! . . . Oh, my heart! . . . And it is no secret that before the elections you . . . There are flashes before my eyes! . . . Where is my hat?

NATALYA: It's mean! It's dishonest! It's disgusting!

TCHUBUKOV: And you yourself are a viperish, double-faced, mischief-making man. Yes, indeed!

LOMOV: Here is my hat. . . . My heart! . . . Which way am I

to go? Where's the door? Oh! I believe I am dying. I've lost the use of my leg. *(Goes toward the door)*

TCHUBUKOV *(calling after him)*: Never set foot within my door again!

NATALYA: Take it into court! We shall see!

(Lomov goes out, staggering)

TCHUBUKOV: Damnation take him! *(Walks about in excitement)*

NATALYA: What a wretch! How is one to believe in good neighbors after that!

TCHUBUKOV: Blackguard! Scarecrow!

NATALYA: The object! Collars other people's land—then abuses them!

TCHUBUKOV: And that noodle—that eyesore—had the face to make a proposal, and all the rest of it. Just fancy, a proposal!

NATALYA: What proposal?

TCHUBUKOV: Why, he came here on purpose to propose to you!

NATALYA: To propose? To me? Why didn't you tell me so before?

TCHUBUKOV: And he had got himself up in his dress coat on purpose! The sausage! The shrimp!

NATALYA: To me? A proposal! Ah! *(She falls into an armchair and moans)* Bring him back! Bring him back! Oh, bring him back!

TCHUBUKOV: Bring whom back?

NATALYA: Make haste, make haste! I feel faint! Bring him back! *(Hysterics)*

TCHUBUKOV: What is it! What's the matter? *(Clutches at his head)* I do have a life of it! I shall shoot myself! I shall hang myself! They'll be the death of me!

NATALYA: I am dying! Bring him back!

TCHUBUKOV: Tfoo! Directly. Don't howl. *(Runs off)*

NATALYA *(alone, moans)*: What have we done! Bring him back! Bring him back!

TCHUBUKOV *(runs in)*: He is just coming in, and all the rest of it. Damnation take him! Ough! Talk to him yourself, I don't want to. . . .

NATALYA *(moans)*: Bring him back!

TCHUBUKOV *(shouts)*: He is coming, I tell you! What a task

it is, O Lord, to be the father of a grown-up daughter!
I shall cut my throat! I shall certainly cut my throat!
We've abused the man, put him to shame, kicked him
out, and it is all your doing—your doing!

NATALYA: No, it was yours!

TCHUBUKOV: Oh, it's my fault, so that's it! (LOMOV *appears
at the door*) Well, talk to him yourself. (*Goes out*)

(*Enter* LOMOV *in a state of collapse*)

LOMOV: Fearful palpitations! My leg is numb . . . there's
a stitch in my side. . . .

NATALYA: Forgive us; we were too hasty, Ivan Vassilyevitch.
I remember now: the Volovyi meadows really are yours.

LOMOV: My heart is throbbing frightfully. . . . The meadows
are mine. . . . There's a twitching in both my eyelids.

NATALYA: Yes, they are yours, they are. Sit down. (*They sit
down*) We were wrong.

LOMOV: I acted from principle. . . . I do not value the land,
but I value the principle. . . .

NATALYA: Just so, the principle. . . . Let us talk of something else.

LOMOV: Especially as I have proofs. My aunt's grandmother
gave the peasants of your father's grandfather . . .

NATALYA: Enough, enough about that. . . . (*Aside*) I don't
know how to begin. (*To him*) Shall you soon be going
shooting?

LOMOV: I expect to go grouse-shooting after the harvest,
honored Natalya Stepanovna. Oh! did you hear? Only
fancy, I had such a misfortune! My Tracker, whom I
think you know, has fallen lame.

NATALYA: What a pity! How did it happen?

LOMOV: I don't know. . . . He must have put his paw out of
joint, or perhaps some other dog bit it. . . . (*Sighs*) My
very best dog, to say nothing of the money I have spent
on him! You know I paid Mironov a hundred and twenty-
five rubles for him.

NATALYA: You gave too much, Ivan Vassilyevitch!

LOMOV: Well, to my mind it was very cheap. He is a delightful dog.

NATALYA: Father gave eighty-five rubles for his Backer, and
Backer is a much better dog than your Tracker.

LOMOV: Backer a better dog than Tracker? What nonsense! *(Laughs)* Backer a better dog than Tracker!

NATALYA: Of course he is better. It's true that Backer is young yet—he is hardly a full-grown dog—but for points and cleverness even Voltchanetsky hasn't one to beat him.

LOMOV: Excuse me, Natalya Stepanovna, but you forget that your Backer has a pug jaw, and a dog with a pug jaw is never any good for gripping.

NATALYA: A pug jaw! That's the first time I've heard so.

LOMOV: I assure you the lower jaw is shorter than the upper.

NATALYA: Why, have you measured?

LOMOV: Yes. He is all right for coursing, no doubt, but for gripping he'd hardly do.

NATALYA: In the first place, our Backer is a pedigree dog, son of Harness and Chisel, but you can't even tell what breed your spotty piebald is. . . . Then he is as old and ugly as a broken-down horse.

LOMOV: He is old, but I wouldn't exchange him for half a dozen of your Backers. . . . How could I? Tracker is a dog, but Backer—there can be no question about it. Every huntsman has packs and packs of dogs like your Backer. Twenty-five rubles would be a good price for him.

NATALYA: There is a demon of contradictoriness in you today, Ivan Vassilyevitch. First you make out that the meadows are yours, then that your Tracker is a better dog than Backer. I don't like a man to say what he does not think. You know perfectly well that Backer is worth a hundred of your . . . stupid Trackers. Why, then, say the opposite?

LOMOV: I see, Natalya Stepanovna, that you think I am blind or a fool. Do you understand that your Backer has a pug jaw?

NATALYA: It's not true!

LOMOV: It is!

NATALYA *(shouts)*: It's not true!

LOMOV: Why are you shouting, madam?

NATALYA: Why do you talk nonsense? This is revolting! It's time your Tracker was shot—and you compare him to Backer!

LOMOV: Excuse me, I cannot continue this argument. I have palpitations.

NATALYA: I have noticed that men argue most about hunting who know least about it.

LOMOV: Madam, I beg you to be silent. My heart is bursting. *(Shouts)* Be silent!

NATALYA: I will not be silent till you own that Backer is a hundred times better than your Tracker.

LOMOV: A hundred times worse. Plague take your Backer! My temples . . . my eyes . . . my shoulder. . . .

NATALYA: There's no need for plague to take your fool of a Tracker—he is as good as dead already.

LOMOV *(weeping)*: Be silent! My heart is bursting!

NATALYA: I won't be silent.

(Enter TCHUBUKOV*)*

TCHUBUKOV *(coming in)*: What now?

NATALYA: Papa, tell me truly, on your conscience, which is the better dog—our Backer or his Tracker?

LOMOV: Stepan Stepanovitch, I implore you to tell me one thing only: has your Backer a pug jaw or not? Yes or no?

TCHUBUKOV: And what if he has? It's of no consequence. Anyway, there's no better dog in the whole district, and all the rest of it.

LOMOV: But my Tracker is better, isn't he? Honestly?

TCHUBUKOV: Don't excite yourself, my precious. Your Tracker certainly has his good qualities. . . . He is a well-bred dog, has good legs, and is well set-up, and all the rest of it. But the dog, if you care to know, my beauty, has two serious defects: he is old and is snub-nosed.

LOMOV: Excuse me, I have palpitations. . . . Let us take the facts. . . . If you will kindly remember, at Maruskin's my Tracker kept shoulder to shoulder with the Count's Swinger, while your Backer was a good half-mile behind.

TCHUBUKOV: Yes, he was, because the Count's huntsman gave him a crack with his whip.

LOMOV: He deserved it. All the other dogs were after the fox, but Backer got hold of a sheep.

TCHUBUKOV: That's not true! . . . Darling, I am hot-tempered, and I beg you to drop this conversation. He lashed him because everyone is jealous of another man's dog. . . . Yes, they are all envious! And you are not free from blame on that score either, sir. As soon as you notice, for instance, that someone's dog is better than your Tracker, at once you begin with this and that, and all the rest of it. I remember it all!

LOMOV: I remember it too!

TCHUBUKOV (*mimics him*): "I remember it too!" And what do you remember?

LOMOV: Palpitations! . . . My leg has no feeling in it. I can't . . .

NATALYA (*mimicking him*): "Palpitations!". . . A fine sportsman! You ought to be lying on the stove in the kitchen squashing black beetles instead of hunting foxes. Palpitations!

TCHUBUKOV: Yes, you are a fine sportsman, really! With your palpitations you ought to stay at home, instead of jolting in the saddle. It wouldn't matter if you hunted, but you only ride out to wrangle and interfere with other men's dogs, and all the rest of it. I am hot-tempered; let us drop this subject. You are not a sportsman at all.

LOMOV: And you—are you a sportsman? You only go to the hunt to intrigue and make up to the Count. . . . My heart! . . . You are an intriguer!

TCHUBUKOV: What? Me an intriguer? (*Shouts*) Hold your tongue!

LOMOV: Intriguer!

TCHUBUKOV: Milksop! Puppy!

LOMOV: Old rat! Jesuit!

TCHUBUKOV: Hold your tongue, or I'll shoot you with a filthy gun like a partridge! Noodle!

LOMOV: Everyone knows—oh, my heart—that your wife used to beat you. . . . My leg . . . my forehead . . . my eyes! . . . I shall drop! I shall drop!

TCHUBUKOV: And you go in terror of your housekeeper!

LOMOV: Oh, oh, oh! My heart has burst! I can't feel my shoulder—what has become of my shoulder? I am dying! (*Falls into an armchair*) A doctor! (*Swoons*)

TCHUBUKOV: Puppy! Milksop! Noodle! I feel faint! (*Drinks water*) Faint!

NATALYA: You are a fine sportsman! You don't know how to sit on your horse. (*To her father*) Papa, what's the matter with him? Papa! Look, Papa! (*Shrieks*) Ivan Vassilyevitch! He is dead!

TCHUBUKOV: I feel faint! I can't breathe! Give me air!

NATALYA: He is dead! (*Shakes* LOMOV *by the sleeve*) Ivan

Vassilyevitch! Ivan Vassilyevitch! What have we done! He is dead! *(Falls into an armchair)* A doctor! A doctor! *(Hysterics)*

TCHUBUKOV: Och! What is it? What do you want?

NATALYA *(moans)*: He is dead! He is dead!

TCHUBUKOV: Who is dead? *(Looking at* LOMOV) He really is dead! Holy Saints! Water! A doctor! *(Holds a glass of water to* LOMOV's *lips)* Drink! . . . No, he won't drink. So he is dead, and all the rest of it. Why don't I put a bullet through my brains? Why is it I haven't cut my throat? What am I waiting for? Give me a knife! Give me a pistol! *(LOMOV makes a slight movement)* I believe he is reviving. . . . Have a drink of water. That's right.

LOMOV: Flashes—dizziness—where am I?

TCHUBUKOV: You'd better make haste and get married—and go to the devil! She consents. *(Joins the hands of* LOMOV *and his daughter)* She accepts you, and all the rest of it. I give you my blessing, and so on. Only leave me in peace.

LOMOV: Eh? What? *(Getting up)* Who?

TCHUBUKOV: She accepts you. Well? Kiss each other and , , , be damned to you!

NATALYA *(moans)*: He is alive! Yes, yes, I accept.

TCHUBUKOV: Kiss!

LOMOV: Eh? Whom? *(Kisses* NATALYA STEPANOVNA) Delighted! Excuse me, what's the point? Oh, yes, I understand! Palpitations . . . dizziness . . . I am happy, Natalya Stepanovna. *(Kisses her hand)* My leg is numb!

NATALYA: I . . . I, too, am happy.

TCHUBUKOV: It's a load off my heart! Ough!

NATALYA: But . . . still you must admit now that Tracker is not as good a dog as Backer.

LOMOV: He is better!

NATALYA: He is worse!

TCHUBUKOV: Well, here's the beginning of family happiness! Champagne!

LOMOV: He is better!

NATALYA: He is not! He is not! He is not!

TCHUBUKOV *(trying to shout them down)*: Champagne! Champagne!

CURTAIN

The Man of
Destiny

by GEORGE BERNARD SHAW

George Bernard Shaw (1856–1950)

Although Shaw himself laid claim to fifteen reputations —critic of drama, art and music; Fabian Socialist; Irish iconoclast, novelist, etc.—it is Shaw the dramatist, probably the greatest since Shakespeare, who interests us today. After championing the musical and dramatic rebels Wagner and Ibsen in his books *The Perfect Wagnerite* and *The Quintessence of Ibsenism,* Shaw began his career as a playwright by writing two controversial problem plays, *Widower's Houses* (1892) and *Mrs. Warren's Profession* (1893). His first stage successes were the satirical comedies *Arms and the Man* and *Candida,* written in 1894. In the autumn of the following year he wrote *The Man of Destiny,* "a bravura piece to display the virtuosity of the two principal performers."

Shaw hoped that Ellen Terry, the famous leading lady in Sir Henry Irving's Lyceum Theatre, would play the part of The Strange Lady. (Shaw had already begun his love affair with her by correspondence.) But because as a drama critic, he had attacked the romantic melodramas produced at the Lyceum and the histrionic self-glorification of Irving in his lead roles, Sir Henry, after a two years' delay, finally rejected the play. It was also turned down by the popular actor Richard Mansfield, who had introduced Shaw to the American stage with *Arms and the Man. The Man of Destiny* was finally presented in a poorly improvised performance at the Grand Theatre in Croyden on July 1, 1897. Shaw himself was present on this disastrous first night when a "rowdy little kitten, fluffy but disreputable" twice strayed onto the stage. In spite of this unhappy debut, the play has been successfully performed all over the world as Shaw's first treatment of an important historical figure, to be followed by his greater characterizations in his full-length chronicle plays, *Caesar and Cleopatra* (1898) and *Saint Joan* (1923).

As Shaw in *Arms and the Man* had deglamorized the romantic notions of war—whether found in Shakespeare's historical plays or in *Othello,* in countless Victorian melodramas, or in conventional operas—so he humanized the historical hero (and heroine) by creating him in his own image. Napoleon, Caesar, and Joan of Arc were presented as recognizable people possessed of intelligence, of self-confidence that derived from self-knowledge, of humor combined with practicality. Their early trials have given them a self-sufficiency and faith in their destiny to be honest leaders who use their power to destroy the outmoded conventions of their times. All history, Shaw believed, can only be understood in subjective terms; human beings and their motivations have not changed through the centuries. He denied the commonly accepted Victorian concept of progress in historical development. In his notes to *Caesar and Cleopatra* he shrewdly observed, "All the savagery, barbarism, dark ages and the rest of it which we have any record as existing in the past exists at the present moment." Although his historical heroes possess the charismatic appeal that easily attracts followers, they are not supermen. We can readily identify with them because of their common-sense rationality.

The young Napoleon in *The Man of Destiny* has a realistic understanding of human nature and of the power of gunpowder. He is a prodigious worker, with a remarkable knowledge of geography and logistics. Unhampered by the classic, traditional methods of warfare, he has no difficulty in defeating "the respectable regular army" of the Austrians. Only in The Strange Lady does he encounter a worthy antagonist who recognizes that the secret of his power lies in his faith combined with the courage to follow his own destiny.

Like many of Shaw's plays, *The Man of Destiny* is an antiromantic satire built on the framework of a melodrama. Exposing the folly of traditional warfare (a horse won the battle of Lodi), the hypocrisy of the moral and respectable English, and the infidelity of Napoleon's wife, Josephine, the play utilizes the conventional trappings of melodrama— the clash of wills between two wily opponents, the stolen letter, the suspected spy, the phony disguise, etc. But Shaw has mastered the successful theatrical device of pouring new wine into old bottles. The play is redeemed by its brilliant characterizations, its clever, paradoxical dialogue, and the mutual puncturing of the heroic poses of the two antagonists. *The Man of Destiny* is an excellent example of Louis Kronenberger's concept of comedy. "Comedy is criticism, then, because it exposes human beings for what they are in contrast to what they profess to be."*

---

* *The Thread of Laughter* (New York: Alfred A. Knopf, 1952), p. 5.

CHARACTERS

Napoleon Bonaparte

Giuseppe Grandi

The Strange Lady

The Lieutenant

The twelfth of May, 1796, in north Italy, at Tavazzano, on the road from Lodi to Milan. The afternoon sun is blazing serenely over the plains of Lombardy, treating the Alps with respect and the anthills with indulgence, neither disgusted by the basking of the swine in the villages nor hurt by its cool reception in the churches, but ruthlessly disdainful of two hordes of mischievous insects which are the French and Austrian armies. Two days before, at Lodi, the Austrians tried to prevent the French from crossing the river by the narrow bridge there; but the French, commanded by a general aged 27, Napoleon Bonaparte, who does not respect the rules of war, rushed the fireswept bridge, supported by a tremendous cannonade in which the young general assisted with his own hands. Cannonading is his technical speciality: he has been trained in the artillery under the old régime, and made perfect in the military arts of shirking his duties, swindling the paymaster over travelling expenses, and dignifying war with the noise and smoke of cannon, as depicted in all military portraits. He is, however, an original observer, and has perceived, for the first time since the invention of gunpowder, that a cannon ball, if it strikes a man, will kill him. To a thorough grasp of this remarkable discovery he adds a highly evolved faculty for physical geography and for the calculation of times and distances. He has prodigious powers of work, and a clear realistic knowledge of human nature in public affairs, having seen it exhaustively tested in that department during the French Revolution. He is imaginative without illusions, and creative without religion, loyalty, patriotism or any of the common ideals. Not that he is incapable of these ideals: on the contrary, he has swallowed them all in his boyhood, and now, having a keen dramatic faculty, is extremely clever at playing upon them by the arts of the actor and stage manager. Withal, he is no spoiled child. Poverty, ill-luck, the shifts of impecunious shabby-gentility, repeated failure as a would-be author, humiliation as a rebuffed time server, reproof and punishment as an incompetent and dishonest officer, an escape from dismissal from the service so narrow that if the emigration of the nobles had not raised the value of even the most rascally lieutenant to the famine price of a general he would have been swept contemptuously from the army: these trials have ground his conceit out of him, and forced him to be self-sufficient and to understand that to such men as he is the world will give nothing that he cannot take from it by force. In this the world is not free from cowardice and folly; for Napoleon, as a merciless cannonader of political rubbish, is making himself useful: indeed, it is even now impossible to live in England without sometimes feeling how much that country lost in not being conquered by him as well as by Julius Caesar.

However, on this May afternoon in 1796, it is early days with him. He has but recently been promoted general, partly by using his wife to seduce the Directory (then governing France); partly by the scarcity of officers caused by the emigration as aforesaid; partly by his faculty of knowing a country, with all its roads, rivers, hills and valleys, as he knows the palm of his hand; and largely by that new faith of his in the efficacy of firing cannons at people. His army is, as to discipline, in a state which has so greatly shocked some modern writers before whom the following story has been enacted, that they, impressed with the later glory of "L'Empereur," have altogether refused to credit it. But Napoleon is not L'Empereur yet: his men call him Le Petit Caporal, as he is still in the stage of gaining influence over them by displays of pluck. He is not in a position to force his will on them in orthodox military fashion by the cat o' nine tails. The French Revolution, which has escaped suppression solely through the monarchy's habit of being at least four years in arrear with its soldiers in the matter of pay, has substituted for that habit, as far as possible, the habit of not paying at all, except in promises and patriotic flatteries which are not compatible with martial law of the Prussian type. Napoleon has therefore approached the Alps in command of men without money, in rags, and consequently in-

disposed to stand much discipline, especially from upstart generals. This circumstance, which would have embarrassed an idealist soldier, has been worth a thousand cannon to Napoleon. He has said to his army "You have patriotism and courage; but you have no money, no clothes, and hardly anything to eat. In Italy there are all these things, and glory as well, to be gained by a devoted army led by a general who regards loot as the natural right of the soldier. I am such a general. En avant, mes enfants!" The result has entirely justified him. The army conquers Italy as the locusts conquered Cyprus. They fight all day and march all night, covering impossible distances and appearing in incredible places, not because every soldier carries a field marshal's baton in his knapsack, but because he hopes to carry at least half a dozen silver forks there next day.

It must be understood, by the way, that the French army does not make war on the Italians. It is there to rescue them from the tyranny of their Austrian conquerors, and confer republican institutions on them; so that in incidentally looting them it merely makes free with the property of its friends, who ought to be grateful to it, and perhaps would be if ingratitude were not the proverbial failing of their country. The Austrians, whom it fights, are a thoroughly respectable regular army, well disciplined, commanded by gentlemen versed in orthodox campaigning: at the head of them Beaulieu, practising the classic art of war under orders from Vienna, and getting horribly beaten by Napoleon, who acts on his own responsibility in defiance of professional precedents or orders from Paris. Even when the Austrians win a battle, all that is necessary is to wait until their routine obliges them to return to their quarters for afternoon tea, so to speak, and win it back again from them: a course pursued later on with brilliant success at Marengo. On the whole, with his foe handicapped by Austrian statesmanship, classic generalship, and the exigencies of the aristocratic social structure of Viennese society, Napoleon finds it possible to be irresistible without working heroic miracles. The world, however, likes miracles and heroes, and is quite incapable of conceiving the action of such forces as academic militarism or Viennese drawing-roomism. Hence it has already begun to manufacture "L'Empereur," and thus to make it difficult for the romanticists of a hundred years later to credit the hitherto unrecorded little scene now in question at Tavazzano.

The best quarters in Tavazzano are at a little inn, the first house reached by travellers passing through the place from Milan to Lodi. It stands in a vineyard; and its principal room, a pleasant refuge from the summer heat, is open so widely at the back to this vineyard that it is almost a large veranda. The bolder children, much excited by the alarums and excursions of the past few days, and by an irruption of French troops at six o'clock, know that the French commander has quartered himself in this room, and are divided between a craving to peep in at the front windows, and a mortal dread of the sentinel, a young gentleman-soldier who, having no natural moustache, has had a most ferocious one painted on his face with boot blacking by his sergeant. As his heavy uniform, like all the uniforms of that day, is designed for parade without the least reference to his health or comfort, he perspires profusely in the sun; and his painted moustache has run in little streaks down his chin and round his neck, except where it has dried in stiff japanned flakes and had its sweeping outline chipped off in grotesque little bays and headlands, making him unspeakably ridiculous in the eye of History a hundred years later, but monstrous and horrible to the contemporary north Italian infant, to whom nothing would seem more natural than that he should relieve the monotony of his guard by pitchforking a stray child up on his bayonet, and eating it uncooked. Nevertheless one girl of bad character, in whom an instinct of privilege with soldiers is already stirring, does peep in at the safest window for a moment before a glance and a clink from the sentinel sends her flying. Most of what she sees she has seen before: the vineyard àt the back, with the old winepress and a cart among the vines; the door close on her right leading to the street entry; the landlord's best sideboard, now in full action for dinner, further back on the same side; the fireplace on the other side with a couch near it; another door, leading to the inner rooms, between it and the vineyard; and the table in the middle set out with a repast of Milanese risotto, cheese, grapes, bread, olives, and a big wickered flask of red wine.

The landlord, Giuseppe Grandi, she knows well. He is a swarthy vivacious shrewdly cheerful black-curled bullet

*headed grinning little innkeeper of forty. Naturally an ex-
cellent host, he is in the highest spirits this evening at his
good fortune in having as his guest the French commander
to protect him against the license of the troops. He actually
sports a pair of gold earrings which would otherwise have
been hidden carefully under the winepress with his little
equipment of silver plate.*

*Napoleon, sitting facing her on the further side of the
table, she sees for the first time. He is working hard, partly
at his meal, which he has discovered how to dispatch in
ten minutes by attacking all the courses simultaneously
(this practice is the beginning of his downfall), and partly
at a military map on which he from time to time marks the
position of the forces by taking a grapeskin from his mouth
and planting it on the map with his thumb like a wafer.
There is no revolutionary untidiness about his dress or
person; but his elbow has displaced most of the dishes and
glasses; and his long hair trails into the risotto when he
forgets it and leans more intently over the map.*

GIUSEPPE: Will your excellency——
NAPOLEON (*intent on his .map, but cramming himself me-
chanically with his left hand*): Dont talk. I'm busy.
GIUSEPPE (*with perfect good humor*): Excellency: I obey.
NAPOLEON: Some red ink.
GIUSEPPE: Alas! excellency, there is none.
NAPOLEON (*with Corsican facetiousness*): Kill something and
bring me its blood.
GIUSEPPE (*grinning*): There is nothing but your excellency's
horse, the sentinel, the lady upstairs, and my wife.
NAPOLEON: Kill your wife.
GIUSEPPE: Willingly, your excellency; but unhappily I am
not strong enough. She would kill me.
NAPOLEON: That will do equally well.
GIUSEPPE: Your excellency does me too much honor.
(*Stretching his hand towards the flask*). Perhaps some wine
will answer your excellency's purpose.
NAPOLEON (*hastily protecting the flask, and becoming quite
serious*): Wine! No: that would be waste. You are all the
same: waste! waste! waste! (*He marks the map with gravy,
using his fork as a pen*). Clear away. (*He finishes his wine;*

pushes back his chair; and uses his napkin, stretching his legs and leaning back, but still frowning and thinking).

GIUSEPPE *(clearing the table and removing the things to a tray on his sideboard)*: Every man to his trade, excellency. We innkeepers have plenty of cheap wine: we think nothing of spilling it. You great generals have plenty of cheap blood: you think nothing of spilling it. Is it not so, excellency?

NAPOLEON: Blood costs nothing: wine costs money. *(He rises and goes to the fireplace).*

GIUSEPPE: They say you are careful of everything except human life, excellency.

NAPOLEON: Human life, my friend, is the only thing that takes care of itself. *(He throws himself at his ease on the couch).*

GIUSEPPE *(admiring him)*: Ah, excellency, what fools we all are beside you! If I could only find out the secret of your success!

NAPOLEON: You would make yourself Emperor of Italy, eh?

GIUSEPPE: Too troublesome, excellency: I leave all that to you. Besides, what would become of my inn if I were Emperor? See how you enjoy looking on at me whilst I keep the inn for you and wait on you! Well, I shall enjoy looking on at you whilst you become Emperor of Europe, and govern the country for me. *(As he chatters, he takes the cloth off deftly without removing the map, and finally takes the corners in his hands and the middle in his mouth, to fold it up).*

NAPOLEON: Emperor of Europe, eh? Why only Europe?

GIUSEPPE: Why, indeed? Emperor of the world, excellency! Why not? *(He folds and rolls up the cloth, emphasizing his phrase by the steps of the process).* One man is like another *(fold)*: one country is like another *(fold)*: one battle is like another. *(At the last fold, he slaps the cloth on the table and deftly rolls it up, adding, by way of peroration)* Conquer one: conquer all. *(He takes the cloth to the sideboard, and puts it in a drawer).*

NAPOLEON: And govern for all; fight for all; be everybody's servant under cover of being everybody's master. Giuseppe.

GIUSEPPE *(at the sideboard)*: Excellency?

NAPOLEON: I forbid you to talk to me about myself.

GIUSEPPE (*coming to the foot of the couch*): Pardon. Your excellency is so unlike other great men. It is the subject they like best.

NAPOLEON: Well, talk to me about the subject they like next best, whatever that may be.

GIUSEPPE (*unabashed*): Willingly, your excellency. Has your excellency by any chance caught a glimpse of the lady upstairs?

NAPOLEON (*sitting up promptly*): How old is she?

GIUSEPPE: The right age, excellency.

NAPOLEON: Do you mean seventeen or thirty?

GIUSEPPE: Thirty, excellency.

NAPOLEON: Goodlooking?

GIUSEPPE: I cannot see with your excellency's eyes: every man must judge that for himself. In my opinion, excellency, a fine figure of a lady. (*Slyly*). Shall I lay the table for her collation here?

NAPOLEON (*brusquely, rising*): No: lay nothing here until the officer for whom I am waiting comes back. (*He looks at his watch, and takes to walking to and fro between the fireplace and the vineyard*).

GIUSEPPE (*with conviction*): Excellency: believe me, he has been captured by the accursed Austrians! He dare not keep you waiting if he were at liberty.

NAPOLEON (*turning at the edge of the shadow of the veranda*): Giuseppe: if that turns out to be true, it will put me into such a temper that nothing short of hanging you and your whole household, including the lady upstairs, will satisfy me.

GIUSEPPE: We are all cheerfully at your excellency's disposal, except the lady. I cannot answer for her; but no lady could resist you, General.

NAPOLEON (*sourly, resuming his march*): Hm! You will never be hanged. There is no satisfaction in hanging a man who does not object to it.

GIUSEPPE (*sympathetically*): Not the least in the world, excellency: is there? (NAPOLEON *again looks at his watch, evidently growing anxious*). Ah, one can see that you are a great man, General: you know how to wait. If it were a corporal now, or a sub-lieutenant, at the end of three minutes he would be swearing, fuming, threatening, pulling the house about our ears.

NAPOLEON: Giuseppe: your flatteries are insufferable. Go and talk outside. *(He sits down again at the table, with his jaws in his hands, and his elbows propped on the map, poring over it with a troubled expression).*

GIUSEPPE: Willingly, your excellency. You shall not be disturbed. *(He takes up the tray and prepares to withdraw).*

NAPOLEON: The moment he comes back, send him to me.

GIUSEPPE: Instantaneously, your excellency.

A LADY'S VOICE *(calling from some distant part of the inn):* Giusep-pe! *(The voice is very musical, and the two final notes make an ascending interval).*

NAPOLEON *(startled):* Who's that?

GIUSEPPE: The lady, excellency.

NAPOLEON: The lady upstairs?

GIUSEPPE: Yes, excellency. The strange lady.

NAPOLEON: Strange? Where does she come from?

GIUSEPPE *(with a shrug):* Who knows? She arrived here just before your excellency in a hired carriage belonging to the Golden Eagle at Borghetto. By herself, excellency. No servants. A dressing bag and a trunk: that is all. The postillion says she left a horse at the Golden Eagle. A charger, with military trappings.

NAPOLEON: A woman with a charger! French or Austrian?

GIUSEPPE: French, excellency.

NAPOLEON: Her husband's charger, no doubt. Killed at Lodi, poor fellow.

THE LADY'S VOICE *(the two final notes now making a peremptory descending interval):* Giuseppe!

NAPOLEON *(rising to listen):* Thats not the voice of a woman whose husband was killed yesterday.

GIUSEPPE: Husbands are not always regretted, excellency. *(Calling).* Coming, lady, coming. *(He makes for the inner door).*

NAPOLEON *(arresting him with a strong hand on his shoulder):* Stop. Let h e r come.

VOICE: Giuseppe!! *(Impatiently).*

GIUSEPPE: Let me go, excellency. It is my point of honor as an innkeeper to come when I am called. I appeal to you as a soldier.

A MAN'S VOICE *(outside, at the inn door, shouting):* Here, someone. Hollo! Landlord! Where are you?

(Somebody raps vigorously with a whip handle on a bench in the passage).

NAPOLEON *(suddenly becoming the commanding officer again and throwing GIUSEPPE off)*: My man at last. *(Pointing to the inner door).* Go. Attend to your business: the lady is calling you. *(He goes to the fireplace and stands with his back to it with a determined military air).*

GIUSEPPE *(with bated breath, snatching up his tray)*: Certainly, excellency. *(He hurries out by the inner door).*

THE MAN'S VOICE *(impatiently)*: Are you all asleep here?

> *The other door is kicked rudely open. A dusty sub-lieutenant bursts into the room. He is a tall chuckle-headed young man of twenty-four, with the complexion and style of a man of rank, and a self-assurance on that ground which the French Revolution has failed to shake in the smallest degree. He has a thick silly lip, an eager credulous eye, an obstinate nose, and a loud confident voice. A young man without fear, without reverence, without imagination, without sense, hopelessly insusceptible to the Napoleonic or any other idea, stupendously egotistical, eminently qualified to rush in where angels fear to tread, yet of a vigorous babbling vitality which bustles him into the thick of things. He is just now boiling with vexation, attributable by a superficial observer to his impatience at not being promptly attended to by the staff of the inn, but in which a more discerning eye can perceive a certain moral depth, indicating a more permanent and momentous grievance. On seeing NAPOLEON, he is sufficiently taken aback to check himself and salute; but he does not betray by his manner any of that prophetic consciousness of Marengo and Austerlitz, Waterloo and St Helena, or the Napoleonic pictures of Delaroche and Meissonier, which later ages expect from him.*

NAPOLEON *(watch in hand)*: Well, sir, you have come at last. Your instructions were that I should arrive here at six, and find you waiting for me with my mail from Paris and with despatches. It is now twenty minutes to eight. You were sent on this service as a hard rider with the fastest horse in the camp. You arrived a hundred minutes late, on foot. Where is your horse?

THE LIEUTENANT (*moodily pulling off his gloves and dashing them with his cap and whip on the table*): Ah! where indeed? Thats just what I should like to know, General. (*With emotion*). You dont know how fond I was of that horse.

NAPOLEON (*angrily sarcastic*): Indeed! (*With sudden misgiving*). Where are the letters and despatches?

THE LIEUTENANT (*importantly, rather pleased than otherwise at having some remarkable news*): I dont know.

NAPOLEON (*unable to believe his ears*): You dont know!

LIEUTENANT: No more than you do, General. Now I suppose I shall be court-martialled. Well, I dont mind being court-martialled; but (*with solemn determination*). I tell you, General, if ever I catch that innocent looking youth, I'll spoil his beauty, the slimy little liar! I'll make a picture of him. I'll——

NAPOLEON (*advancing from the hearth to the table*): What innocent looking youth? Pull yourself together, sir, will you; and give an account of yourself.

LIEUTENANT (*facing him at the opposite side of the table, leaning on it with his fists*): Oh, I'm all right, General: I'm perfectly ready to give an account of myself. I shall make the court-martial thoroughly understand that the fault was not mine. Advantage has been taken of the better side of my nature; and I'm not ashamed of it. But with all respect to you as my commanding officer, General, I say again that if ever I set eyes on that son of Satan, I'll——

NAPOLEON (*angrily*): So you said before.

LIEUTENANT (*drawing himself upright*): I say it again. Just wait until I catch him. Just wait: thats all. (*He folds his arms resolutely, and breathes hard, with compressed lips*).

NAPOLEON: I a m waiting, sir. For your explanation.

LIEUTENANT (*confidently*): Youll change your tone, General, when you hear what has happened to me.

NAPOLEON: Nothing has happened to you, sir: you are alive and not disabled. Where are the papers entrusted to you?

LIEUTENANT: Nothing happened to me! Nothing!! He swore eternal brotherhood with me. Was that nothing? He said my eyes reminded him of his sister's eyes. Was that nothing? He cried—actually cried—over the story of my separation from Angelica. Was that nothing? He paid for both bottles of wine, though he only ate bread and grapes himself. Perhaps you call that nothing. He gave me his pistols and his horse and his despatches—most important despatches—and let me go away with them. (*Triumphantly, seeing that he has reduced* NAPOLEON *to blank stupefaction*). Was t h a t nothing?

NAPOLEON (*enfeebled by astonishment*): What did he do that for?

LIEUTENANT (*as if the reason were obvious*): To shew his confidence in me, of course. (NAPOLEON'- *jaw does not exactly drop; but its hinges become nerveless*). And I was worthy of his confidence: I brought them all back honorably. But would you believe it? when I trusted him with m y pistols, and m y horse, and m y despatches——

NAPOLEON: What the devil did you do that for?

LIEUTENANT: I'm telling you: to shew my confidence in him. And he betrayed it! abused it! never came back again! The thief! the swindler! the heartless treacherous little blackguard! You call that nothing, I suppose. But look here, General: (*again resorting to the table with his fist for greater emphasis*), y o u may put up with this outrage from the Austrians if you like; but speaking for myself personally, I tell you that if ever I catch——

NAPOLEON (*turning on his heel in disgust and irritably resuming his march to and fro*): Yes: you have said that more than once already.

LIEUTENANT (*excitedly*): More than once! I'll say it fifty times; and whats more, I'll do it. Youll see, General. I ' l l shew my confidence in him, so I will. I ' l l——

NAPOLEON: Yes, yes, sir: no doubt you will. What kind of man was he?

LIEUTENANT: Well, I should think you ought to be able to tell from his conduct the kind of man he was.

NAPOLEON: Pshaw! What was he like?

LIEUTENANT: Like! He was like—well, you ought to have just seen the fellow: that will give you a notion of what he was like. He wont be like it five minutes after I catch him; for I tell you that if ever——

NAPOLEON (*shouting furiously for the innkeeper*): Giuseppe! (*To the* LIEUTENANT, *out of all patience*). Hold your tongue, sir, if you can.

LIEUTENANT (*plaintively*): I warn you it's no use trying to put the blame on me. How was I to know the sort of fellow he was? (*He takes a chair from between the sideboard and the outer door; places it near the table; and sits down*). If you only knew how hungry and tired I am, youd have more consideration.

GIUSEPPE (*returning*): What is it, excellency?

NAPOLEON (*struggling with his temper*): Take this—this officer. Feed him; and put him to bed, if necessary. When he is in his right mind again, find out what has happened to him and bring me word. (*To the* LIEUTENANT). Consider yourself under arrest, sir.

LIEUTENANT (*with sulky stiffness*): I was prepared for that. It takes a gentleman to understand a gentleman. (*He throws his sword on the table*).

GIUSEPPE (*with sympathetic concern*): Have you been attacked by the Austrians, lieutenant? Dear! dear! dear!

LIEUTENANT (*contemptuously*): Attacked! I could have broken his back between my finger and thumb. I wish I had, now. No: it was by appealing to the better side of my nature: thats what I cant get over. He said he'd never met a man he liked so much as me. He put his handkerchief round my neck because a gnat bit me, and my stock was chafing it. Look! (*He pulls a handkerchief from his stock.* GIUSEPPE *takes it and examines it*).

GIUSEPPE (*to* NAPOLEON): A lady's handkerchief, excellency. (*He smells it*). Perfumed.

NAPOLEON: Eh? (*He takes it and looks at it attentively*). Hm! (*He smells it*). Ha! (*He walks thoughtfully across the room, looking at the handkerchief, which he finally sticks in the breast of his coat*).

LIEUTENANT: Good enough for him, anyhow. I noticed that he had a woman's hands when he touched my neck, with his coaxing fawning ways, the mean effeminate little hound. (*Lowering his voice with thrilling intensity*). But mark my words, General. If ever——

THE LADY'S VOICE (*outside, as before*): Giuseppe!

LIEUTENANT (*petrified*): What was that?

GIUSEPPE: Only a lady upstairs, lieutenant, calling me.

LIEUTENANT: Lady!

VOICE: Giuseppe, Giuseppe: where a r e you?

LIEUTENANT (*murderously*): Give me that sword. (*He snatches up the sword and draws it*).

GIUSEPPE (*rushing forward and seizing his right arm*): What are you thinking of, lieutenant? It's a lady: dont you hear? It's a woman's voice.

LIEUTENANT: It's h i s voice, I tell you. Let me go. (*He breaks away, and rushes to the edge of the veranda, where he posts himself, sword in hand, watching the door like a cat watching a mousehole*).

> *It opens; and the* STRANGE LADY *steps in. She is tall and extraordinarily graceful, with a delicately intelligent, apprehensive, questioning face: perception in the brow, sensitiveness in the nostrils, character in the chin: all keen, refined, and original. She is very feminine, but by no means weak: the lithe tender figure is hung on a strong frame: the hands and feet, neck and shoulders, are useful vigorous members, of full size in proportion to her stature, which perceptibly exceeds that of* NAPOLEON *and the innkeeper, and leaves her at no disadvantage with the* LIEUTENANT. *Only, her elegance and radiant charm keep the secret of her size and strength. She is not, judging by her dress, an admirer of the latest fashions of the Directory; or perhaps she uses up her old dresses for travelling. At all events she wears no jacket with extravagant lappels, no Greco-Tallien sham chiton, nothing, indeed, that the Princess de Lamballe might not have worn. Her dress of flowered silk is long waisted, with a Watteau pleat behind, but with the paniers reduced to mere rudiments, as she is too tall for them. It is cut low in the neck, where it is eked out by a creamy fichu. She is fair, with golden brown hair and grey eyes.*
>
> *She enters with the self-possession of a woman accustomed to the privileges of rank and beauty. The innkeeper, who has excellent natural manners, is highly appreciative of her.* NAPOLEON *is smitten self-conscious. His color deepens: he becomes stiffer and less at ease than before. She is advancing in an infinitely well bred manner to pay her respects to him when the* LIEUTENANT *pounces on her and seizes her right*

wrist. As she recognizes him, she becomes deadly pale. There is no mistaking her expression: a revelation of some fatal error, utterly unexpected, has suddenly appalled her in the midst of tranquillity, security, and victory. The next moment a wave of angry color rushes up from beneath the creamy fichu and drowns her whole face. One can see that she is blushing all over her body. Even the LIEUTENANT, *ordinarily incapable of observation, can see a thing when it is painted red for him. Interpreting the blush as the involuntary confession of black deceit confronted with its victim, he addresses her in a loud crow of retributive triumph.*

LIEUTENANT: So Ive got you, my lad. So youve disguised yourself, have you? *(In a voice of thunder, releasing her wrist).* Take off that skirt.

GIUSEPPE *(remonstrating)*: Oh, lieutenant!

LADY *(affrighted, but highly indignant at his having dared to touch her)*: Gentlemen: I appeal to you. *(To* NAPOLEON*).* You, sir, are an officer: a general. You will protect me, will you not?

LIEUTENANT: Never you mind him, General. Leave me to deal with him.

NAPOLEON: With him! With whom, sir? Why do you treat this lady in such a fashion?

LIEUTENANT: Lady! Hes a man! the man I shewed my confidence in. *(Raising his sword).* Here, you——

LADY *(running behind* NAPOLEON *and in her agitation clasping to her breast the arm which he extends before her as a fortification)*: Oh, thank you, General. Keep him away.

NAPOLEON: Nonsense, sir. This is certainly a lady *(she suddenly drops his arm and blushes again)*; and you are under arrest. Put down your sword, sir, instantly.

LIEUTENANT: General: I tell you hes an Austrian spy. He passed himself off on me as one of General Masséna's staff this afternoon; and now hes passing himself off on you as a woman. Am I to believe my own eyes or not?

LADY: General: it must be my brother. He is on General Masséna's staff. He is very like me.

LIEUTENANT *(his mind giving way)*: Do you mean to say that youre not your brother, but your sister? the sister who was so like me? who had my beautiful blue eyes? It's a lie: your eyes are not like mine: theyre exactly like your own.

NAPOLEON (*with contained exasperation*): Lieutenant: will you obey my orders and leave the room, since you are convinced at last that this is no gentleman?

LIEUTENANT: Gentleman! I should think not. No gentleman would have abused my confid——

NAPOLEON (*out of all patience*): That will do, sir: do you hear? Will you leave the room? I order you to leave the room.

LADY: Oh pray let me go instead.

NAPOLEON (*drily*): Excuse me, madam. With all possible respect for your brother, I do not yet understand what an officer on General Masséna's staff wants with my letters. I have some questions to put to you.

GIUSEPPE (*discreetly*): Come, lieutenant. (*He opens the door*).

LIEUTENANT: Im off. General: take warning by me: be on your guard against the better side of your nature. (*To the* LADY). Madam: my apologies. I thought you were the same person, only of the opposite sex; and that naturally misled me.

LADY (*recovering her good humor*): It was not your fault, was it? Im so glad youre not angry with me any longer, lieutenant. (*She offers her hand*).

LIEUTENANT (*bending gallantly to kiss it*): Oh, madam, not the lea—— (*Checking himself and looking at it*). You have your brothers hand. And the same sort of ring!

LADY (*sweetly*): We are twins.

LIEUTENANT: That accounts for it. (*He kisses her hand*). A thousand pardons. I didnt mind about the despatches at all: thats more the General's affair than mine: it was the abuse of my confidence through the better side of my nature. (*Taking his cap, gloves and whip from the table and going*). Youll excuse my leaving you, General, I hope. Very sorry, Im sure. (*He talks himself out of the room.* GIUSEPPE *follows him and shuts the door*).

NAPOLEON (*looking after them with concentrated irritation*): Idiot!

The STRANGE LADY *smiles sympathetically. He comes frowning down the room between the table and the*

> *fireplace, all his awkwardness gone now that he is alone with her.*

LADY: How can I thank you, General, for your protection?

NAPOLEON *(turning on her suddenly)*: My despatches: come! *(He puts out his hand for them).*

LADY: General! *(She involuntarily puts her hands on her fichu as if to protect something there).*

NAPOLEON: You tricked that blockhead out of them. You disguised yourself as a man. I want my despatches. They are there in the bosom of your dress, under your hands.

LADY *(quickly removing her hands)*: Oh how unkindly you are speaking to me! *(She takes her handkerchief from her fichu)*. You frighten me. *(She touches her eyes as if to wipe away a tear).*

NAPOLEON: I see you dont know me, madam, or you would save yourself the trouble of pretending to cry.

LADY *(producing an effect of smiling through her tears)*: Yes, I do know you. Yóu are the famous General Buonaparte. *(She gives the name a marked Italian pronunciation: Bwawna-parr-te).*

NAPOLEON *(angrily, with the French pronunciation)*: Bonaparte, Madam, Bonaparte. The papers, if you please.

LADY: But I assure you—— *(He snatches the handkerchief rudely)*. General! *(Indignantly).*

NAPOLEON *(taking the other handkerchief from his breast)*: You lent one of your handkerchiefs to my lieutenant when you robbed him. *(He looks at the two handkerchiefs)*. They match one another. *(He smells them)*. The same scent. *(He flings them down on the table)*: I am waiting for my despatches. I shall take them, if necessary, with as little ceremony as I took the handkerchief.

LADY *(in dignified reproof)*: General: do you threaten women?

NAPOLEON *(bluntly)*: Yes.

LADY *(disconcerted, trying to gain time)*: But I dont understand. I——

NAPOLEON: You understand perfectly. You came here because your Austrian employers calculated that I was six leagues away. I am always to be found where my enemies dont expect me. You have walked into the lion's den. Come! You are a brave woman. Be a sensible one: I have no time to waste. The papers. (*He advances a step ominously*).

LADY (*breaking down in the childish rage of impotence, and throwing herself in tears on the chair left beside the table by the* LIEUTENANT): *I* brave! How little you know! I have spent the day in an agony of fear. I have a pain here from the tightening of my heart at every suspicious look, every threatening movement. Do you think everyone is as brave as you? Oh, why will not you brave people do the brave things? Why do you leave them to us, who have no courage at all? I'm not brave: I shrink from violence: danger makes me miserable.

NAPOLEON (*interested*): Then why have you thrust yourself into danger?

LADY: Because there is no other way: I can trust nobody else. And now it is all useless: all because of you, who have no fear because you have no heart, no feeling, no—— (*She breaks off, and throws herself on her knees*). Ah, General, let me go: let me go without asking any questions. You shall have your despatches and letters: I swear it.

NAPOLEON (*holding out his hand*): Yes: I am waiting for them.

> *She gasps, daunted by his ruthless promptitude into despair of moving him by cajolery. She looks up perplexedly at him, racking her brains for some device to outwit him. He meets her regard inflexibly.*

LADY (*rising at last with a quiet little sigh*): I will get them for you. They are in my room. (*She turns to the door*).

NAPOLEON: I shall accompany you, madam.

LADY (*drawing herself up with a noble air of offended delicacy*): I cannot permit you, General, to enter my chamber.

NAPOLEON: Then you shall stay here, madam, whilst I have your chamber searched for my papers.

LADY (*spitefully; openly giving up her plan*): You may save yourself the trouble. They are not there.

NAPOLEON: No: I have already told you where they are. (*Pointing to her breast*).

LADY (*with pretty piteousness*): General: I only want to keep one little private letter. Only one. Let me have it.

NAPOLEON (*cold and stern*): Is that a reasonable demand, madam?

LADY (*encouraged by his not refusing point-blank*): No; but that is why you must grant it. Are your own demands reasonable? thousands of lives for the sake of your victories, your ambitions, your destiny! And what I ask is such a little thing. And I am only a weak woman, and you a brave man. (*She looks at him with her eyes full of tender pleading, and is about to kneel to him again*).

NAPOLEON (*brusquely*): Get up, get up. (*He turns moodily away and takes a turn across the room, pausing for a moment to say, over his shoulder*). Youre talking nonsense; and you know it. (*She sits down submissively on the couch. When he turns and sees her despair, he feels that his victory is complete, and that he may now indulge in a little play with his victim. He comes back and sits beside her. She looks alarmed and moves a little away from him; but a ray of rallying hope beams from her eye. He begins like a man enjoying some secret joke*). How do you know I am a brave man?

LADY (*amazed*): You! General Buonaparte. (*Italian pronunciation*).

NAPOLEON: Yes, I, General Bonaparte. (*Emphasizing the French pronunciation*).

LADY: Oh, how can you ask such a question? you! who stood only two days ago at the bridge at Lodi, with the air full of death, fighting a duel with cannons across the river! (*Shuddering*) Oh, you d o brave things.

NAPOLEON: So do you.

LADY: I! (*With a sudden odd thought*). Oh! Are you a coward?

NAPOLEON (*laughing grimly and slapping his knees*): That is the one question you must never ask a soldier. The sergeant asks after the recruit's height, his age, his wind, his limb, but never after his courage.

LADY (*as if she had found it no laughing matter*): Ah, you can laugh at fear. Then you dont know what fear is.

NAPOLEON: Tell me this. Suppose you could have got that letter by coming to me over the bridge at Lodi the day before yesterday! Suppose there had been no other way, and that this was a sure way—if only you escaped the cannon! (*She shudders and covers her eyes for a moment with her hands*). Would you have been afraid?

LADY: Oh, horribly afraid, agonizingly afraid. (*She presses her hands on her heart*). It hurts only to imagine it.

NAPOLEON (*inflexibly*): Would you have come for the despatches?

LADY (*overcome by the imagined horror*): Dont ask me. I m u s t have come.

NAPOLEON: Why?

LADY: Because I must. Because there would have been no other way.

NAPOLEON (*with conviction*): Because you would have wanted my letter enough to bear your fear. (*He rises suddenly, and deliberately poses for an oration*). There is only one universal passion: fear. Of all the thousand qualities a man may have, the only one you will find as certainly in the youngest drummer boy in my army as in me, is fear. It is fear that makes men fight: it is indifference that makes them run away: fear is the mainspring of war. Fear! I know fear well, better than you, better than any woman. I once saw a regiment of good Swiss soldiers massacred by a mob in Paris because I was afraid to interfere: I felt myself a coward to the tips of my toes as I looked on at it. Seven months ago I revenged my shame by pounding that mob to death with cannon balls. Well, what of that? Has fear ever held a man back from anything he really wanted —or a woman either? Never. Come with me; and I will shew you twenty thousand cowards who will risk death every day for the price of a glass of brandy. And do you think there are no women in the army, braver than the men, though their lives are worth more? Pshaw! I think nothing of your fear or your bravery. If you had had to come across to me at Lodi, you would not have been afraid: once on the bridge, every other feeling would have gone down before the necessity—the n e c e s s i t y—for making your way to my side and getting what you wanted.

And now, suppose you had done all this! suppose you had come safely out with that letter in your hand, knowing that when the hour came, your fear had tightened, not your heart, but your grip of your own purpose! that it had ceased to be fear, and had become strength, penetration, vigilance, iron resolution! how would you answer then if you were asked whether you were a coward?

LADY (*rising*): Ah, you are a hero, a real hero.

NAPOLEON: Pooh! theres no such thing as a real hero. (*He*

strolls about the room, making light of her enthusiasm, but by no means displeased with himself for having evoked it).

LADY: Ah yes, there is. There is a difference between what you call my bravery and yours. You wanted to win the battle of Lodi for yourself and not for anyone else, didnt you?

NAPOLEON: Of course. *(Suddenly recollecting himself).* Stop: no. *(He pulls himself piously together, and says, like a man conducting a religious service).* I am only the servant of the French republic, following humbly in the footsteps of the heroes of classical antiquity. I win battles for humanity: for my country, not for myself.

LADY *(disappointed)*: Oh, then you are only a womanish hero after all. *(She sits down again, all her enthusiasm gone).*

NAPOLEON *(greatly astonished)*: Womanish!

LADY *(listlessly)*: Yes, like me. *(With deep melancholy).* Do you think that if I wanted those despatches only for myself, I dare venture into a battle for them? No: if that were all, I should not have the courage to ask to see you at your hotel, even. My courage is mere slavishness: it is of no use to me for my own purposes. It is only through love, through pity, through the instinct to save and protect someone else, that I can do the things that terrify me.

NAPOLEON *(contemptuously)*: Pshaw! *(He turns slightingly away from her).*

LADY: Aha! now you see that I'm not really brave. *(Relapsing into petulant listlessness).* But what right have you to despise me if you only win your battles for others? for your country! through patriotism! That is what I call womanish: it is so like a Frenchman!

NAPOLEON *(furiously)*: I am no Frenchman.

LADY *(innocently)*: I thought you said you won the battle of Lodi for your country, General Bu—— shall I pronounce it in Italian or French?

NAPOLEON: You are presuming on my patience, madam. I was born a French subject, but not in France.

LADY *(affecting a marked access of interest in him)*: You were not born a subject at all, I think.

NAPOLEON *(greatly pleased)*: Eh? Eh? You think not.

LADY: I am sure of it.

NAPOLEON: Well, well, perhaps not. *(The self-complacency of his assent catches his own ear. He stops short, redden-*

ing. Then, composing himself into a solemn attitude, modelled on the heroes of classical antiquity, he takes a high moral tone). But we must not live for ourselves alone, little one. Never forget that we should always think of others, and work for others, and lead and govern them for their own good. Self-sacrifice is the foundation of all true nobility of character.

LADY *(again relaxing her attitude with a sigh)*: Ah, it is easy to see that you have never tried it, General.

NAPOLEON *(indignantly, forgetting all about Brutus and Scipio)*: What do you mean by that speech, madam?

LADY: Havent you noticed that people always exaggerate the value of the things they havent got? The poor think they need nothing but riches to be quite happy and good. Everybody worships truth, purity, unselfishness, for the same reason: because they have no experience of them. Oh, if they only knew!

NAPOLEON *(with angry derision)*: If they only knew! Pray do y o u know?

LADY: Yes. I had the misfortune to be born good. *(Glancing up at him for a moment).* And it i s a misfortune, I can tell you, General. I really am truthful and unselfish and all the rest of it; and it's nothing but cowardice; want of character; want of being really, strongly, positively oneself.

NAPOLEON: Ha? *(Turning to her quickly with a flash of strong interest).*

LADY *(earnestly, with rising enthusiasm)*: What is the secret of your power? Only that you believe in yourself. You can fight and conquer for yourself and for nobody else. You are not afraid of your own destiny. You teach us what we all might be if we had the will and courage; and that *(suddenly sinking on her knees before him)* is why we all begin to worship you. *(She kisses his hands).*

NAPOLEON *(embarrassed)*: Tut tut! Pray rise, madam.

LADY: Do not refuse my homage: it is your right. You will be Emperor of France——

NAPOLEON *(hurriedly)*: Take care. Treason!

LADY *(insisting)*: Yes. Emperor of France; then of Europe; perhaps of the world. I am only the first subject to swear allegiance. *(Again kissing his hand).* My Emperor!

NAPOLEON *(overcome, raising her)*: Pray! pray! No, no: this is folly. Come: be calm, be calm. (*Petting her*). There! there! my girl.

LADY (*struggling with happy tears*): Yes, I know it is an impertinence in me to tell you what you must know far better than I do. But you are not angry with me, are you?

NAPOLEON: Angry! No, no: not a bit, not a bit. Come: you are a very clever and sensible and interesting woman. (*He pats her on the cheek*). Shall we be friends?

LADY (*enraptured*): Your friend! You will let me be your friend! Oh! (*She offers him both her hands with a radiant smile*). You see: I shew my confidence in you.

> *This incautious echo of the* LIEUTENANT *undoes her,* NAPOLEON *starts: his eyes flash: he utters a yell of rage.*

NAPOLEON: What! ! !

LADY: Whats the matter?

NAPOLEON: Shew your confidence in me! So that I may shew my confidence in you in return by letting you give me the slip with the despatches, eh? Ah, Dalila, Dalila, you have been trying your tricks on me; and I have been as gross a gull as my jackass of a lieutenant. (*Menacingly*). Come: the despatches. Quick: I am not to be trifled with now.

LADY (*flying round the couch*): General——

NAPOLEON: Quick, I tell you. (*He passes swiftly up the middle of the room and intercepts her as she makes for the vineyard*).

LADY (*at bay, confronting him and giving way to her temper*): You dare address me in that tone.

NAPOLEON: Dare!

LADY: Yes, dare. Who are you that you should presume to speak to me in that coarse way? Oh, the vile, vulgar Corsican adventurer comes out in you very easily.

NAPOLEON (*beside himself*): You she devil! (*Savagely*). Once more, and only once, will you give me those papers or shall I tear them from you?—by force!

LADY: Tear them from me: by force!

> *As he glares at her like a tiger about to spring, she crosses her arms on her breast in the attitude of a martyr. The gesture and pose instantly awaken his*

theatrical instinct: he forgets his rage in the desire to shew her that in acting, too, she has met her match. He keeps her a moment in suspense; then suddenly clears up his countenance; puts his hands behind him with provoking coolness; looks at her up and down a couple of times; takes a pinch of snuff; wipes his fingers carefully and puts up his handerchief, her heroic pose becoming more and more ridiculous all the time.

NAPOLEON (*at last*): Well?

LADY (*disconcerted, but with her arms still crossed devotedly*): Well: what are you going to do?

NAPOLEON: Spoil your attitude.

LADY: You brute! (*Abandoning the attitude, she comes to the end of the couch, where she turns with her back to it, leaning against it and facing him with her hands behind her*).

NAPOLEON: Ah, thats better. Now listen to me. I like you. Whats more, I value your respect.

LADY: You value what you have not got, then

NAPOLEON: I shall have it presently. Now attend to me. Suppose I were to allow myself to be abashed by the respect due to your sex, your beauty, your heroism and all the rest of it! Suppose I, with nothing but such sentimental stuff to stand between these muscles of mine and those papers which you have about you, and which I want and mean to have! suppose I, with the prize within my grasp, were to falter and sneak away with my hands empty; or, what would be worse, cover up my weakness by playing the magnanimous hero, and sparing you the violence I dared not use! would you not despise me from the depths of your woman's soul? Would any woman be such a fool? Well, Bonaparte can rise to the situation and act like a woman when it is necessary. Do you understand?

The LADY, *without speaking, stands upright, and takes a packet of papers from her bosom. For a moment she has an intense impulse to dash them in his face. But her good breeding cuts her off from any vulgar method of relief. She hands them to him politely, only averting her head. The moment he takes them, she hurries*

> *across to the other side of the room; sits down; and covers her face with her hands.*

NAPOLEON (*gloating over the papers*): Aha! Thats right. Thats right. (*Before he opens them, he looks at her and says*) Excuse me. (*He sees that she is hiding her face*). Very angry with me, eh? (*He unties the packet, the seal of which is already broken, and puts it on the table to examine its contents*).

LADY (*quietly, taking down her hands and shewing that she is not crying, but only thinking*): No. You were right. But I am sorry for you.

NAPOLEON (*pausing in the act of taking the uppermost paper from the packet*): Sorry for me! Why?

LADY: I am going to see you lose your honor.

NAPOLEON: Hm! Nothing worse than that? (*He takes up the paper*).

LADY: And your happiness.

NAPOLEON: Happiness! Happiness is the most tedious thing in the world to me. Should I be what I am if I cared for happiness? Anything else?

LADY: Nothing.

NAPOLEON: Good.

LADY: Except that you will cut a very foolish figure in the eyes of France.

NAPOLEON (*quickly*): What? (*The hand unfolding the paper involuntarily stops. The lady looks at him enigmatically, in tranquil silence. He throws the letter down and breaks out into a torrent of scolding*). What do you mean? Eh? Are you at your tricks again? Do you think I dont know what these papers contain? I'll tell you. First, my information as to Beaulieu's retreat. There are only two things he can do—leather-brained idiot that he is!—shut himself up in Mantua or violate the neutrality of Venice by taking Peschiera. You are one of old Leatherbrain's spies: he has discovered that he has been betrayed, and has sent you to intercept the information at all hazards. As if that could save him from m e, the old fool! The other papers are only my private letters from Paris, of which you know nothing.

LADY (*prompt and businesslike*): General: let us make a fair division. Take the information your spies have sent you about the Austrian army; and give me the Paris correspondence. That will content me.

NAPOLEON (*his breath taken away by the coolness of the proposal*): A fair di—— (*He gasps*). It seems to me, madam, that you have come to regard my letters as your own property, of which I am trying to rob you.

LADY (*earnestly*): No: on my honor I ask for no letter of yours: not a word that has been written by you or to you. That packet contains a stolen letter: a letter written by a woman to a man: a man not her husband: a letter that means disgrace, infamy——

NAPOLEON: A love letter?

LADY (*bitter-sweetly*): What else but a love letter could stir up so much hate?

NAPOLEON: Why is it sent to me? To put the husband in my power, eh?

LADY: No, no: it can be of no use to you: I swear that it will cost you nothing to give it to me. It has been sent to you out of sheer malice: solely to injure the woman who wrote it.

NAPOLEON: Then why not send it to her husband instead of to me?

LADY (*completely taken aback*): Oh! (*Sinking back into the chair*). I——I dont know. (*She breaks down*).

NAPOLEON: Aha! I thought so: a little romance to get the papers back. Per Bacco, I cant help admiring you. I wish I could lie like that. It would save me a great deal of trouble.

LADY (*wringing her hands*): Oh, how *I* wish I really had told you some lie! You would have believed me then. The truth is the one thing that nobody will believe.

NAPOLEON (*with coarse familiarity, treating her as if she were a vivandière*): Capital! Capital! (*He puts his hands behind him on the table, and lifts himself on to it, sitting with his arms akimbo and his legs wide apart*). Come: I am a true Corsican in my love for stories. But I could tell them better than you if I set my mind to it. Next time you are asked why a letter compromising a wife should not be sent to her husband, answer simply that the husband wouldnt read it. Do you suppose, you goose, that a man wants to be compelled by public opinion to make a scene, to fight a duel, to break up his household, to injure his career by a scandal, when he can avoid it all by taking care not to know?

LADY (*revolted*): Suppose that packet contained a letter about your own wife?

NAPOLEON (*offended, coming off the table*): You are impertient, madam.

LADY (*humbly*): I beg your pardon. Caesar's wife is above suspicion.

NAPOLEON (*with a deliberate assumption of superiority*): You have committed an indiscretion. I pardon you. In future, do not permit yourself to introduce real persons in your romances.

LADY (*politely ignoring a speech which is to her only a breach of good manners*): General: there really is a woman's letter there. (*Pointing to the packet*). Give it to me.

NAPOLEON (*with brute conciseness*): Why?

LADY: She is an old friend: we were at school together. She has written to me imploring me to prevent the letter falling into your hands.

NAPOLEON: Why has it been sent to me?

LADY: Because it compromises the director Barras.

NAPOLEON (*frowning, evidently startled*): Barras! (*Haughtily*). Take care, madam. The director Barras is my attached personal friend.

LADY (*nodding placidly*): Yes. You became friends through your wife.

NAPOLEON: Again! Have I not forbidden you to speak of my wife? (*She keeps looking curiously at him, taking no account of the rebuke. More and more irritated, he drops his haughty manner, of which he is himself somewhat impatient, and says suspiciously, lowering his voice*). Who is this woman with whom you sympathize so deeply?

LADY: Oh, General! How could I tell you that?

NAPOLEON (*ill humoredly, beginning to walk about again in angry perplexity*): Ay, ay: stand by one another. You are all the same, you women.

LADY (*indignantly*): We are not all the same, any more than you are. Do you think that if *I* loved another man, I should pretend to go on loving my husband, or be afraid to tell him or all the world? But this woman is not made that way. She governs men by cheating them; and they like it, and let her govern them. (*She turns her back to him in disdain*).

NAPOLEON (*not attending to her*): Barras? Barras? (*Very threateningly, his face darkening*). Take care. Take care: do you hear? You may go too far.

LADY (*innocently turning her face to him*): Whats the matter?

NAPOLEON: What are you hinting at? Who is this woman?

LADY (*meeting his angry searching gaze with tranquil indifference as she sits looking up at him*): A vain, silly, extravagant creature, with a very able and ambitious husband who knows her through and through: knows that she has lied to him about her age, her income, her social position, about everything that silly women lie about: knows that she is incapable of fidelity to any principle or any person; and yet can not help loving her—can not help his man's instinct to make use of her for his own advancement with Barras.

NAPOLEON (*in a stealthy coldly furious whisper*): This is your revenge, you she cat, for having had to give me the letters.

LADY: Nonsense! Or do you mean that y o u are that sort of man?

NAPOLEON (*exasperated, clasps his hands behind him, his fingers twitching, and says, as he walks irritably away from her to the fireplace*): This woman will drive me out of my senses. (*To her*). Begone.

LADY (*seated immovably*): Not without that letter.

NAPOLEON: Begone, I tell you. (*Walking from the fireplace to the vineyard and back to the table*). You shall have no letter. I dont like you. Youre a detestable woman, and as ugly as Satan. I dont choose to be pestered by strange women. Be off. (*He turns his back on her. In quiet amusement, she leans her cheek on her hand and laughs at him. He turns again, angrily mocking her*). Ha! ha! ha! What are you laughing at?

LADY: At you, General. I have often seen persons of your sex getting into a pet and behaving like children; but I never saw a really great man do it before.

NAPOLEON (*brutally, flinging the words in her face*): Pshaw! Flattery! Flattery! Coarse, impudent flattery!

LADY (*springing up with a bright flush in her cheeks*): Oh, you are too bad. Keep your letters. Read the story of your

own dishonor in them; and much good may they do you.
Goodbye. (*She goes indignantly towards the inner door*).

NAPOLEON: My own——! Stop. Come back. Come back, I
order you. (*She proudly disregards his savagely peremptory
tone and continues on her way to the door. He rushes at
her; seizes her by the arm; and drags her back*). Now, what
do you mean? Explain. Explain. I tell you, or—— (*Threatening her. She looks at him with unflinching defiance*).
Rrrr! you obstinate devil, you. (*Throwing her arm away*).
Why cant you answer a civil question?

LADY (*deeply offended by his violence*): Why do you ask me?
You have the explanation.

NAPOLEON: Where?

LADY (*pointing to the letters on the table*): There. You have
only to read it.

> He snatches the packet up; hesitates; looks at her suspiciously; and throws it down again.

NAPOLEON: You seem to have forgotten your solicitude for
the honor of your old friend.

LADY: I do not think she runs any risk now. She does not
quite understand her husband.

NAPOLEON: I am to read the letter, then? (*He stretches out
his hand as if to take up the packet again, with his eye on
her*).

LADY: I do not see how you can very well avoid doing so
now. (*He instantly withdraws his hand*). Oh, dont be afraid.
You will find many interesting things in it.

NAPOLEON: For instance?

LADY: For instance, a duel with Barras, a domestic scene, a
broken household, a public scandal, a checked career, all
sorts of things.

NAPOLEON: Hm! (*He looks at her; takes up the packet and
looks at it, pursing his lips and balancing it in his hand;
looks at her again; passes the packet into his left hand and
puts it behind his back, raising his right to scratch the back
of his head as he turns and goes up to the edge of the
vineyard, where he stands for a moment looking out into
the vines, deep in thought. The LADY watches him in
silence, somewhat slightingly. Suddenly he turns and comes
back again, full of force and decision*). I grant your request, madam. Your courage and resolution deserve to suc-

ceed. Take the letters for which you have fought so well; and remember henceforth that you found the vile vulgar Corsican adventurer as generous to the vanquished after the battle as he was resolute in the face of the enemy before it. *(He offers her the packet)*.

LADY *(without taking it, looking hard at him)*: What are you at now, I wonder? *(He dashes the packet furiously to the floor)*. Aha! Ive spoilt t h a t attitude, I think. *(She makes him a pretty mocking curtsey)*.

NAPOLEON *(snatching it up again)*: Will you take the letters and begone? *(Advancing and thrusting them upon her)*.

LADY *(escaping round the table)*: No: I don't want your letters.

NAPOLEON: Ten minutes ago, nothing else would satisfy you.

LADY *(keeping the table carefully between them)*: Ten minutes ago you had not insulted me beyond all bearing.

NAPOLEON: I—— *(swallowing his spleen)*. I apologize.

LADY *(coolly)*: Thanks. *(With forced politeness he offers her the packet across the table. She retreats a step out of its reach and says)* But dont you want to know whether the Austrians are at Mantua or Peschiera?

NAPOLEON: I have already told you that I can conquer my enemies without the aid of spies, madam.

LADY: And the letter? dont you want to read that?

NAPOLEON: You have said that it is not addressed to me. I am not in the habit of reading other people's letters. *(He again offers the packet)*.

LADY: In that case there can be no objection to your keeping it. All I wanted was to prevent your reading it. *(Cheerfully)* G o o d afternoon, General. *(She turns coolly towards the inner door)*.

NAPOLEON *(angrily flinging the packet on the couch)*: Heaven grant me patience! *(He goes determinedly to the door, and places himself before it)*. Have you any sense of personal danger? Or are you one of those women who like to be beaten black and blue?

LADY: Thank you, General: I have no doubt the sensation is very voluptuous; but I had rather not. I simply want to go home: thats all. I was wicked enough to steal your despatches; but you have got them back; and you have forgiven me, because *(delicately reproducing his rhetorical cadence)* you are as generous to the vanquished after the battle as you are resolute in the face of the enemy before it. Wont you say goodbye to me? (*She offers her hand sweetly*).

NAPOLEON (*repulsing the advance with a gesture of concentrated rage, and opening the door to call fiercely*): Giuseppe! (*Louder*). Giuseppe! (*He bangs the door to, and comes to the middle of the room. The* LADY *goes a little way into the vineyard to avoid him*).

GIUSEPPE (*appearing at the door*): Excellency?

NAPOLEON: Where is that fool?

GIUSEPPE: He has had a good dinner, according to your instructions, excellency, and is now doing me the honor to gamble with me to pass the time.

NAPOLEON: Send him here. B r i n g him here. Come with him. (GIUSEPPE, *with unruffled readiness, hurries off.* NAPOLEON *turns curtly to the* LADY, *saying*) I must trouble you to remain some moments longer, madam. (*He comes to the couch*).

She comes from the vineyard along the opposite side of the room to the sideboard, and posts herself there, leaning against it, watching him. He takes the packet from the couch and deliberately buttons it carefully into his breast pocket, looking at her meanwhile with an expression which suggests that she will soon find out the meaning of his proceedings, and will not like it. Nothing more is said until the LIEUTENANT *arrives followed by* GIUSEPPE, *who stands modestly in attendance at the table. The* LIEUTENANT, *without cap, sword or gloves, and much improved in temper and spirits by his meal, chooses the* LADY's *side of the room, and waits, much at his ease, for* NAPOLEON *to begin.*

NAPOLEON: Lieutenant.

LIEUTENANT (*encouragingly*): General.

NAPOLEON: I cannot persuade this lady to give me much information; but there can be no doubt that the man who tricked you out of your charge was, as she admitted to you, her brother.

LIEUTENANT (*triumphantly*): What did I tell you, General! What did I tell you!

NAPOLEON: You must find that man. Your honor is at stake; and the fate of the campaign, the destiny of France, of

Europe, of humanity, perhaps, may depend on the information those despatches contain.

LIEUTENANT: Yes, I suppose they really are rather serious. (*As if this had hardly occurred to him before*).

NAPOLEON (*energetically*): They are so serious, sir, that if you do not recover them, you will be degraded in the presence of your regiment.

LIEUTENANT: Whew! The regiment wont like that, I can tell you.

NAPOLEON: Personally I am sorry for you. I would willingly hush up the affair if it were possible. But I shall be called to account for not acting on the despatches. I shall have to prove to all the world that I never received them, no matter what the consequences may be to you. I am sorry; but you see that I cannot help myself.

LIEUTENANT (*goodnaturedly*): Oh, dont take it to heart, General: it's really very good of you. Never mind what happens to me: I shall scrape through somehow; and well beat the Austrians for you, despatches or no despatches. I hope you wont insist on my starting off on a wild goose chase after the fellow now. I havnt a notion where to look for him.

GIUSEPPE (*deferentially*): You forget, Lieutenant: he has your horse.

LIEUTENANT (*starting*): I forgot that. (*Resolutely*). I'll go after him, General: I'll find that horse if it's alive anywhere in Italy. And I shant forget the despatches: never fear. Giuseppe: go and saddle one of those mangy old posthorses of yours while I get my cap and sword and things. Quick march. Off with you. (*Bustling him*).

GIUSEPPE: Instantly, Lieutenant, instantly. (*He disappears in the vineyard, where the light is now reddening with the sunset*).

LIEUTENANT (*looking about him on his way to the inner door*): By the way, General, did I give you my sword or did I not? Oh, I remember now. (*Fretfully*). It's all that nonsense about putting a man under arrest: one never knows where to find —— (*He talks himself out of the room*).

LADY (*still at the sideboard*): What does all this mean, General?

NAPOLEON: He will not find your brother.

LADY: Of course not. Theres no such person.

NAPOLEON: The despatches will be irrevocably lost.

LADY: Nonsense! They are inside your coat.

NAPOLEON: You will find it hard, I think, to prove that wild statement. (*The* LADY *starts. He adds, with clinching emphasis*) Those papers are lost.

LADY (*anxiously, advancing to the corner of the table*): And that unfortunate young man's career will be sacrificed?

NAPOLEON: H i s career! The fellow is not worth the gunpowder it would cost to have him shot. (*He turns contemptuously and goes to the hearth, where he stands with his back to her*).

LADY (*wistfully*): You are very hard. Men and women are nothing to you but things to be used, even if they are broken in the use.

NAPOLEON (*turning on her*): Which of us has broken this fellow? I or you? Who tricked him out of the despatches? Did you think of his career then?

LADY (*conscience-stricken*): Oh, I never thought of that. It was wicked of me; but I couldnt help it, could I? How else could I have got the papers? (*Supplicating*). General: you will save him from disgrace.

NAPOLEON (*laughing sourly*): Save him yourself, since you are so clever: it was you who ruined him. (*With savage intensity*). I h a t e a bad soldier.

> He goes out determinedly through the vineyard. She follows him a few steps with an appealing gesture, but is interrupted by the return of the LIEUTENANT, gloved and capped, with his sword on, ready for the road. He is crossing to the outer door when she intercepts him.

LADY: Lieutenant.

LIEUTENANT (*importantly*): You mustnt delay me, you know. Duty, madam, duty.

LADY (*imploringly*): Oh, sir, what are you going to do to my poor brother?

LIEUTENANT: Are you very fond of him?

LADY: I should die if anything happened to him. You must spare him. (*The* LIEUTENANT *shakes his head gloomily*). Yes, yes: you must: you shall: he is not fit to die. Listen to me. If I tell you where to find him—if I undertake to place him in your hands a prisoner, to be delivered up by you to General Bonaparte—will you promise me on your honor as an officer and a gentleman not to fight with him or treat him unkindly in any way?

LIEUTENANT: But suppose he attacks me. He has my pistols.

LADY: He is too great a coward.

LIEUTENANT: I dont feel so sure about that. Hes capable of anything.

LADY: If he attacks you, or resists you in any way, I release you from your promise.

LIEUTENANT: My promise! I didnt mean to promise. Look here: youre as bad as he is: youve taken an advantage of me through the better side of my nature. What about my horse?

LADY: It is part of the bargain that you are to have your horse and pistols back.

LIEUTENANT: Honor bright?

LADY: Honor bright. (*She offers her hand*).

LIEUTENANT (*taking it and holding it*): All right: I'll be as gentle as a lamb with him. His sister's a very pretty woman. (*He attempts to kiss her*).

LADY (*slipping away from him*): Oh, Lieutenant! You forget: your career is at stake—the destiny of Europe—of humanity.

LIEUTENANT: Oh, bother the destiny of humanity! (*Making for her*). Only a kiss.

LADY (*retreating round the table*): Not until you have regained your honor as an officer. Remember: you have not captured my brother yet.

LIEUTENANT (*seductively*): Youll tell me where he is, wont you?

LADY: I have only to send him a certain signal; and he will be here in quarter of an hour.

LIEUTENANT: He's not far off, then.

LADY: No: quite close. Wait here for him: when he gets my message he will come here at once and surrender himself to you. You understand?

LIEUTENANT (*intellectually overtaxed*): Well, it's a little complicated; but I daresay it will be all right.

LADY: And now, whilst youre waiting, dont you think you had better make terms with the General?

LIEUTENANT: Oh, look here: this is getting frightfully complicated. What terms?

LADY: Make him promise that if you catch my brother he

will consider that you have cleared your character as a soldier. He will promise anything you ask on that condition.

LIEUTENANT: Thats not a bad idea. Thank you: I think I'll try it.

LADY: Do. And mind, above all things, dont let him see how clever you are.

LIEUTENANT: I understand. Hed be jealous.

LADY: Dont tell him anything except that you are resolved to capture my brother or perish in the attempt. He wont believe you. Then you will produce my brother——

LIEUTENANT (*interrupting as he masters the plot*): And have the laugh at him! I say: what a jolly clever woman you are! (*Shouting*). Giuseppe!

LADY: Sh! Not a word to Giuseppe about me. (*She puts her finger on her lips. He does the same. They look at one another warningly. Then, with a ravishing smile, she changes the gesture into wafting him a kiss, and runs out through the inner door. Electrified, he bursts into a volley of chuckles*).

GIUSEPPE *comes back by the outer door.*

GIUSEPPE: The horse is ready, Lieutenant.

LIEUTENANT: Im not going just yet. Go and find the General and tell him I want to speak to him.

GIUSEPPE (*shaking his head*): That will never do, Lieutenant.

LIEUTENANT: Why not?

GIUSEPPE: In this wicked world a general may send for a lieutenant; but a lieutenant must not send for a general.

LIEUTENANT: Oh, you think he wouldnt like it. Well, perhaps youre right: one has to be awfully particular about that sort of thing now we're a republic.

NAPOLEON *reappears, advancing from the vineyard, buttoning the breast of his coat, pale and full of gnawing thoughts.*

GIUSEPPE (*unconscious of NAPOLEON's approach*): Quite true, Lieutenant, quite true. You are all like innkeepers now in France: you have to be polite to everybody.

NAPOLEON (*putting his hand on GIUSEPPE's shoulder*): And that destroys the whole value of politeness, eh?

LIEUTENANT: The very man I wanted! See here, General: suppose I catch that fellow for you!

NAPOLEON *(with ironical gravity)*: You will not catch him, my friend.

LIEUTENANT: Aha! you think so; but youll see. Just wait. Only, if I do catch him and hand him over to you, will you cry quits? Will you drop all this about degrading me in the presence of my regiment? Not that *I* mind, you know; but still no regiment likes to have all the other regiments laughing at it.

NAPOLEON *(a cold ray of humor striking pallidly across his gloom)*: What shall we do with this officer, Giuseppe? Everything he says is wrong.

GIUSEPPE *(promptly)*: Make him a general, excellency; and then everything he says will be right.

LIEUTENANT *(crowing)*: Haw-aw! *(He throws himself ecstatically on the couch to enjoy the joke)*.

NAPOLEON *(laughing and pinching GIUSEPPE's ear)*: You are thrown away in this inn, Giuseppe. *(He sits down and places GIUSEPPE before him like a schoolmaster with a pupil)*. Shall I take you away with me and make a man of you?

GIUSEPPE *(shaking his head rapidly and repeatedly)*: No no no no no no no. All my life long people have wanted to make a man of me. When I was a boy, our good priest wanted to make a man of me by teaching me to read and write. Then the organist at Melegnano wanted to make a man of me by teaching me to read music. The recruiting sergeant would have made a man of me if I had been a few inches taller. But it always meant making me work; and I am too lazy for that, thank Heaven! So I taught myself to cook and became an innkeeper; and now I keep servants to do the work, and have nothing to do myself except talk, which suits me perfectly.

NAPOLEON *(looking at him thoughtfully)*: You are satisfied?

GIUSEPPE *(with cheerful conviction)*: Quite, excellency.

NAPOLEON: And you have no devouring devil inside you who must be fed with action and victory: gorged with them night and day: who makes you pay, with the sweat of your brain and body, weeks of Herculean toil for ten minutes of enjoyment: who is at once your slave and your tyrant, your genius and your doom: who brings you a crown in one hand and the oar of a galley slave in the other: who shews you all the kingdoms of the earth and offers to make you their master on condition that you become their servant! have you nothing of that in you?

GIUSEPPE: Nothing of it! Oh, I assure you, excellency, m y devouring devil is far worse than that. He offers me no crowns and kingdoms: he expects to get everything for nothing: sausages! omelettes! grapes! cheese! polenta! wine! three times a day, excellency: nothing less will content him.

LIEUTENANT: Come: drop it. Giuseppe: youre making me feel hungry again.

> GIUSEPPE, *with an apologetic shrug, retires from the conversation.*

NAPOLEON *(turning to the* LIEUTENANT *with sardonic politeness)*: I hope *I* have not been making you feel ambitious.

LIEUTENANT: Not at all: I dont fly so high. Besides, I'm better as I am: men like me are wanted in the army just now. The fact is, the Revolution was all very well for civilians; but it wont work in the army. You know what soldiers are, General: they w i l l have men of family for their officers. A subaltern must be a gentleman, because he's so much in contact with the men. But a general. or even a colonel, may be any sort of riff-raff if he understands his job well enough. A lieutenant is a gentleman: all the rest is chance. Why, who do you suppose won the battle of Lodi? I'll tell you. My horse did.

NAPOLEON *(rising)*: Your folly is carrying you too far, sir. Take care.

LIEUTENANT: Not a bit of it. You remember all that red-hot cannonade across the river: the Austrians blazing away at you to keep you from crossing, and you blazing away at them to keep them from setting the bridge on fire? Did you notice where I was then?

NAPOLEON: I am sorry. I am afraid I was rather occupied at the moment.

GIUSEPPE *(with eager admiration)*: They say you jumped off your horse and worked the big guns with your own hands, General.

LIEUTENANT: That was a mistake: an officer should never let himself down to the level of his men. (NAPOLEON *looks at him dangerously, and begins to walk tigerishly to and fro).* But you might have been firing away at the Austrians still if we cavalry fellows hadnt found the ford and got across and turned old Beaulieu's flank for you. You know you didnt dare give the order to charge the bridge until you saw us on the other side. Consequently, I say that whoever found that ford won the battle of Lodi. Well, who found it? I was the first man to cross; and I know. It was my horse that found it. (*With conviction, as he rises from the couch*). That horse is the true conqueror of the Austrians.

NAPOLEON (*passionately*): You idiot: I'll have you shot for losing those despatches: I'll have you blown from the mouth of a cannon: nothing less could make any impression on you. (*Baying at him*). Do you hear? Do you understand?

A French officer enters unobserved, carrying his sheathed sabre in his hand.

LIEUTENANT (*unabashed*): If I dont capture him, General. Remember the if.

NAPOLEON: If!! Ass: there is no such man.

THE OFFICER (*suddenly stepping between them and speaking in the unmistakable voice of the* STRANGE LADY): Lieutenant: I am your prisoner. (*She offers him her sabre*).

NAPOLEON *gazes at her for a moment thunderstruck; then seizes her by the wrist and drags her roughly to him, looking closely and fiercely at her to satisfy himself as to her identity; for it now begins to darken rapidly into night, the red glow over the vineyard giving way to clear starlight.*

NAPOLEON: Pah! (*He flings her hand away with an exclamation of disgust, and turns his back on her with his hand in his breast, his brow lowering and his toes twitching*).

LIEUTENANT (*triumphantly, taking the sabre*): No such man! eh, General? (*To the* LADY). I say: wheres my horse?

LADY: Safe at Borghetto, waiting for you, Lieutenant.

NAPOLEON (*turning on them*): Where are the despatches?

LADY: You would never guess. They are in the most unlikely place in the world. Did you meet my sister here, any of you?

LIEUTENANT: Yes. Very nice woman. She's wonderfully like you; but of course she's better-looking.

LADY (*mysteriously*): Well, do you know that she is a witch?

GIUSEPPE (*in terror, crossing himself*): Oh, no, no, no. It is not safe to jest about such things. I cannot have it in my house, excellency.

LIEUTENANT: Yes, drop it. Youre my prisoner, you know. Of course I dont believe in any such rubbish; but still it's not a proper subject for joking.

LADY: But this is very serious. My sister has bewitched the General. (GIUSEPPE *and the* LIEUTENANT *recoil from* NAPOLEON). General: open your coat: you will find the despatches in the breast of it. (*She puts her hand quickly on his breast*). Yes: there they are: I can feel them. Eh? (*She looks up into his face half coaxingly, half mockingly*). Will you allow me, General? (*She takes a button as if to unbutton his coat, and pauses for permission*).

NAPOLEON (*inscrutably*): If you dare.

LADY: Thank you. (*She opens his coat and takes out the despatches*). There! (*To* GIUSEPPE, *shewing him the despatches*). See!

GIUSEPPE (*flying to the outer door*): No, in Heaven's name! Theyre bewitched.

LADY (*turning to the* LIEUTENANT): Here, Lieutenant: you are not afraid of them.

LIEUTENANT (*retreating*): Keep off. (*Seizing the hilt of the sabre*). Keep off, I tell you.

LADY (*to* NAPOLEON): They belong to you, General. Take them.

GIUSEPPE: Dont touch them, excellency. Have nothing to do with them.

LIEUTENANT: Be careful, General: be careful.

GIUSEPPE: Burn them. And burn the witch too.

LADY (*to* NAPOLEON): Shall I burn them?

NAPOLEON (*thoughtfully*): Yes, burn them. Giuseppe: go and fetch a light.

GIUSEPPE (*trembling and stammering*): Do you mean go alone? in the dark? with a witch in the house?

NAPOLEON: Pshaw! Youre a poltroon. (*To the* LIEUTENANT). Oblige me by going, Lieutenant.

LIEUTENANT (*remonstrating*): Oh, I say, General! No, look here, you know: nobody can say I'm a coward after Lodi. But to ask me to go into the dark by myself without a candle after such an awful conversation is a little too much. How would you like to do it yourself?

NAPOLEON (*irritably*): You refuse to obey my order?

LIEUTENANT (*resolutely*): Yes I do. It's not reasonable. But I'll tell you what I'll do. If Giuseppe goes, I'll go with him and protect him.

NAPOLEON (*to* GIUSEPPE): There! will that satisfy you? Be off, both of you.

GIUSEPPE (*humbly, his lips trembling*): W-willingly, your excellency. (*He goes reluctantly towards the inner door*). Heaven protect me! (*To the* LIEUTENANT). After you, Lieutenant.

LIEUTENANT: Youd better go first: I dont know the way.

GIUSEPPE: You cant miss it. Besides (*imploringly, laying his hand on his sleeve*) I am only a poor innkeeper: you are a man of family.

LIEUTENANT: Theres something in that. Here: you neednt be in such a fright. Take my arm (GIUSEPPE *does so*). Thats the way. (*They go out, arm in arm*).

> *It is now starry night. The* LADY *throws the packet on the table and seats herself at her ease on the couch, enjoying the sensation of freedom from petticoats.*

LADY: Well, General: Ive beaten you.

NAPOLEON (*walking about*): You are guilty of indelicacy: of unwomanliness. Is that costume proper?

LADY: It seems to me much the same as yours.

NAPOLEON: Pshaw! I blush for you.

LADY (*naïvely*): Yes: soldiers blush so easily. (*He growls and turns away. She looks mischievously at him, balancing the despatches in her hand*). Wouldnt you like to read these before theyre burnt, General? You must be dying with curiosity. Take a peep. (*She throws the packet on the table, and turns her face away from it*). I wont look.

NAPOLEON: I have no curiosity whatever, madam. But since you are evidently burning to read them, I give you leave to do so.

LADY: Oh, Ive read them already.

NAPOLEON (*starting*): What!

LADY: I read them the first thing after I rode away on that poor lieutenant's horse. So you see I know whats in them; and you dont.

NAPOLEON: Excuse me. I read them when I was out there in the vineyard ten minutes ago.

LADY: Oh! *(jumping up)*. Oh, General: Ive not beaten you after all. I do admire you so. *(He laughs and pats her cheek)*. This time, really and truly without shamming, I do you homage. *(Kissing his hand)*.

NAPOLEON *(quickly withdrawing it)*: Brr! Dont do that. No more witchcraft.

LADY: I want to say something to you; only you would misunderstand it.

NAPOLEON: Need that stop you?

LADY: Well, it is this. I adore a man who is not afraid to be mean and selfish.

NAPOLEON *(indignantly)*: I am neither mean nor selfish.

LADY: Oh, you dont appreciate yourself. Besides, I dont really mean meanness and selfishness.

NAPOLEON: Thank you. I thought perhaps you did.

LADY: Well, of course I d o. But what I mean is a certain strong simplicity about you.

NAPOLEON: Thats better.

LADY: You didnt want to read the letters; but you were curious about what was in them. So you went into the garden and read them when no one was looking, and then came back and pretended you hadnt. Thats the meanest thing I ever knew any man do; but it exactly fulfilled your purpose; and so you werent a bit afraid or ashamed to do it.

NAPOLEON *(abruptly)*: Where did you pick up all these vulgar scruples? this *(with contemptuous emphasis)* conscience of yours? I took you for a lady: an aristocrat. Was your grandfather a shopkeeper, pray?

LADY: No: he was an Englishman.

NAPOLEON: That accounts for it. The English are a nation of shopkeepers. Now I understand why youve beaten me.

LADY: Oh, I havnt beaten you. And I'm not English.

NAPOLEON: Yes you are: English to the backbone. Listen to me: I will explain the English to you.

LADY *(eagerly)*: Do. *(With a lively air of anticipating an intellectual treat, she sits down on the couch and composes herself to listen to him. Secure of his audience, he at once nerves himself for a performance. He considers a little before he begins; so as to fix her attention by a moment of suspense. His style is at first modelled on Talma's in Corneille's Cinna; but it is somewhat lost in the dark-*

ness, and Talma presently gives way to NAPOLEON, *the voice coming through the gloom with startling intensity).*

NAPOLEON: There are three sorts of people in the world: the low people, the middle people, and the high people. The low people and the high people are alike in one thing: they have no scruples, no morality. The low are beneath morality, the high above it. I am not afraid of either of them; for the low are unscrupulous without knowledge, so that they make an idol of me; whilst the high are unscrupulous without purpose, so that they go down before my will. Look you: I shall go over all the mobs and all the courts of Europe as a plough goes over a field. It is the middle people who are dangerous: they have both knowledge and purpose. But they, too, have their weak point. They are full of scruples: chained hand and foot by their morality and respectability.

LADY: Then you will beat the English; for all shopkeepers are middle people.

NAPOLEON: No, because the English are a race apart. No Englishman is too low to have scruples: no Englishman is high enough to be free from their tyranny. But every Englishman is born with a certain miraculous power that makes him master of the world. When he wants a thing, he never tells himself that he wants it. He waits patiently until there comes into his mind, no one knows how, a burning conviction that it is his moral and religious duty to conquer those who possess the thing he wants. Then he becomes irresistible. Like the aristocrat, he does what pleases him and grabs what he covets: like the shopkeeper, he pursues his purpose with the industry and steadfastness that come from strong religious conviction and deep sense of moral responsibility. He is never at a loss for an effective moral attitude. As the great champion of freedom and national independence, he conquers and annexes half the world, and calls it Colonization. When he wants a new market for his adulterated Manchester goods, he sends a missionary to teach the natives the Gospel of Peace. The natives kill the missionary: he flies to arms in defence of Christianity; fights for it; conquers for it; and takes the market as a reward from heaven. In defence of his island shores, he puts a chaplain on board his ship; nails a flag with a cross on it to his top-gallant mast; and sails to the ends of the earth, sinking, burning, and destroying all who dispute the empire of the seas with him. He boasts that a slave is free the moment his foot touches British soil; and he sells the children of his poor at six years of age to work under the lash in his factories for sixteen hours a day. He makes two revolutions, and then declares war on our one in the name of law and order. There is nothing so bad or so good that you will not find Englishmen doing it; but you will never find an Englishman in the wrong. He does everything on principle. He fights you on patriotic principles; he robs you on business principles; he enslaves you on imperial principles; he bullies you on manly principles; he supports his king on loyal principles and cuts off his king's head on republican principles. His watchword is always Duty, and he never forgets that the nation which lets its duty get on the opposite side to its interest is lost. He——

LADY: W-w-w-w-w-wh! Do stop a moment. I want to know how you make me out to be English at this rate.

NAPOLEON (*dropping his rhetorical style*): It's plain enough. You wanted some letters that belonged to me. You have spent the morning in stealing them: yes, stealing them, by highway robbery. And you have spent the afternoon in putting me in the wrong about them: in assuming that it was *I* who wanted to steal y o u r letters: in explaining that it all came about through my meanness and selfishness, and your goodness, your devotion, your self-sacrifice. Thats English.

LADY: Nonsense! I am sure I am not a bit English. The English are a very stupid people.

NAPOLEON: Yes, too stupid sometimes to know when theyre beaten. But I grant that your brains are not English. You see, though your grandfather was an Englishman, your grandmother was—what? A Frenchwoman?

LADY: Oh no. An Irishwoman.

NAPOLEON (*quickly*): Irish! (*Thoughtfully*). Yes: I forgot the Irish. An English army led by an Irish general: that might be a match for a French army led by an Italian general. (*He pauses, and adds, half jestingly, half moodily*) At all events, y o u have beaten me; and what beats a man first will beat him last. (*He goes meditatively into the moonlit vineyard and looks up*).

She steals out after him. She ventures to rest her hand on his shoulder, overcome by the beauty of the night and emboldened by its obscurity.

LADY (*softly*): What are you looking at?

NAPOLEON (*pointing up*): My star.

LADY: You believe in that?

NAPOLEON: I do.

They look at it for a moment, she leaning a little on his shoulder.

LADY: Do you know that the English say that a man's star is not complete without a woman's garter?

NAPOLEON (*scandalized: abruptly shaking her off and coming back into the room*): Pah! the hypocrites! If the French said that, how they would hold up their hands in pious horror! (*He goes to the inner door and holds it open, shouting*) Hallo! Giuseppe! Wheres that light, man? (*He comes between the table and the sideboard, and moves the second chair to the table, beside his own*). We have still to burn the letter. (*He takes up the packet*).

GIUSEPPE comes back, pale and still trembling, carrying in one hand a branched candlestick with a couple of candles alight, and a broad snuffers tray in the other.

GIUSEPPE (*piteously, as he places the light on the table*): Excellency: what were you looking up at just now? Out there! (*He points across his shoulder to the vineyard, but is afraid to look round*).

NAPOLEON (*unfolding the packet*): What is that to you?

GIUSEPPE: Because the witch is gone: vanished; and no one saw her go out.

LADY (*coming behind him from the vineyard*): We were watching her riding up to the moon on your broomstick, Giuseppe. You will never see her again.

GIUSEPPE: Gesu Maria! (*He crosses himself and hurries out*).

NAPOLEON (*throwing down the letters in a heap on the table*): Now! (*He sits down at the table in the chair which he has just placed*).

LADY: Yes; but you know you have THE letter in your pocket. (*He smiles; takes a letter from his pocket; and tosses it on*

top of the heap. She holds it up and looks at him, saying)
About Caesar's wife.

NAPOLEON: Caesar's wife is above suspicion. Burn it.

LADY *(taking up the snuffers and holding the letter to the candle flame with it)*: I wonder would Caesar's wife be above suspicion if she saw us here together!

NAPOLEON *(echoing her, with his elbows on the table and his cheeks on his hands, looking at the letter)*: I wonder!

> THE STRANGE LADY *puts the letter down alight on the snuffers tray, and sits down beside* NAPOLEON, *in the same attitude, elbows on table, cheeks on hands, watching it burn. When it is burnt, they simultaneously turn their eyes and look at one another. The curtain steals down and hides them.*

Interior

by MAURICE MAETERLINCK

*Translated from the French
by WILLIAM ARCHER*

Maurice Maeterlinck (1862–1949)

Although Maurice Maeterlinck—symbolist poet, essayist, philosophic mystic, and dramatist—was born in Ghent, Belgium, he spent most of his life in France and was influenced by its culture. Encouraged by his family to study law, he was admitted to the bar in 1886. During a stay in Paris he was inspired by his study of the symbolist poets Paul Verlaine, Stéphane Mallarmé, and August Villiers de l'Isle Adam and determined to become a writer. After publishing two volumes of imitative poetry, he wrote a play, *La Princesse Malaine*, which was highly praised by the important critic Octave Mirbeau. From 1890 to 1894 Maeterlinck wrote four plays which established him as the leader of a new type of drama. Three short plays—*The Intruder* (1890), *The Blind* (1891), *Interior* (1894)—and his full-length *Pelléas and Mélisande* (1892) were antinaturalistic dramas that had a profound influence on the theater for a generation.

In his essays in *The Treasure of the Humble*, published in 1896, he propounded his theory of a static, symbolistic drama. The realistic and naturalistic plays popular in the second half of the nineteenth century, he felt, dealt only superficially with life by depicting in their complicated plots the struggles of articulate characters. (Brunetière's theory that drama was essentially a clash of wills was the accepted concept.) To Maeterlinck the mystic, life was a mystery whose inexplicable pattern could only be suggested by creating a mood by the use of symbols. The reality behind the commonplace could be evoked by "interior dialogue": short musical speeches, pauses, and silences to evoke emotions and soulstates of the characters. Plotless plays avoiding theatrical violence could best express the infinite mysteries and realities of birth, life, and death. In an oft-quoted passage, he declared,

173

"I have grown to believe that an old man, seated in his arm chair, waiting patiently with his lamp beside him, giving unconscious ear to all the external laws that reign about his house, interpreting, without comprehending, the silence of doors and windows and the quivering voice of the light, submitting with bent head to the presence of his soul and his destiny . . . motionless as he is, does yet in reality live a deeper, more human, and more universal life than the lover who strangles his mistress, the captain who conquers in battle, or 'the husband who avenges his honor.'"*

The Intruder is an excellent example of Maeterlinck's dramatic skill in communicating the ineffable mystery of the approach of Death. Although the characters with their terse, fragmentary speeches are not involved in any violent action, the play does build up considerable emotional tension as they intuitively sense the arrival of the mysterious intruder. The blind old grandfather, alerted by his other sharpened senses, sees as the uncle realizes "better than we can." The dramatist's use of concrete symbolic details—the hushed nightingales, the frightened swans, the silent dogs, the mysterious opening of the glass door, the cold wind, the sound of the gardener sharpening his scythe, the dimming of the lamp—all contribute to the tragic atmosphere.

Interior, like *The Intruder*, deals with the inexplicable mystery of death. The wraithlike, passive characters, speaking in cadenced prose that evokes the mood of a dirge, discuss in hushed whispers how they should break the news of the drowning of a beautiful young girl to her family. Maeterlinck symbolizes the tenuous separation between death and life by using darkness and light dramatically. The compassionate group—The Old Man, his two granddaughters, and The Stranger—aware of the tragedy, are huddled in the dark garden in the shadow of great trees, while the silent, unwitting personages in the house are bathed in the light of a lamp. The tranquil family is separated from man's greatest enemy, Death, "by only a few poor panes of glass." Although there is little action in his static drama, Maeterlinck skillfully creates emotional tensions, as when The Old Man enters the room

---

* *The Treasure of the Humble*, trans. Alfred Sutro (London: George Allen and Unwin, 1897).

as the bearer of ill tidings. The quiet but effective climax of the play is the slow affirmative nod that he gives the questioning family.

The Old Man, sorrowed and perplexed by the sudden death of the girl, sees the world in a different light. "Men understand nothing until after all is over." Recognizing the unfathomable nature of the human soul and the helplessness of man to avert misfortune, he is oppressed by the tragic sense of life. Maeterlinck symbolizes man's powerlessness in an immense, mysterious universe by the winding procession of the villagers lost in the herbage and by the final tableau of the starry sky, the moonlight on the lawn, and the lonely, sleeping child.

CHARACTERS

In the garden

THE OLD MAN
THE STRANGER
MARTHA }
MARY } Granddaughters of the Old Man
A PEASANT
THE CROWD

In the house

THE FATHER
THE MOTHER
THE TWO DAUGHTERS } Silent personages
THE CHILD

*An old garden planted with willows.
At the back, a house, with three of
the ground-floor windows lighted up.
Through them a family is pretty distinctly visible, gathered for the evening
around the lamp.* THE FATHER *is seated
at the chimney corner.* THE MOTHER
*resting one elbow on the table, is gazing
into vacancy. Two young girls, dressed
in white, sit at their embroidery, dreaming and smiling in the tranquility of the
room. A* CHILD *is asleep, his head resting
on his mother's left arm. When one of
them rises, walks, or makes a gesture,
the movements appear grave, slow,
apart, and as though spiritualized by the
distance, the light, and the transparent
film of the windowpanes.*

THE OLD MAN *and* THE STRANGER *enter
the garden cautiously.*

THE OLD MAN: Here we are in the part of the garden that
lies behind the house. They never come here. The doors
are on the other side. They are closed and the shutters
shut. But there are no shutters on this side of the house,
and I saw the light. . . . Yes, they are still sitting up in
the lamplight. It is well that they have not heard us; the
mother or the girls would perhaps have come out, and
then what should we have done?
THE STRANGER: What are we going to do?
THE OLD MAN: I want first to see if they are all in the room.

177

Yes, I see the father seated at the chimney corner. He is doing nothing, his hands resting on his knees. The mother is leaning her elbow on the table . . .

THE STRANGER: She is looking at us.

THE OLD MAN: No, she is looking at nothing; her eyes are fixed. She cannot see us; we are in the shadow of the great trees. But do not go any nearer. . . . There, too, are the dead girl's two sisters; they are embroidering slowly. And the little child has fallen asleep. It is nine on the clock in the corner. . . . They divine no evil, and they do not speak.

THE STRANGER: If we were to attract the father's attention, and make some sign to him? He has turned his head this way. Shall I knock at one of the windows? One of them will have to hear of it before the others. . . .

THE OLD MAN: I do not know which to choose. . . . We must be very careful. The father is old and ailing—the mother too—and the sisters are too young. . . . And they all loved her as they will never love again. I have never seen a happier household. . . . No, no! do not go up to the window; that would be the worst thing we could do. It is better that we should tell them of it as simply as we can, as though it were a commonplace occurrence; and we must not appear too sad, else they will feel that their sorrow must exceed ours, and they will not know what to do. . . . Let us go around to the other side of the garden. We will knock at the door, and go in as if nothing had happened. I will go in first: they will not be surprised to see me; I sometimes look in of an evening, to bring them some flowers or fruit, and to pass an hour or two with them.

THE STRANGER: Why do you want me to go with you? Go alone; I will wait until you call me. They have never seen me—I am only a passerby, a stranger. . . .

THE OLD MAN: It is better that I should not be alone. A misfortune announced by a single voice seems more definite and crushing. I thought of that as I came along. . . . If I go in alone, I shall have to speak at the very first moment; they will know all in a few words; I shall have nothing more to say; and I dread the silence which follows the last words that tell of a misfortune. It is then that the heart is torn. If we enter together, I shall go roundabout to work; I shall tell them, for example: "They found her thus, or thus . . . She was floating on the stream, and her hands were clasped . . ."

THE STRANGER: Her hands were not clasped; her arms were floating at her sides.

THE OLD MAN: You see, in spite of ourselves we begin to talk—and the misfortune is shrouded in its details. Otherwise, if I go in alone, I know them well enough to be sure that the very first words would produce a terrible effect, and Gods knows what would happen. But if we speak to them in turns, they will listen to us, and will forget to look the evil tidings in the face. Do not forget that the mother will be there, and that her life hangs by a thread . . . It is well that the first wave of sorrow should waste its strength in unnecessary words. It is wisest to let people gather round the unfortunate and talk as they will. Even the most indifferent carry off, without knowing it, some portion of the sorrow. It is dispersed without effort and without noise, like air or light. . . .

THE STRANGER: Your clothes are soaked and are dripping on the flagstones.

THE OLD MAN: It is only the skirt of my mantle that has trailed a little in the water. You seem to be cold. Your coat is all muddy. . . . I did not notice it on the way, it was so dark.

THE STRANGER: I went into the water up to my waist.

THE OLD MAN: Had you found her long when I came up?

THE STRANGER: Only a few moments. I was going toward the village; it was already late, and the dusk was falling on the river bank. I was walking along with my eyes fixed on the river, because it was lighter than the road, when I saw something strange close by a tuft of reeds. . . . I drew nearer, and I saw her hair, which had floated up almost into a circle round her head, and was swaying hither and thither with the current. . . . (*In the room the two young girls turn their heads toward the window.*)

THE OLD MAN: Did you see her two sisters' hair trembling on their shoulders?

THE STRANGER: They turned their heads in our direction— they simply turned their heads. Perhaps I was speaking too loudly. (*The two girls resume their former position.*) They have turned away again already. . . . I went into the water up to my waist, and then I managed to grasp her hand and easily drew her to the bank. She was as beautiful as her sisters. . . .

THE OLD MAN: I think she was more beautiful. . . . I do not know why I have lost all my courage. . . .

THE STRANGER: What courage do you mean? We did all that man could do. She had been dead for more than an hour.

THE OLD MAN: She was living this morning! I met her coming out of the church. She told me that she was going away; she was going to see her grandmother on the other side of the river in which you found her. She did not know when I should see her again. . . . She seemed to be on the point of asking me something; then I suppose she did not dare, and she left me abruptly. But now that I think of it—and I noticed nothing at the time!—she smiled as people smile who want to be silent, or who fear that they will not be understood. . . . Even hope seemed like a pain to her; her eyes were veiled, and she scarcely looked at me.

THE STRANGER: Some peasants told me that they saw her wandering all the afternoon on the bank. They thought she was looking for flowers. . . . It is possible that her death . . .

THE OLD MAN: No one can tell. . . . What can anyone know? She was perhaps one of those who shrink from speech, and everyone bears in his breast more than one reason for ceasing to live. You cannot see into the soul as you see into that room. They are all like that—they say nothing but trivial things, and no one dreams that there is aught amiss. You live for months by the side of one who is no longer of this world, and whose soul cannot stoop to to it; you answer her unthinkingly; and you see what happens. They look like lifeless puppets, and all the time so many things are passing in their souls. They do not themselves know what they are. She might have lived as the others live. She might have said to the day of her death: "Sir, or Madam, it will rain this morning," or, "We are going to lunch; we shall be thirteen at table," or "The fruit is not yet ripe." They speak smilingly of the flowers that have fallen, and they weep in the darkness. An angel from heaven would not see what ought to be seen; and men understand nothing until after all is over. . . . Yesterday evening she was there, sitting in the lamplight like her sisters; and you would not see them now as they ought to be seen if this had not happened. . . . I seem to see her for the first time. . . . Something new must come into our ordinary life before we can understand it. They are at your side day and night; and you do not really see them until the moment when they depart forever. And yet, what a strange little soul she must have had—what a poor little, artless, unfathomable soul she must have had—to have said what she must have said, and done what she must have done!

THE STRANGER: See, they are smiling in the silence of the room. . . .

THE OLD MAN: They are not at all anxious—they did not expect her this evening.

THE STRANGER: They sit motionless and smiling. But see, the father puts his fingers to his lips. . . .

THE OLD MAN: He points to the child asleep on its mother's breast. . . .

THE STRANGER: She dares not raise her head for fear of disturbing it. . . .

THE OLD MAN: They are not sewing anymore. There is a dead silence. . . .

THE STRANGER: They have let fall their skein of white silk. . . .

THE OLD MAN: They are looking at the child. . . .

THE STRANGER: They do not know that others are looking at them. . . .

THE OLD MAN: We, too, are watched. . . .

THE STRANGER: They have raised their eyes. . . .

THE OLD MAN: And yet they can see nothing. . . .

THE STRANGER: They seem to be happy, and yet there is something—I cannot tell what. . . .

THE OLD MAN: They think themselves beyond the reach of danger. They have closed the doors, and the windows are barred with iron. They have strengthened the walls of the old house; they have shot the bolts of the three oaken doors. They have foreseen everything that can be foreseen. . . .

THE STRANGER: Sooner or later we must tell them. Someone might come in and blurt it out abruptly. There was a crowd of peasants in the meadow where we left the dead girl—if one of them were to come and knock at the door. . . .

THE OLD MAN: Martha and Mary are watching the little body. The peasants were going to make a litter of branches, and I told my eldest granddaughter to hurry on and let us know the moment they made a start. Let us wait till she

comes; she will go with me. . . . I wish we had not been
able to watch them in this way. I thought there was nothing
to do but to knock at the door, to enter quite simply, and
to tell all in a few phrases. . . . But I have watched them
too long, living in the lamplight. . . . *(Enter MARY.)*

MARY: They are coming, grandfather.

THE OLD MAN: Is that you? Where are they?

MARY: They are at the foot of the last slope.

THE OLD MAN: They are coming silently.

MARY: I told them to pray in a low voice. Martha is with
them.

THE OLD MAN: Are there many of them?

MARY: The whole village is around the bier. They had brought
lanterns; I bade them put them out.

THE OLD MAN: What way are they coming?

MARY: They are coming by the little path. They are moving
slowly.

THE OLD MAN: It is time. . . .

MARY: Have you told them, grandfather?

THE OLD MAN: You can see that we have told them nothing.
There they are, still sitting in the lamplight. Look, my child,
look: you will see what life is. . . .

MARY: Oh! how peaceful they seem! I feel as though I were
seeing them in a dream.

THE STRANGER: Look there—I saw the two sisters give a start.

THE OLD MAN: They are rising. . . .

THE STRANGER: I believe they are coming to the windows.

> *(At this moment, one of the two sisters comes up to the
> first window, the other to the third; and resting their
> hands against the panes, they stand gazing into the
> darkness.)*

THE OLD MAN: No one comes to the middle window.

MARY: They are looking out; they are listening. . . .

THE OLD MAN: The elder is smiling at what she does not see.

THE STRANGER: The eyes of the second are full of fear.

THE OLD MAN: Take care: who knows how far the soul may
extend around the body. . . . *(A long silence. MARY nestles
close to THE OLD MAN's breast and kisses him.)*

MARY: Grandfather!

THE OLD MAN: Do not weep, my child; our turn will come.
(A pause.)

THE STRANGER: They are looking long. . . .

THE OLD MAN: Poor things, they would see nothing though they looked for a hundred thousand years—the night is too dark. They are looking this way; and it is from the other side that misfortune is coming.

THE STRANGER: It is well that they are looking this way. Something, I do not know what, is approaching by way of the meadows.

MARY: I think it is the crowd; they are too far off for us to see clearly.

THE STRANGER: They are following the windings of the path —there they come in sight again on that moonlit slope.

MARY: Oh! how many they seem to be. Even when I left, people were coming up from the outskirts of the town. They are taking a very roundabout way. . . .

THE OLD MAN: They will arrive at last, nonetheless. I see them, too—they are crossing the meadows—they look so small that one can scarcely distinguish them among the herbage. You might think them children playing in the moonlight; if the girls saw them, they would not understand. Turn their backs to it as they may, misfortune is approaching step by step, and has been looming larger for more than two hours past. They cannot bid it stay; and those who are bringing it are powerless to stop it. It has mastered them, too, and they must needs serve it. It knows its goal, and it takes its course. It is unwearying, and it has but one idea. They have to lend it their strength. They are sad, but they draw nearer. Their hearts are full of pity, but they must advance. . . .

MARY: The elder has ceased to smile, grandfather.

THE STRANGER: They are leaving the windows. . . .

MARY: They are kissing their mother. . . .

THE STRANGER: The elder is stroking the child's curls without wakening it.

MARY: Ah! the father wants them to kiss him, too. . . .

THE STRANGER: Now there is silence. . . .

MARY: They have returned to their mother's side.

THE STRANGER: And the father keeps his eyes fixed on the great pendulum of the clock. . . .

MARY: They seem to be praying without knowing what they do. . . .

THE STRANGER: They seem to be listening to their own souls. . . . *(A pause.)*

MARY: Grandfather, do not tell them this evening!

THE OLD MAN: You see, you are losing courage, too. I knew you ought not to look at them. I am nearly eighty-three years old, and this is the first time that the reality of life has come home to me. I do not know why all they do appears to me so strange and solemn. There they sit awaiting the night, simply, under their lamp, as we should under our own; and yet I seem to see them from the altitude of another world, because I know a little fact which as yet they do not know . . . Is it so, my children? Tell me, why are you, too, pale? Perhaps there is something else that we cannot put in words, and that makes us weep? I did not know that there was anything so sad in life, or that it could strike such terror to those who look on at it. And even if nothing had happened, it would frighten me to see them sit there so peacefully. They have too much confidence in this world. There they sit, separated from the enemy by only a few poor panes of glass. They think that nothing will happen because they have closed their doors, and they do not know that it is in the soul that things always happen, and that the world does not end at their house door. They are so secure of their little life, and do not dream that so many others know more of it than they, and that I, poor old man, at two steps from their door, hold all their little happiness, like a wounded bird, in the hollow of my old hands, and dare not open them. . . .

MARY: Have pity on them, grandfather. . . .

THE OLD MAN: We have pity on them, my child, but no one has pity on us.

MARY: Tell them tomorrow, grandfather; tell them when it is light, then they will not be so sad.

THE OLD MAN: Perhaps you are right, my child. . . . It would be better to leave all this in the night. And the daylight is sweet to sorrow. . . . But what would they say to us tomorrow? Misfortune makes people jealous; those upon whom it has fallen want to know of it before strangers—they do not like to leave it in unknown hands. We should seem to have robbed them of something.

THE STRANGER: Besides, it is too late now; already I can hear the murmur of prayers.

MARY: They are here—they are passing behind the hedges. *(Enter* MARTHA.*)*

MARTHA: Here I am. I have guided them hither—I told them to wait in the road. *(Cries of children are heard.)* Ah! the children are still crying. I forbade them to come, but they want to see, too, and the mothers would not obey me. I will go and tell them—no, they have stopped crying. Is everything ready? I have brought the little ring that was found upon her. I have some fruit, too, for the child. I laid her to rest myself upon the bier. She looks as though she were sleeping. I had a great deal of trouble with her hair—I could not arrange it properly. I made them gather marguerites—it is a pity there were no other flowers. What are you doing here? Why are you not with them? *(She looks in at the windows.)* They are not weeping! They—you have not told them!

THE OLD MAN: Martha, Martha, there is too much life in your soul; you cannot understand. . . .

MARTHA: Why should I not understand? *(After a silence, and in a tone of grave reproach.)* You really ought not to have done that, grandfather. . . .

THE OLD MAN: Martha, you do not know. . . .

MARTHA: I will go and tell them.

THE OLD MAN: Remain here, my child, and look for a moment.

MARTHA: Oh, how I pity them! They must wait no longer. . . .

THE OLD MAN: Why not?

MARTHA: I do not know, but it is not possible!

THE OLD MAN: Come here, my child. . . .

MARTHA: How patient they are!

THE OLD MAN: Come here, my child. . . .

MARTHA *(turning)*: Where are you, grandfather? I am so unhappy, I cannot see you anymore. I do not myself know now what to do. . . .

THE OLD MAN: Do not look anymore; until they know all. . . .

MARTHA: I want to go with you. . . .

THE OLD MAN: No, Martha, stay here. Sit beside your sister on this old stone bench against the wall of the house, and do not look. You are too young, you would never be able to forget it. You cannot know what a face looks like at the moment when Death is passing into its eyes. Perhaps they will cry out, too . . . Do not turn around. Perhaps there will be no sound at all. Above all things, if there is no sound, be sure you do not turn and look. One can never foresee the course that sorrow will take. A few little sobs wrung from the depths, and generally that is all. I do not know myself what I shall do when I hear them—they do not belong to this life. Kiss me, my child, before I go. *(The murmur of prayers has gradually drawn nearer. A portion of the crowd forces its way into the garden. There is a sound of deadened footfalls and of whispering.)*

THE STRANGER *(to the crowd)*: Stop here—do not go near the window. Where is she?

A PEASANT: Who?

THE STRANGER: The others—the bearers.

A PEASANT: They are coming by the avenue that leads up to the door.

> *(THE OLD MAN goes out. MARTHA and MARY have seated themselves on the bench, their backs to the windows. Low murmurings are heard among the crowd.)*

THE STRANGER: Hush! Do not speak. *(In the room the taller of the two sisters rises, goes to the door, and shoots the bolts.)*

MARTHA: She is opening the door!

THE STRANGER: On the contrary, she is fastening it. *(A pause.)*

MARTHA: Grandfather has not come in?

THE STRANGER: No. She takes her seat again at her mother's side. The others do not move, and the child is still sleeping. *(A pause.)*

MARTHA: My little sister, give me your hands.

MARY: Martha! *(They embrace and kiss each other.)*

THE STRANGER: He must have knocked—they have all raised their heads at the same time—they are looking at each other.

MARTHA: Oh! oh! my poor little sister! I can scarcely help crying out, too. *(She smothers her sobs on her sister's shoulder.)*

THE STRANGER: He must have knocked again. The father is looking at the clock. He rises. . . .

MARTHA: Sister, sister, I must go in too—they cannot be left alone.

MARY: Martha, Martha! *(She holds her back.)*

THE STRANGER: The father is at the door—he is drawing the bolts—he is opening it cautiously.

MARTHA: Oh!—you do not see the . . .

THE STRANGER: What?

MARTHA: The bearers . . .

THE STRANGER: He has only opened it a very little. I see nothing but a corner of the lawn and the fountain. He keeps his hand on the door—he takes a step back—he seems to be saying, "Ah, it is you!" He raises his arms. He carefully closes the door again. Your grandfather has entered the room . . . (*The crowd has come up to the window.* MARTHA *and* MARY *half rise from their seat, then rise altogether and follow the rest toward the windows, pressing close to each other.* THE OLD MAN *is seen advancing into the room. The two* SISTERS *rise; the* MOTHER *also rises, and carefully settles the* CHILD *in the armchair which she has left, so that from outside the little one can be seen sleeping, his head a little bent forward, in the middle of the room. The* MOTHER *advances to meet* THE OLD MAN, *and holds out her hand to him, but draws it back again before he has had time to take it. One of the girls wants to take off the visitor's mantle, and the other pushes forward an armchair for him. But* THE OLD MAN *makes a little gesture of refusal. The* FATHER *smiles with an air of astonishment.* THE OLD MAN *looks toward the windows.*)

THE STRANGER: He dares not tell them. He is looking toward us. (*Murmurs in the crowd.*)

THE STRANGER: Hush! (THE OLD MAN, *seeing faces at the windows, quickly averts his eyes. As one of the girls is still offering him the armchair, he at last sits down and passes his right hand several times over his forehead.*)

THE STRANGER: He is sitting down. . . . (*The others who are in the room also sit down, while the* FATHER *seems to be speaking volubly. At last* THE OLD MAN *opens his mouth, and the sound of his voice seems to arouse their attention. But the* FATHER *interrupts him.* THE OLD MAN *begins to speak again, and little by little the others grow tense with apprehension. All of a sudden the* MOTHER *starts and rises.*)

MARTHA: Oh! the mother begins to understand! (*She turns away and hides her face in her hands. Renewed murmurs among the crowd. They elbow each other. Children cry*

*to be lifted up, so that they may see too. Most of the
mothers do as they wish.)*

THE STRANGER: Hush! he has not told them yet. . . . *(The
MOTHER is seen to be questioning THE OLD MAN with anxiety. He says a few more words; then, suddenly, all the
others rise, too, and seem to question him. Then he slowly
makes an affirmative movement of his head.)*

THE STRANGER: He has told them—he has told them all at
once!

VOICES IN THE CROWD: He has told them! he has told them!

THE STRANGER: I can hear nothing. . . . *(THE OLD MAN also
rises, and, without turning, makes a gesture indicating the
door, which is behind him. The MOTHER, the FATHER, and
the two DAUGHTERS rush to this door, which the FATHER
has difficulty in opening. THE OLD MAN tries to prevent
the MOTHER from going out.)*

VOICES IN THE CROWD: They are going out! they are going
out! *(Confusion among the crowd in the garden. All hurry
to the other side of the house and disappear, except THE
STRANGER, who remains at the windows. In the room, the
folding door is at last thrown wide open; all go out at the
same time. Beyond can be seen the starry sky, the lawn
and the fountain in the moonlight; while, left alone in the
middle of the room, the CHILD continues to sleep peacefully in the armchair. A pause)*

THE STRANGER: The child has not wakened! *(He also goes
out.)*

CURTAIN

The Tenor

by FRANK WEDEKIND

*Translated from the German
by ANDRÉ TRIDON*

In 1888, when his father died, Wedekind was a serious

Frank Wedekind (1864–1918)

Frank Wedekind, the father of expressionism and the prophet of sexuality in the modern drama, was like his father—a restless, revolutionary wanderer. Dr. Friedrich Wedekind was a German liberal who migrated to Constantinople, where for ten years he was the physician to the Sultan of Turkey. After traveling with various expeditions to the Tigris and Euphrates Rivers, he practiced medicine in Palermo, Rome, and Paris until the autumn of 1847. Hating the Junkers and Prussianism, he returned to Germany to participate in the Revolution of 1848. After its failure he escaped to America and settled in San Francisco. There, at the age of forty-six, he married a German actress, Emilie Kammerer, who was half his age. In 1864 they returned to Hanover, Germany, where their second child, christened Benjamin Franklin, was born.

Independently wealthy, Dr. Wedekind gave up medicine and plunged into politics. Disenchanted with Bismarck's new Reich, he emigrated to Switzerland, where his two sons received an excellent education from private tutors and in boarding schools. Frank was particularly interested in biology and literature, but was encouraged at the age of nineteen to enter the University of Zurich law school. He quickly abandoned his legal studies and went to Munich, where he joined a group of political and literary radicals and began contributing articles to the local papers. Through Gerhart Hauptmann he became familiar with *Wozzeck*, the tragedy of an inarticulate Slavic soldier, written by an early nineteenth-century German playwright, Georg Büchner. (In 1925 the play was turned into a powerful opera by the modernist composer Alban Berg). This play and the naturalistic dramas of Strindberg exerted a strong influence on Wedekind's later works.

In 1888, when his father died, Wedekind led a restless

191

bohemian life, wandering through many European cities as the manager of a circus troupe. Later, like Bertholt Brecht, he recited poems, sang ballads in cafés and cabarets, and acted in theaters in Leipzig and Munich. The publication of his first tragedy, *The Awakening of Spring*, in 1891, created a furor as great as Ibsen's *Ghosts*. The play, unperformed for fifteen years because of censorship, was an indictment of middle-class parents and teachers who fail to give honest answers to adolescents faced with sexual problems. The evasions and hypocrisies of the elders result in the death of a girl by abortion and a youth by suicide. The play, didactic in tone and a strange mixture of expressionism and romanticism in technique, marked Wedekind as a controversial dramatist and helped usher in the sexual revolution of our time. Like Thomas Hardy, Émile Zola, and D. H. Lawrence, he pleaded for an honest approach to sex, but his frankness was denounced as a corruption of youth.

For two years during a sojourn in Paris, he plunged into a life of sensual debauchery and proclaimed his views on the Morality of the Flesh, that erotic love is an elemental force that enslaves us, that society hypocritically covers up our enslavement instead of recognizing that the flesh is its own spirit. Unlike D. H. Lawrence who saw sex as a liberating force, Wedekind, the moralist, saw it as a destructive force as well. In his two Lulu plays, *Earth Spirit* (1895) and *Pandora's Box* (1904), he created a mythlike embodiment of the eternal female whose erotic passion, feeding her ego, brings about the death of several husbands and, in the end, her own at the hands of Jack the Ripper.

Iconoclast in politics, morality, and drama, Wedekind naturally became a controversial and persecuted figure. In 1899 he was imprisoned for writing satirical poems on politics in the comic magazine *Simplicissimus*. Censorship postponed the production of several of his plays, and he was brought to trial for *Pandora's Box*.

In 1908 he married an actress and made his home in Munich. However, he frequently traveled to Berlin to produce his own plays at Max Reinhardt's Neues Theater. Two of Wedekind's successful plays are *The Marquis of Keith* (1901) and *Such Is Life* (1902). The first is a sardonic satire on bourgeois society and morality; its scheming, ruthless protagonist, when exposed, instead of committing suicide, concludes, "Life is one switchback after another" and determines to continue riding the roller coaster of life. The second is a bitter autobiographical allegory with poetic overtones of a king who at first is misunderstood and rejected by his people and who is finally accepted as a national jester.

Wedekind's mordant one-act tragi-comedy *The Tenor* (1897) is an ironic study of a conceited, calculating singer who rationalizes his ruthlessness by depicting himself as a slave to his art. As men driven by sexuality are attracted to Lulu, so girls and women are to the popular Wagnerian tenor Gerardo. With unconscious hypocrisy he first rejects the infatuated young English girl by telling her to sacrifice herself to music, not the performer, and then rejects Professor Duhring, who for fifty years has been a willing victim of "the tyranny of art." Gerardo despises the bourgeois audiences who really do not appreciate or understand his art, yet he proclaims himself as an "artist first and a man next." Cloaking his cowardice in the false rectitude of artistic integrity, he spurns the sacrificial love of Helen Marova, who has deserted her husband and children to be with him. When she kills herself, he hastens to catch his train for Brussels, where he is to sing *Tristan and Isolde* the next night.

CHARACTERS

GERARDO,
  Wagnerian tenor, thirty-six years old

HELEN MAROVA,
  a beautiful dark-haired woman of twenty-five

PROFESSOR DUHRING,
  sixty, the typical "misunderstood genius"

MISS ISABEL COEURNE,
  a blonde English girl of sixteen

MULLER,
  hotel manager

A VALET

A BELL BOY

AN UNKNOWN WOMAN

TIME: The present

PLACE: A city in Austria

SCENE: *A large hotel room. There are doors at the right and in the center, and at the left a window with heavy portières. Behind a grand piano at the right stands a Japanese screen which conceals the fireplace. There are several large trunks, open; bunches of flowers are all over the room; many bouquets are piled up on the piano.*

VALET (*entering from the adjoining room carrying an armful of clothes which he proceeds to pack in one of the trunks. There is a knock at the door*): Come in.

BELL BOY: There is a lady who wants to know if the Maestro is in.

VALET: He isn't in. (*Exit* BELL BOY. *The* VALET *goes into the adjoining room and returns with another armful of clothes. There is another knock at the door. He puts the clothes on a chair and goes to the door.*) What's this again? (*He opens the door and someone hands him several large bunches of flowers, which he places carefully on the piano; then he goes back to his packing. There is another knock. He opens the door and takes a handful of letters. He glances at the addresses and reads aloud.*) "Mister Gerardo. Monsieur Gerardo. Gerardo Esquire. Signor Gerardo." (*He drops the letters on a tray and resumes his packing.*)

(*Enter* GERARDO.)

GERARDO: Haven't you finished packing yet? How much longer will it take you?

VALET: I'll be through in a minute, sir.

GERARDO: Hurry! I still have things to do. Let me see. (*He*

195

reaches for something in a trunk.) God Almighty! Don't you know how to fold a pair of trousers? *(Taking the trousers out.)* This is what you call packing! Look here! You still have something to learn from me, after all. You take the trousers like this. . . . You lock this up here. . . . Then you take hold of these buttons. Watch these buttons here, that's the important thing. Then—you pull them straight. . . . There. . . . There. . . . Then you fold them here. . . . See. . . . Now these trousers would keep their shape for a hundred years.

VALET *(respectfully, with downcast eyes)*: You must have been a tailor once, sir.

GERARDO: What! Well, not exactly. . . . *(He gives the trousers to the* VALET.) Pack those up, but be quick about it. Now about that train. You are sure this is the last one we can take?

VALET: It is the only one that gets you there in time, sir. The next train does not reach Brussels until ten o'clock.

GERARDO: Well, then, we must catch this one. I will just have time to go over the second act. Unless I go over that. . . . Now don't let anybody. . . . I am out to everybody.

VALET: All right, sir. There are some letters for you, sir.

GERARDO: I have seen them.

VALET: And flowers!

GERARDO: Yes, all right. *(He takes the letters from the tray and throws them on a chair before the piano. Then he opens the letters, glances over them with beaming eyes, crumples them up and throws them under the chair.)* Remember! I am out to everybody.

VALET: I know, sir. *(He locks the trunks.)*

GERARDO: To everybody.

VALET: You needn't worry, sir. *(Giving him the trunk keys.)* Here are the keys, sir.

GERARDO *(pocketing the keys)*: To everybody!

VALET: The trunks will be taken down at once. *(He goes out.)*

GERARDO *(looking at his watch)*: Forty minutes. *(He pulls the score of* Tristan *from underneath the flowers on the piano and walks up and down humming.)* "Isolde! Geliebte! Bist du mein? Hab' ich dich wieder? Darf ich dich fassen?" *(He clears his throat, strikes a chord on the piano and starts again.)* "Isolde! Geliebte! Bist du mein? Hab' ich dich *wieder? . . ."* (He clears his throat.) The air is dead here. (He sings.) *"Isolde! Geliebte. . . ."* It's oppressive here. Let's have a little fresh air. (He goes to the window at the left and fumbles for the curtain cord.) Where is the thing? On the other side! Here! (He pulls the cord and throws his head back with an annoyed expression when he sees MISS COEURNE.)

MISS COEURNE (in three-quarter length skirt, her blonde hair down her back, holding a bunch of red roses; she speaks with an English accent and looks straight at GERARDO): Oh, please don't send me away.

GERARDO: What else can I do? God knows, I haven't asked you to come here. Do not take it badly, dear young lady, but I have to sing to-morrow night in Brussels. I must confess, I hoped I would have this half-hour to myself. I had just given positive orders not to let anyone, whoever it might be, come up to my rooms.

MISS COEURNE (coming down stage): Don't send me away. I heard you yesterday in *Tannhäuser*, and I was just bringing you these roses, and——

GERARDO: And—and what?

MISS COEURNE: And myself. . . . I don't know whether you understand me.

GERARDO (holding the back of a chair; he hesitates, then shakes his head): Who are you?

MISS COEURNE: My name is Miss Coeurne.

GERARDO: Yes. . . . Well?

MISS COEURNE: I am very silly.

GERARDO: I know. Come here, my dear girl. (He sits down in an armchair and she stands before him.) Let's have a good earnest talk, such as you have never had in your life —and seem to need. An artist like myself—don't misunderstand me; you are—how old are you?

MISS COEURNE: Twenty-two.

GERARDO: You are sixteen or perhaps seventeen. You make yourself a little older so as to appear more—tempting. Well? Yes, you are very silly. It is really none of my business, as an artist, to cure you of your silliness. . . . Don't take this badly. . . . Now then! Why are you staring away like this?

MISS COEURNE: I said I was very silly, because I thought you Germans liked that in a young girl.

GERARDO: I am not a German, but just the same. . . .

MISS COEURNE: What! I am not as silly as all that.

GERARDO: Now look here, my dear girl—you have your tennis court, your skating club; you have your riding class, your dances; you have all a young girl can wish for. What on earth made you come to me?

MISS COEURNE: Because all those things are awful, and they bore me to death.

GERARDO: I will not dispute that. Personally, I must tell you, I know life from an entirely different side. But, my child, I am a man; I am thirty-six. The time will come when you, too, will claim a fuller existence. Wait another two years and there will be some one for you, and then you won't need to—hide yourself behind curtains, in my room, in the room of a man who—never asked you, and whom you don't know any better than—the whole continent of Europe knows him—in order to look at life from his— wonderful point of view. (MISS COEURNE *sighs deeply*.) Now then. . . . Many thanks from the bottom of my heart for your roses. (*He presses her hand.*) Will this do for to-day?

MISS COEURNE: I had never in all my life thought of a man, until I saw you on the stage last night in *Tannhäuser*. And I promise you——

GERARDO: Oh, don't promise me anything, my child. What good could your promise do me? The burden of it would all fall upon you. You see, I am talking to you as lovingly as the most loving father could. Be thankful to God that with your recklessness you haven't fallen into the hands of another artist. (*He presses her hand again.*) Let this be a lesson to you and never try it again.

MISS COEURNE (*holding her handkerchief to her face but shedding no tears*): Am I so homely?

GERARDO: Homely! Not homely, but young and indiscreet. (*He rises nervously, goes to the right, comes back, puts his arm around her waist and takes her hand.*) Listen to me, child. You are not homely because I have to be a singer, because I have to be an artist. Don't misunderstand me, but I can't see why I should simply, because I am an artist, have to assure you that I appreciate your youthful freshness and beauty. It is a question of time. Two hundred, maybe three hundred, nice, lovely girls of your age saw me last night in the rôle of Tannhäuser. Now if every one of those girls made the same demands upon me which you are making—what would become of my singing? What would become of my voice? What would become of my art?

(MISS COEURNE *sinks into a seat, covers her face and weeps.*)

GERARDO (*leaning over the back of her chair, in a friendly tone*): It is a crime for you, child, to weep over the fact that you are still so young. Your whole life is ahead of you. Is it my fault if you fell in love with me? They all do. That is what I am for. Now won't you be a good girl and let me, for the few minutes I have left, prepare myself for to-morrow's appearance?

MISS COEURNE (*rising and drying her tears*): I can't believe that any other girl would have acted the way I have.

GERARDO (*leading her to the door*): No, dear child.

MISS COEURNE (*with sobs in her voice*): At least, not if——

GERARDO: If my valet had stood before the door.

MISS COEURNE: If——

GERARDO: If the girl had been as beautiful and youthfully fresh as you.

MISS COEURNE: If——

GERARDO: If she had heard me only once in *Tannhäuser.*

MISS COEURNE (*indignantly*): If she were as respectable as I am!

GERARDO (*pointing to the piano*): Before saying good-by to me, child, have a look at all those flowers. May this be a warning to you in case you feel tempted again to fall in love with a singer. See how fresh they all are. And I have to let them wither, dry up, or I give them to the porter. And look at those letters. (*He takes a handful of them from a tray.*) I don't know any of these women. Don't worry; I leave them all to their fate. What else could I do? But I'll wager with you that every one of your lovely young friends sent in her little note.

MISS COEURNE: Well, I promise not to do it again, not to hide myself behind your curtains. But don't send me away.

GERARDO: My time, my time, dear child. If I were not on the point of taking a train! I have already told you, I am very sorry for you. But my train leaves in twenty-five minutes. What do you expect?

MISS COEURNE: A kiss.

GERARDO *(stiffening up)*: From me?

MISS COEURNE: Yes.

GERARDO *(holding her around the waist and looking very serious)*: You rob Art of its dignity, my child. I do not wish to appear an unfeeling brute, and I, am going to give you my picture. Give me your word that after that you will leave me.

MISS COEURNE: Yes.

GERARDO: Good. *(He sits at the table and autographs one of his pictures.)* You should try to become interested in the operas themselves instead of the men who sing them. You would probably derive much greater enjoyment.

MISS COEURNE *(to herself)*: I am too young yet.

GERARDO: Sacrifice yourself to music. *(He comes down stage and gives her the picture.)* Don't see in me a famous tenor but a mere tool in the hands of a noble master. Look at all the married women among your acquaintances. All Wagnerians. Study Wagner's works; learn to understand his *leit motifs*. That will save you from further foolishness.

MISS COEURNE: I thank you.

(GERARDO leads her out and rings the bell. He takes up his piano score again. There is a knock at the door.)

VALET *(coming in out of breath)*: Yes, sir.

GERARDO: Are you standing at the door?

VALET: Not just now, sir.

GERARDO: Of course not! Be sure not to let anybody come up here.

VALET: There were three ladies who asked for you, sir.

GERARDO: Don't you dare to let any one of them come up, whatever she may tell you.

VALET: And then here are some more letters.

GERARDO: Oh, all right. *(The VALET places the letters on a tray.)* And don't you dare to let any one come up.

VALET *(at the door)*: No, sir.

GERARDO: Even if she offers to settle a fortune upon you.

VALET: No, sir. *(He goes out.)*

GERARDO *(singing)*: "Isolde! Geliebte! Bist du . . ." Well, if women don't get tired of me— Only the world is so full of them; and I am only one man. Every one has his burden to carry. *(He strikes a chord on the piano.)*

(PROFESSOR DUHRING, *dressed all in black, with a long white beard, a red hooked nose, gold spectacles, Prince Albert coat and silk hat, an opera score under his arm, enters without knocking.*)

GERARDO: What do you want?

DUHRING: Maestro—I—I—have—an opera.

GERARDO: How did you get in?

DUHRING: I have been watching for two hours for a chance to run up the stairs unnoticed.

GERARDO: But, my dear good man, I have no time.

DUHRING: Oh, I will not play the whole opera for you.

GERARDO: I haven't the time. My train leaves in forty minutes.

DUHRING: You haven't the time! What should I say? You are thirty and successful. You have your whole life to live yet. Just listen to your part in my opera. You promised to listen to it when you came to this city.

GERARDO: What is the use? I am not a free agent——

DUHRING: Please! Please! Please! Maestro! I stand before you an old man, ready to fall on my knees before you; an old man who has never cared for anything in the world but his art. For fifty years I have been a willing victim to the tyranny of art——

GERARDO (*interrupting him*): Yes, I understand; I understand, but—

DUHRING (*excitedly*): No, you don't understand. You could not understand. How could you, the favorite of fortune, you understand what fifty years of bootless work means? But I will try to make you understand it. You see, I am too old to take my own life. People who do that do it at twenty-five, and I let the time pass by. I must now drag along to the end of my days. Please, sir, please don't let these moments pass in vain for me, even if you have to lose a day thereby, a week even. This is in your own interest. A week ago, when you first came for your special appearances, you promised to let me play my opera for you. I have come here every day since; either you had a rehearsal or a woman caller. And now you are on the point of going away. You have only to say one word: I will sing the part of Hermann —and they will produce my opera. You will then thank God for my insistence. . . . Of course you sing Siegfried, you sing Florestan—but you have no role like Hermann in your repertoire, no role better suited to your middle register.

(GERARDO *leans against the mantelpiece; while drumming on the top with his right hand, he discovers something behind the screen; he suddenly stretches out his arm and pulls out a woman in a gray gown, whom he leads out of the room through the middle door; after closing the door, he turns to* DUHRING.)

GERARDO: Oh, are you still there?

DUHRING (*undisturbed*): This opera is good; it is dramatic; it *is* a financial success. I can show you letters from Liszt, from Wagner, from Rubinstein, in which they consider me as a superior man. And why hasn't my opera ever been produced? Because I am not crying wares on the marketplace. And then you know our directors: they will revive ten dead men before they give a live man a chance. Their walls are well guarded. At thirty you are in. At sixty I am still out. One word from you and I shall be in, too. This is why I have come, and (*Raising his voice*) if you are not an unfeeling brute, if success has not killed in you the last spark of artistic sympathy, you will not refuse to hear my work.

GERARDO: I will give you an answer in a week. I will go over your opera. Let me have it.

DUHRING: No, I am too old, Maestro. In a week, in what you call a week, I shall be dead and buried. In a week—that is what they all say; and then they keep it for years.

GERARDO: I am very sorry but——

DUHRING: To-morrow perhaps you will be on your knees before me; you will boast of knowing me . . . and today, in your sordid lust for gold, you cannot even spare the half-hour which would mean the breaking of my fetters.

GERARDO: No, really, I have only thirty-five minutes left, and unless I go over a few passages. . . . You know I sing Tristan in Brussels to-morrow night. (*He pulls out his watch. I haven't even half an hour. . . .*

DUHRING: Half an hour. . . . Oh, then, let me play to you your big aria at the end of the first act. (*He attempts to sit down on the piano bench.* GERARDO *restrains him.*)

GERARDO: Now, frankly, my dear sir . . . I am a singer; I am not a critic. If you wish to have your opera produced, address yourself to those gentlemen who are paid to know what is good and what is not. People scorn and ignore my opinions in such matters as completely as they appreciate and admire my singing.

DUHRING: My dear Maestro, you may take it from me that I myself attach no importance whatever to your judgment. What do I care about your opinions? I know you tenors; I would like to play my score for you so that you could say: "I would like to sing the role of Hermann."

GERARDO: If you only knew how many things I would like to do and which I have to renounce, and how many things I must do for which I do not care in the least! Half a million a year does not repay me for the many joys of life which I must sacrifice for the sake of my profession. I am not a free man. But you were a free man all your life. Why didn't you go to the market-place and cry your wares?

DUHRING: Oh, the vulgarity of it. . . . I have tried it a hundred times. I am a composer, Maestro, and nothing more.

GERARDO: By which you mean that you have exhausted all your strength in the writing of your operas and kept none of it to secure their production.

DUHRING: That is true.

GERARDO: The composers I know reverse the process. They get their operas written somehow and then spend all their strength in an effort to get them produced.

DUHRING: That is the type of artist I despise.

GERARDO: Well, I despise the type of man that wastes his life in useless endeavor. What have you done in those fifty years of struggle, for yourself or for the world? Fifty years of useless struggle! That should convince the worst blockhead of the impracticability of his dreams. What have you done with your life? You have wasted it shamefully. If I had wasted my life as you have wasted yours—of course I am only speaking for myself—I don't think I should have the courage to look anyone in the face.

DUHRING: I am not doing it for myself; I am doing it for my art.

GERARDO (*scornfully*): Art, my dear man! Let me tell you that art is quite different from what the papers tell us it is.

DUHRING: To me it is the highest thing in the world.

GERARDO: You may believe that, but nobody else does. We

artists are merely a luxury for the use of the *bourgeoisie*. When I stand there on the stage I feel absolutely certain that not one solitary human being in the audience takes the slightest interest in what we, the artists, are doing. If they did, how could they listen to *Die Walküre*, for instance? Why, it is an indecent story which could not be mentioned anywhere in polite society. And yet, when I sing Siegmund, the most puritanical mothers bring their fourteen-year-old daughters to hear me. This, you see, is the meaning of whatever you call art. This is what you have sacrificed fifty years of your life to. Find out how many people came to hear me sing and how many came to gape at me as they would at the Emperor of China if he should turn up here tomorrow. Do you know what the artistic wants of the public consist in? To applaud, to send flowers, to have a subject for conversation, to see and be seen. They pay me half a million, but then I make business for hundreds of cabbies, writers, dressmakers, restaurant keepers. It keeps money circulating; it keeps blood running. It gets girls engaged, spinsters married, wives tempted, old cronies supplied with gossip; a woman loses her pocketbook in the crowd, a fellow becomes insane during the performance. Doctors, lawyers made. . . . *(He coughs.)* And with this I must sing Tristan in Brussels to-morrow night! I tell you all this, not out of vanity, but to cure you of your delusions. The measure of a man's worth is the world's opinion of him, not the inner belief which one finally adopts after brooding over it for years. Don't imagine that you are a misunderstood genius. There are no misunderstood geniuses.

DUHRING: Let me just play to you the first scene of the second act. A park landscape as in the painting, "Embarkation for the Isle of Cythera."

GERARDO: I repeat to you I have no time. And furthermore, since Wagner's death the need for new operas has never been felt by anyone. If you come with new music, you set against yourself all the music schools, the artists, the public. If you want to succeed just steal enough out of Wagner's works to make up a whole opera. Why should I cudgel my brains with your new music when I have cudgeled them cruelly with the old?

DUHRING *(holding out his trembling hand)*: I am afraid I am too old to learn how to steal. Unless one begins very young, one can never learn it.

GERARDO: Don't feel hurt. My dear sir—if I could. . . . The thought of how you have to struggle. . . . I happen to have received some five hundred marks more than my fee. . . .

DUHRING (*turning to the door*): Don't! Please don't! Do not say that. I did not try to show you my opera in order to work a touch. No, I think too much of this child of my brain. . . . No, Maestro.

(He goes out through the center door.)

GERARDO (*following him to the door*): I beg your pardon. . . . Pleased to have met you.

(He closes the door and sinks into an armchair. A voice is heard outside: "I will not let that man step in my way." HELEN rushes into the room followed by the VALET. She is an unusually beautiful young woman in street dress.)

HELEN: That man stood there to prevent me from seeing you!

GERARDO: Helen!

HELEN: You knew that I would come to see you.

VALET (*rubbing his cheek*): I did all I could, sir, but this lady actually——

HELEN: Yes,—I slapped his face.

GERARDO: Helen!

HELEN: Should I have let him insult me?

GERARDO (*to the* VALET): Please leave us.

(The VALET *goes out.)*

HELEN (*placing her muff on a chair*): I can no longer live without you. Either you take me with you or I will kill myself.

GERARDO: Helen!

HELEN: Yes, kill myself. A day like yesterday, without even seeing you—no, I could not live through that again. I am not strong enough. I beseech you, Oscar, take me with you.

GERARDO: I couldn't.

HELEN: You could if you wanted to. You can't leave me without killing me. These are not mere words. This isn't a threat. It is a fact: I will die if I can no longer have you.

You must take me with you—it is your duty—if only for a short time.

GERARDO: I give you my word of honor, Helen, I can't—I give you my word.

HELEN: You must, Oscar. Whether you can or not, you must bear the consequences of your acts. I love life, but to me life and you are one and the same thing. Take me with you, Oscar, if you don't want to have my blood on your hands.

GERARDO: Do you remember what I said to you the first day we were together here?

HELEN: I remember, but what good does that do me?

GERARDO: I said that there couldn't be any question of love between us.

HELEN: I can't help that. I didn't know you then. I never knew what a man could be to me until I met you. You knew very well that it would come to this, otherwise you wouldn't have obliged me to promise not to make you a parting scene.

GERARDO: I simply cannot take you with me.

HELEN: Oh, God! I knew you would say that! I knew it when I came here. That's what you say to every woman. And I am just one of a hundred. I know it. But, Oscar, I am love-sick; I am dying of love. This is your work, and you can save me without any sacrifice on your part, without assuming any burden. Why can't you do it?

GERARDO (*very slowly*): Because my contract forbids me to marry or to travel in the company of a woman.

HELEN (*disturbed*): What can prevent you?

GERARDO: My contract.

HELEN: You cannot . . .

GERARDO: I cannot marry until my contract expires.

HELEN: And you cannot . . .

GERARDO: I cannot travel in the company of a woman.

HELEN: That is incredible. And whom in the world should it concern?

GERARDO: My manager.

HELEN: Your manager! What business is it of his?

GERARDO: It is precisely his business.

HELEN: Is it perhaps because it might—affect your voice?

GERARDO: Yes.

HELEN: That is preposterous. Does it affect your voice?

(GERARDO *chuckles.*)

HELEN: Does your manager believe that nonsense?

GERARDO: No, he doesn't.

HELEN: This is beyond me. I can't understand how a decent man could sign such a contract.

GERARDO: I am an artist first and a man next.

HELEN: Yes, that's what you are—a great artist—an eminent artist. Can't you understand how much I must love you? You are the first man whose superiority I have felt and whom I desired to please, and you despise me for it. I have bitten my lips many a time not to let you suspect how much you meant to me; I was so afraid I might bore you. Yesterday, however, put me in a state of mind which no woman can endure. If I didn't love you so insanely, Oscar, you would think more of me. That is the terrible thing about you—that you must scorn a woman who thinks the world of you.

GERARDO: Helen!

HELEN: Your contract! Don't use your contract as a weapon to murder me with. Let me go with you, Oscar. You will see if your manager ever mentions a breach of contract. He would not do such a thing. I know men. And if he says a word, it will be time then for me to die.

GERARDO: We have no right to do that, Helen. You are just as little free to follow me, as I am to shoulder such a responsibility. I don't belong to myself; I belong to my art.

HELEN: Oh, leave your art alone. What do I care about your art? Has God created a man like you to make a puppet of himself every night? You should be ashamed of it instead of boasting of it. You see, I overlooked the fact that you were merely an artist. What wouldn't I overlook for a god like you? Even if you were a convict, Oscar, my feelings would be the same. I would lie in the dust at your feet and beg for your pity. I would face death as I am facing it now.

GERARDO (*laughing*): Facing death, Helen! Women who are endowed with your gifts for enjoying life don't make away with themselves. You know even better than I do the value of life.

HELEN (*dreamily*): Oscar, I didn't say that I would shoot myself. When did I say that? Where would I find the courage

to do that? I only said that I will die, if you don't take me
with you. I will die as I- would of an illness, for I only live
when I am with you. I can live without my home, without
my children, but not without you, Oscar. I cannot live without you.

GERARDO: Helen, if you don't calm yourself. . . . You put me
in an awful position. . . . I have only ten minutes left. . . .
I can't explain in court that your excitement made me break
my contract. . . . I can only give you ten minutes. . . . If
you don't calm yourself in that time . . . I can't leave you
alone in this condition. Think all you have at stake!

HELEN: As though I had anything else at stake!

GERARDO: You can lose your position in society.

HELEN: I can lose you!

GERARDO: And your family.

HELEN: I care for no one but you.

GERARDO: But I cannot be yours.

HELEN: Then I have nothing to lose but my life.

GERARDO: Your children!

HELEN: Who has taken me from them, Oscar? Who has taken
me from my children?

GERARDO: Did I make any advances to you?

HELEN (*passionately*): No, no. I have thrown myself at you,
and would throw myself at you again. Neither my husband
nor my children could keep me back. When I die, at least
I will have lived; thanks to you, Oscar! I thank you, Oscar,
for revealing me to myself. I thank you for that.

GERARDO: Helen, calm yourself and listen to me.

HELEN: Yes, yes, for ten minutes.

GERARDO: Listen to me. (*Both sit down on the divan.*)

HELEN (*staring at him*): Yes, I thank you for it.

GERARDO: Helen!

HELEN: I don't even ask you to love me. Let me only breathe
the air you breathe.

GERARDO (*trying to be calm*): Helen—a man of my type cannot be swayed by any of the bourgeois ideas. I have known
society women in every country of the world. Some made
parting scenes to me, but at least they all knew what they
owed to their position. This is the first time in my life that
I have witnessed such an outburst of passion. . . . Helen,
the temptation comes to me daily to step with some woman
into an idyllic Arcadia. But every human being has his

duties; you have your duties as I have mine, and the call of duty is the highest thing in the world. . . .

HELEN: I know better than you do what the highest duty is.

GERARDO: What, then? Your love for me? That's what they all say. Whatever a woman has set her heart on winning is to her good; whatever crosses her plans is evil. It is the fault of our playwrights. To draw full houses they set the world upside down, and when a woman abandons her children and her family to follow her instincts they call that—oh, broadmindedness. I personally wouldn't mind living the way turtle doves live. But since I am a part of this world I must obey my duty first. Then whenever the opportunity arises I quaff of the cup of joy. Whoever refuses to do his duty has no right to make any demands upon another fellow being.

HELEN (*staring absent-mindedly*): That does not bring the dead back to life.

GERARDO (*nervously*): Helen, I will give you back your life. I will give you back what you have sacrificed for me. For God's sake take it. What does it come to, after all? Helen, how can a woman lower herself to that point? Where is your pride? What am I in the eyes of the world? A man who makes a puppet of himself every night! Helen, are you going to kill yourself for a man whom hundreds of women loved before you, whom hundreds of women will love after you without letting their feelings disturb their life one second? Will you, by shedding your warm blood, make yourself ridiculous before God and the world?

HELEN (*looking away from him*): I know I am asking a good deal, but—what else can I do?

GERARDO: Helen, you said I should bear the consequences of my acts. Will you reproach me for not refusing to receive you when you first came here, ostensibly to ask me to try your voice? What can a man do in such a case? You are the beauty of this town. Either I would be known as the bear among artists who denies himself to all women callers, or I might have received you and pretended that I didn't understand what you meant and then pass for a fool. Or the very first day I might have talked to you as frankly as I am talking now. Dangerous business. You would have called me a conceited idiot. Tell me, Helen—what else could I do?

HELEN (*staring at him with imploring eyes, shuddering and*

making an effort to speak): O God! O God! Oscar, what
would you say if to-morrow I should go and be as happy
with another man as I have been with you? Oscar—what
would you say?

GERARDO *(after a silence)*: Nothing. *(He looks at his watch.)*
Helen——

HELEN: Oscar! *(She kneels before him.)* For the last time, I
implore you. . . . You don't know what you are doing. . . . It isn't your fault—but don't let me die. . . . Save
me—save me!

GERARDO *(raising her up)*: Helen, I am not such a wonderful
man. How many men have you known? The more men you
come to know, the lower all men will fall in your estima-
tion. When you know men better you will not take your
life for any one of them. You will not think any more of
them than I do of women.

HELEN: I am not like you in that respect.

GERARDO: I speak earnestly, Helen. We don't fall in love with
one person or another; we fall in love with our type, which
we find everywhere in the world if we only look sharply
enough.

HELEN: And when we meet our type, are we sure then of being loved again?

GERARDO *(angrily)*: You have no right to complain of your
husband. Was any girl ever compelled to marry against her
will? That is all rot. It is only the women who have sold
themselves for certain material advantages and then try to
dodge their obligations who try to make us believe that
nonsense.

HELEN *(smiling)*: They break their contracts.

GERARDO *(pounding his chest)*: When I sell myself at least I
am honest about it.

HELEN: Isn't love honest?

GERARDO: No! Love is a beastly bourgeois virtue. Love is the
last refuge of the mollycoddle, of the coward. In my world
every man has his actual value, and when two human beings make up a pact they know exactly what to expect from
each other. Love has nothing to do with it, either.

HELEN: Won't you lead me into your world, then?

GERARDO: Helen, will you compromise the happiness of your
life and the happiness of your dear ones for just a few days'
pleasure?

HELEN: No.

GERARDO *(much relieved)*: Will you promise me to go home quietly now?

HELEN: Yes.

GERARDO: And will you promise me that you will not die. . . .

HELEN: Yes.

GERARDO: You promise me that?

HELEN: Yes.

GERARDO: And you promise me to fulfill your duties as mother and—as wife?

HELEN: Yes.

GERARDO: Helen!

HELEN: Yes. What else do you want? I will promise anything.

GERARDO: And now may I go away in peace?

HELEN *(rising)*: Yes.

GERARDO: A last kiss?

HELEN: Yes, yes, yes. *(They kiss passionately.)*

GERARDO: In a year I am booked again to sing here, Helen.

HELEN: In a year! Oh, I am glad!

GERARDO *(tenderly)*: Helen!

(HELEN presses his hand, takes a revolver out of her muff, shoots herself and falls.)

GERARDO: Helen! *(He totters and collapses in an armchair.)*

BELL BOY *(rushing in)*: My God! Mr. Gerardo! *(GERARDO remains motionless; the BELL BOY rushes toward HELEN.)*

GERARDO *(jumping up, running to the door and colliding with the manager of the hotel)*: Send for the police! I must be arrested! If I went away now I should be a brute, and if I stay I break my contract. I still have *(Looking at his watch.)* one minute and ten seconds.

MANAGER: Fred, run and get a policeman.

BELL BOY: All right, sir.

MANAGER: Be quick about it. *(To GERARDO)* Don't take it too hard, sir. Those things happen once in a while.

GERARDO *(kneeling before HELEN's body and taking her hand)*: Helen! . . . She still lives—she still lives! If I am arrested I am not wilfully breaking my contract. . . . And my trunks? Is the carriage at the door?

MANAGER: It has been waiting twenty minutes, Mr. Gerardo.

(He opens the door for the porter, who takes down one of the trunks.)

GERARDO *(bending over her)*: Helen! *(To himself.)* Well, after all. . . . *(To* MULLER.*)* Have you called a doctor?

MANAGER: Yes, we had the doctor called at once. He will be here at any minute.

GERARDO *(holding her under the arms)*: Helen! Don't you know me anymore? Helen! The doctor will be here right away, Helen. This is your Oscar.

BELL BOY *(appearing in the door at the center)*: Can't find any policeman, sir.

GERARDO *(letting* HELEN's *body drop back)*: Well, if I can't get arrested, that settles it. I must catch that train and sing in Brussels to-morrow night. *(He takes up his score and runs out through the center door, bumping against several chairs.)*

CURTAIN

Riders to
the Sea

by JOHN MILLINGTON SYNGE

John Millington Synge (1871–1909)

In 1899 the poet William Butler Yeats, a prominent figure in the Irish Literary Renaissance, met John Millington Synge in a cheap students' hotel in Paris. Yeats, six years older than his countryman, found Synge to be a lonely, sick, and unhappy writer who was earning a meager livelihood as a journalist, critic, and translator. After graduating from Dublin's Trinity College in 1892, Synge had continued his musical and literary studies in Germany, Italy, and France. Yeats suggested that Synge—both for his physical and spiritual health —should go to the Aran Islands, off the west coast of Ireland, "to express a life that has never found expression." In the following three years his intermittent stays on the bleak but picturesque islands and his contact with the native fishermen and peasants, steeped in Celtic folkways, initiated Synge into a world far removed from the sophisticated, literary society of Europe. In his book *The Aran Islands* and in his play *Riders to the Sea* he depicted the hard life, the poetic speech, the legends and the superstitions of the primitive people on these rocky islands battered by a relentless sea.

After its first performance in Dublin on February 25, 1904, *Riders to the Sea* was quickly recognized as the supreme example of one-act tragedy. Based on an actual incident observed by Synge on the Aran Islands, the play builds up dramatic tension and sustains its somber mood until Maurya's final speech of religious resignation. Homely, realistic details combined with the rhythmic colloquial speech of the characters create a poetry of the theater that universalizes the experience of everyday living. The hushed conversation of the two daughters, the discovery of Michael's shirt and plain stocking, the white coffin boards, Maurya's vision of Michael at the well spring and Bartley's departure—all contribute to the atmosphere of foreboding. When the dripping body of the last drowned son is carried in, the keening women and the kneeling men compose a ritualistic background of grief for the poignant requiem pronounced by the bereaved mother.

Although some critics have viewed the play as an example of Maeterlinck's "static" drama lacking conflict and Maurya as too passive a character to be a tragic protagonist, all admit its powerful emotional impact on an audience. The few events in the plot do, however, suggest the immemorial conflict of mankind versus the power of the ruthless sea. The unseen sea as an omnipotent antagonist dominates the play. As Maurya reviews the tragic havoc it has wrought in three generations of her family, she becomes a symbol of helpless humanity facing a hostile universe. Having endured the worst and accepted the reality of death, in the muted resolution of her final speech she stands, like other tragic protagonists, ennobled in defeat. Purged of fear and exhausted by unmerited suffering, she accepts the inevitable "calm of mind all passion spent."

In *Riders to the Sea* John Millington Synge (in John Gassner's phrase), "a poet with the eye of a realist," has by brilliant dialogue, stark simplicity of plot, living characters, sustained mood, and a tragic vision of life created an enduring dramatic masterpiece.

CHARACTERS

MAURYA,
   an old woman

BARTLEY,
   her son

CATHLEEN,
   her daughter

NORA,
   a younger daughter

MEN and WOMEN

SCENE: *An Island off the West of Ireland.*

> *Cottage kitchen, with nets, oil-skins, spinning-wheel, some new boards standing by the wall, etc.* CATHLEEN, *a girl of about twenty, finishes kneading cake, and puts it down in the pot-oven by the fire; then wipes her hands, and begins to spin at the wheel.* NORA, *a young girl, puts her head in at the door.*

NORA (*in a low voice*): Where is she?

CATHLEEN: She's lying down, God help her, and may be sleeping, if she's able.

> (NORA *comes in softly, and takes a bundle from under her shawl.*)

CATHLEEN (*spinning the wheel rapidly*): What is it you have?

NORA: The young priest is after bringing them. It's a shirt and a plain stocking were got off a drowned man in Donegal.

> (CATHLEEN *stops her wheel with a sudden movement, and leans out to listen.*)

NORA: We're to find out if it's Michael's they are, some time herself will be down looking by the sea.

CATHLEEN: How would they be Michael's, Nora? How would he go the length of that way to the far north?

NORA: The young priest says he's known the like of it. "If it's Michael's they are," says he, "you can tell herself he's got a clean burial by the grace of God, and if they're not his, let no one say a word about them, for she'll be getting her death," says he, "with crying and lamenting."

> (*The door which* NORA *half closed is blown open by a gust of wind.*)

CATHLEEN (*looking out anxiously*): Did you ask him would he stop Bartley going this day with the horses to the Galway fair?

NORA: "I won't stop him," says he, "but let you not be afraid. Herself does be saying prayers half through the night, and the Almighty God won't leave her destitute," says he, "with no son living."

CATHLEEN: Is the sea bad by the white rocks, Nora?

NORA: Middling bad, God help us. There's a great roaring in the west, and it's worse it'll be getting when the tide's turned to the wind. (*She goes over to the table with the bundle.*) Shall I open it now?

CATHLEEN: Maybe she'd wake up on us, and come in before we'd done. (*Coming to the table.*) It's a long time we'll be, and the two of us crying.

NORA (*goes to the inner door and listens*): She's moving about on the bed. She'll be coming in a minute.

CATHLEEN: Give me the ladder, and I'll put them up in the turf-loft,* the way she won't know of them at all, and maybe when the tide turns she'll be going down to see would he be floating from the east.

(*They put the ladder against the gable of the chimney;* CATHLEEN *goes up a few steps and hides the bundle in the turf-loft.* MAURYA *comes from the inner room.*)

MAURYA (*looking up at* CATHLEEN *and speaking querulously*): Isn't it turf enough you have for this day and evening?

CATHLEEN: There's a cake baking at the fire for a short space (*throwing down the turf*) and Bartley will want it when the tide turns if he goes to Connemara.

(NORA *picks up the turf and puts it round the pot-oven.*)

MAURYA (*sitting down on a stool at the fire*): He won't go this day with the wind rising from the south and west. He won't go this day, for the young priest will stop him surely.

NORA: He'll not stop him, mother, and I heard Eamon Simon and Stephen Pheety and Colum Shawn saying he would go.

MAURYA: Where is he itself?

NORA: He went down to see would there be another boat sailing in the week, and I'm thinking it won't be long till he's

---

* Where slabs of peat used for fuel are stored.

here now, for the tide's turning at the green head, and the hooker's tacking* from the east.

CATHLEEN: I hear someone passing the big stones.

NORA (*looking out*): He's coming now, and he in a hurry.

BARTLEY (*comes in and looks round the room. Speaking sadly and quietly*): Where is the bit of new rope, Cathleen, was bought in Connemara?

CATHLEEN (*coming down*): Give it to him, Nora; it's on a nail by the white boards. I hung it up this morning, for the pig with the black feet was eating it.

NORA (*giving him a rope*): Is that it, Bartley?

MAURYA: You'd do right to leave that rope, Bartley, hanging by the boards. (BARTLEY *takes the rope.*) It will be wanting in this place, I'm telling you, if Michael is washed up tomorrow morning, or the next morning, or any morning in the week, for it's a deep grave we'll make him by the grace of God.

BARTLEY (*beginning to work with the rope*): I've no halter the way I can ride down on the mare, and I must go now quickly. This is the one boat going for two weeks or beyond it, and the fair will be a good fair for horses I heard them saying below.

MAURYA: It's a hard thing they'll be saying below if the body is washed up and there's no man in it to make the coffin, and I after giving a big price for the finest white boards you'd find in Connemara. (*She looks round at the boards.*)

BARTLEY: How would it be washed up, and we after looking each day for nine days, and a strong wind blowing a while back from the west and south?

MAURYA: If it wasn't found itself, that wind is raising the sea, and there was a star up against the moon, and it rising in the night. If it was a hundred horses, or a thousand horses you had itself, what is the price of a thousand horses against a son where there is one son only?

BARTLEY (*working at the halter, to* CATHLEEN): Let you go down each day, and see the sheep aren't jumping in on the rye, and if the jobber comes you can sell the pig with the black feet if there is a good price going.

MAURYA: How would the like of her get a good price for a pig?

---

* A one-masted fishing boat running against the wind.

BARTLEY (*to* CATHLEEN): If the west wind holds with the last bit of the moon let you and Nora get up weed enough for another cock for the kelp.* It's hard set we'll be from this day with no one in it but one man to work.

MAURYA: It's hard set we'll be surely the day you're drown'd with the rest. What way will I live and the girls with me, and I an old woman looking for the grave?

(BARTLEY *lays down the halter, takes off his old coat, and puts on a newer one of the same flannel.*)

BARTLEY (*to* NORA): Is she coming to the pier?

NORA (*looking out*): She's passing the green head and letting fall her sails.

BARTLEY (*getting his purse and tobacco*): I'll have half an hour to go down, and you'll see me coming again in two days, or in three days, or maybe in four days if the wind is bad.

MAURYA (*turning round to the fire, and putting her shawl over her head*): Isn't it a hard and cruel man won't hear a word from an old woman, and she holding him from the sea?

CATHLEEN: It's the life of a young man to be going on the sea, and who would listen to an old woman with one thing and she saying it over?

BARTLEY (*taking the halter*): I must go now quickly. I'll ride down on the red mare, and the grey pony'll run behind me. . . . The blessing of God on you. (*He goes out.*)

MAURYA (*crying out as he is in the door*): He's gone now, God spare us, and we'll not see him again. He's gone now, and when the black night is falling I'll have no son left me in the world.

CATHLEEN: Why wouldn't you give him your blessing and he looking round in the door? Isn't it sorrow enough is on every one in this house without your sending him out with an unlucky word behind him, and a hard word in his ear?

(MAURYA *takes up the tongs and begins raking the fire aimlessly without looking round.*)

NORA (*turning towards her*): You're taking away the turf from the cake.

CATHLEEN (*crying out*): The Son of God forgive us, Nora,

---

* Stacks of dried sea wood are burned into kelp and its ash is used as fertilizer.

we're after forgetting his bit of bread. *(She comes over to the fire.)*

NORA: And it's destroyed* he'll be going till dark night, and he after eating nothing since the sun went up.

CATHLEEN *(turning the cake out of the oven)*: It's destroyed he'll be, surely. There's no sense left on any person in a house where an old woman will be talking for ever.

(MAURYA sways herself on her stool.)

CATHLEEN *(cutting off some of the bread and rolling it in a cloth; to MAURYA)*: Let you go down now to the spring well and give him this and he passing. You'll see him then and the dark word will be broken, and you can say "God speed you," the way he'll be easy in his mind.

MAURYA *(taking the bread)*: Will I be in it as soon as himself?

CATHLEEN: If you go now quickly.

MAURYA *(standing up unsteadily)*: It's hard set I am to walk.

CATHLEEN *(looking at her anxiously)*: Give her the stick, Nora, or maybe she'll slip on the big stones.

NORA: What stick?

CATHLEEN: The stick Michael brought from Connemara.

MAURYA *(taking a stick NORA gives her)*: In the big world the old people do be leaving things after them for their sons and children, but in this place it is the young men do be leaving things behind for them that do be old. *(She goes out slowly. NORA goes over to the ladder.)*

CATHLEEN: Wait, Nora, maybe she'd turn back quickly. She's that sorry, God help her, you wouldn't know the thing she'd do.

NORA: Is she gone round by the bush?

CATHLEEN *(looking out)*: She's gone now. Throw it down quickly, for the Lord knows when she'll be out of it again.

NORA *(getting the bundle from the loft)*: The young priest said he'd be passing tomorrow, and we might go down and speak to him below if it's Michael's they are surely.

CATHLEEN *(taking the bundle)*: Did he say what way they were found?

NORA *(coming down)*: "There were two men," says he, "and they rowing round with poeten† before the cocks crowed,

---

* Half-dead.

† Illegally distilled whisky.

and the oar of one of them caught the body, and they passing the black cliffs of the north."

CATHLEEN (*trying to open the bundle*): Give me a knife, Nora, the string's perished with the salt water, and there's a black knot on it you wouldn't loosen in a week.

NORA (*giving her a knife*): I've heard tell it was a long way to Donegal.

CATHLEEN (*cutting the string*): It is surely. There was a man in here a while ago—the man sold us that knife—and he said if you set off walking from the rocks beyond, it would be seven days you'd be in Donegal.

NORA: And what time would a man take, and he floating?

(CATHLEEN *opens the bundle and takes out a bit of a stocking. They look at them eagerly.*)

CATHLEEN (*in a low voice*): The Lord spare us, Nora! isn't it a queer hard thing to say if it's his they are surely?

NORA: I'll get his shirt off the hook the way we can put the one flannel on the other. (*She looks through some clothes hanging in the corner.*) It's not with them, Cathleen, and where will it be?

CATHLEEN: I'm thinking Bartley put it on him in the morning, for his own shirt was heavy with the salt in it (*pointing to the corner*). There's a bit of a sleeve was of the same stuff. Give me that and it will do.

(NORA *brings it to her and they compare the flannel.*)

CATHLEEN: It's the same stuff, Nora; but if it is itself aren't there great rolls of it in the shops of Galway, and isn't it many another man may have a shirt of it as well as Michael himself?

NORA (*who has taken up the stocking and counted the stitches, crying out*): It's Michael, Cathleen, it's Michael; God spare his soul, and what will herself say when she hears this story, and Bartley on the sea?

CATHLEEN (*taking the stocking*): It's a plain stocking.

NORA: It's the second one of the third pair I knitted, and I put up three score stitches, and I dropped four of them.

CATHLEEN (*counts the stitches*): It's that number is in it (*crying out*). Ah, Nora, isn't it a bitter thing to think of him floating that way to the far north, and no one to keen him but the black hags that do be flying on the sea?

NORA (*swinging herself round, and throwing out her arms on the clothes*): And isn't it a pitiful thing when there is nothing left of a man who was a great rower and fisher, but a bit of an old shirt and a plain stocking?

CATHLEEN (*after an instant*): Tell me is herself coming, Nora? I hear a little sound on the path.

NORA (*looking out*): She is, Cathleen. She's coming up to the door.

CATHLEEN: Put these things away before she'll come in. Maybe it's easier she'll be after giving her blessing to Bartley, and we won't let on we've heard anything the time he's on the sea.

NORA (*helping* CATHLEEN *to close the bundle*): We'll put them here in the corner.

(*They put them into a hole in the chimney corner.* CATHLEEN *goes back to the spinning-wheel.*)

NORA: Will she see it was crying I was?

CATHLEEN: Keep your back to the door the way the light'll not be on you.

(NORA *sits down at the chimney corner, with her back to the door.* MAURYA *comes in very slowly, without looking at the girls, and goes over to her stool at the other side of the fire. The cloth with the bread is still in her hand. The girls look at each other, and* NORA *points to the bundle of bread.*)

CATHLEEN (*after spinning for a moment*): You didn't give him his bit of bread?

(MAURYA *begins to keen softly, without turning round.*)

CATHLEEN: Did you see him riding down?

(MAURYA *goes on keening.*)

CATHLEEN (*a little impatiently*): God forgive you; isn't it a better thing to raise your voice and tell what you seen, than to be making lamentation for a thing that's done? Did you see Bartley, I'm saying to you.

MAURYA (*with a weak voice*): My heart's broken from this day.

CATHLEEN (*as before*): Did you see Bartley?

MAURYA: I seen the fearfulest thing.

CATHLEEN (*leaves her wheel and looks out*): God forgive you; he's riding the mare now over the green head, and the grey pony behind him.

MAURYA (*starts, so that her shawl falls back from her head and shows her white tossed hair. With a frightened voice*): The grey pony behind him.

CATHLEEN (*coming to the fire*): What is it ails you, at all?

MAURYA (*speaking very slowly*): I've seen the fearfulest thing any person has seen, since the day Bride Dara seen the dead man with the child in his arms.

CATHLEEN and NORA: Uah. (*They crouch down in front of the old woman at the fire.*)

NORA: Tell us what it is you seen.

MAURYA: I went down to the spring well, and I stood there saying a prayer to myself. Then Bartley came along, and he riding on the red mare with the grey pony behind him. (*She puts up her hands, as if to hide something from her eyes.*) The Son of God spare us, Nora!

CATHLEEN: What is it you seen?

MAURYA: I seen Michael himself.

CATHLEEN (*speaking softly*): You did not, mother; it wasn't Michael you seen, for his body is after being found in the far north, and he's got a clean burial by the grace of God.

MAURYA (*a little defiantly*): I'm after seeing him this day, and he riding and galloping. Bartley came first on the red mare; and I tried to say "God speed you," but something choked the words in my throat. He went by quickly; and "the blessing of God on you," says he, and I could say nothing. I looked up then, and I crying, at the grey pony, and there was Michael upon it—with fine clothes on him, and new shoes on his feet.

CATHLEEN (*begins to keen*): It's destroyed we are from this day. It's destroyed, surely.

NORA: Didn't the young priest say the Almighty God wouldn't leave her destitute with no son living?

MAURYA (*in a low voice, but clearly*): It's little the like of him knows of the sea. . . . Bartley will be lost now, and let you call in Eamon and make me a good coffin out of the white boards, for I won't live after them. I've had a husband, and a husband's father, and six sons in this house— six fine men, though it was a hard birth I had with every one of them and they coming to the world—and some of them were found and some of them were not found, but they're gone now the lot of them. . . . There were Stephen, and Shawn, were lost in the great wind, and found after in the Bay of Gregory of the Golden Mouth, and carried up the two of them on the one plank, and in by that door. *(She pauses for a moment; the girls start as if they heard something through the door that is half open behind them.)*

NORA *(in a whisper)*: Did you hear that, Cathleen? Did you hear a noise in the north-east?

CATHLEEN *(in a whisper)*: There's someone after crying out by the seashore.

MAURYA *(continues without hearing anything)*: There was Sheamus and his father, and his own father again, were lost in a dark night, and not a stick or sign was seen of them when the sun went up. There was Patch after was drowned out of a curragh* that turned over. I was sitting here with Bartley, and he a baby, lying on my two knees, and I seen two women, and three women, and four women coming in, and they crossing themselves, and not saying a word. I looked out then, and there were men coming after them, and they holding a thing in the half of a red sail, and water dripping out of it—it was a dry day, Nora—and leaving a track to the door. *(She pauses again with her hand stretched out towards the door. It opens softly and old women begin to come in, crossing themselves on the threshold, and kneeling down in front of the stage with red petticoats over their heads.)*

MAURYA *(half in a dream, to* CATHLEEN*)*: Is it Patch, or Michael, or what is it at all?

CATHLEEN: Michael is after being found in the far north, and when he is found there how could he be here in this place?

MAURYA: There does be a power of young men floating round in the sea, and what way would they know if it was Michael they had, or another man like him, for when a man is nine days in the sea, and the wind blowing, it's hard set his own mother would be to say what man was it.

CATHLEEN: It's Michael, God spare him, for they're after sending us a bit of his clothes from the far north. *(She reaches out and hands* MAURYA *the clothes that belonged to*

---

* A small boat made by covering a wicker frame with hide, cloth, or tarpaulin.

MICHAEL. MAURYA *stands up slowly and takes them in her hands.* NORA *looks out.*)

NORA: They're carrying a thing among them and there's water dripping out of it and leaving a track by the big stones.

CATHLEEN (*in a whisper to the women who have come in*): Is it Bartley it is?

ONE OF THE WOMEN: It is surely, God rest his soul.

(*Two younger women come in and pull out the table. Then men carry in the body of* BARTLEY, *laid on a plank, with a bit of a sail over it, and lay it on the table.*)

CATHLEEN (*to the women, as they are doing so*): What way was he drowned?

ONE OF THE WOMEN: The grey pony knocked him into the sea, and he was washed out where there is a great surf on the white rocks.

(MAURYA *has gone over and knelt down at the head of the table. The women are keening softly and swaying themselves with a slow movement.* CATHLEEN *and* NORA *kneel at the other end of the table. The men kneel near the door.*)

MAURYA (*raising her head and speaking as if she did not see the people around her*): They're all gone now, and there isn't anything more the sea can do to me. . . . I'll have no call now to be up crying and praying when the wind breaks from the south, and you can hear the surf is in the east, and the surf is in the west, making a great stir with the two noises, and they hitting one on the other. I'll have no call now to be going down and getting Holy Water in the dark nights after Samhain,* and I won't care what way the sea is when the other women will be keening. (*To* NORA) Give me the Holy Water, Nora, there's a small cup still on the dresser.

(NORA *gives it to her.*)

MAURYA (*drops* MICHAEL's *clothes across* BARTLEY's *feet, and sprinkles the Holy Water over him*): It isn't that I haven't

---

* An annual pagan festival similar to Halloween.

prayed for you, Bartley, to the Almighty God. It isn't that I haven't said prayers in the dark night till you wouldn't know what I'd be saying; but it's a great rest I'll have now, and it's time surely. It's a great rest I'll have now, and great sleeping in the long nights after Samhain, if it's only a bit of wet flour we do have to eat, and maybe a fish that would be stinking. *(She kneels down again, crossing herself, and saying prayers under her breath.)*

CATHLEEN *(to an old man)*: Maybe yourself and Eamon would make a coffin when the sun rises. We have fine white boards herself bought, God help her, thinking Michael would be found, and I have a new cake you can eat while you'll be working.

THE OLD MAN *(looking at the boards)*: Are there nails with them?

CATHLEEN: There are not, Colum; we didn't think of the nails.

ANOTHER MAN: It's a great wonder she wouldn't think of the nails, and all the coffins she's seen made already.

CATHLEEN: It's getting old she is, and broken.

(MAURYA stands up again very slowly and spreads out the pieces of MICHAEL's clothes beside the body, sprinkling them with the last of the Holy Water.)

NORA *(in a whisper to CATHLEEN)*: She's quiet now and easy; but the day Michael was drowned you could hear her crying out from this to the spring well. It's fonder she was of Michael, and would any one have thought that?

CATHLEEN *(slowly and clearly)*: An old woman will be soon tired with anything she will do, and isn't it nine days herself is after crying and keening, and making great sorrow in the house?

MAURYA *(puts the empty cup mouth downwards on the table, and lays her hands together on BARTLEY's feet)*: They're all together this time, and the end is come. May the Almighty God have mercy on Bartley's soul, and on Michael's soul, and on the souls of Sheamus and Patch, and Stephen and Shawn *(bending her head)*; and may He have mercy on my soul, Nora, and on the soul of every one is left living in the world. *(She pauses, and the keen rises a little more loudly from the women, then sinks away.)*

MAURYA *(continuing)*: Michael has a clean burial in the far north, by the grace of the Almighty God. Bartley will have a fine coffin out of the white boards, and a deep grave surely. What more can we want than that? No man at all can be living for ever, and we must be satisfied. *(She kneels down again and the curtain falls slowly.)*

Love of One's Neighbor

A Comedy

by LEONID ANDREYEV

Translated from the Russian
by THOMAS SELTZER

Reprinted by permission of Albert and Charles Boni, Inc.

Leonid Andreyev (1871–1919)

During the first seventeen years of the twentieth century, Russia lived through a turbulent period in her history. She suffered a disastrous defeat in her war with Japan, which, combined with the wretchedness among the peasantry and the autocratic Czarist rule, brought on the abortive rebellion of 1905. The incompetence of the government and the enormous casualties suffered by Russia in World War I precipitated the Kerensky revolution in February 1917, and the Bolshevik seizure of power in October. The wars, assassinations, and uprisings encouraged a mood of cynicism and pessimism, which is reflected in the works of Andreyev written during this tumultuous period.

Leonid Andreyev was born in Orel, in central Russia, in 1871. A neurotic youth, who attempted suicide on several occasions, he studied law in St. Petersburg and Moscow. After receiving his law degree, he turned to free-lance writing. Encouraged by Maxim Gorky, he published two volumes of short stories that brought down upon him a storm of hostile criticism. In 1904 he wrote a powerful antiwar novelette, *The Red Laugh*. After the unsuccessful uprising of 1905, he spent a brief period in prison. Three years later he published another novelette, *The Seven Who Were Hanged*, a psychological study of the tragic hopelessness of idealistic martyrdom in a revolutionary era. Andreyev, after the triumph of the Soviet regime, became a rabid anti-Bolshevist. Depressed at the hopelessness of conditions in his native land, he exiled himself to Finland, where he spent the rest of his life. He died there in 1919.

From 1905 to 1917 he wrote twenty-seven plays of unequal merit. The best known are *The Life of Man* (1906), an allegory about the futility of goodness in an evil world, and *He Who Gets Slapped* (1916), a symbolic play of the

230

tragic betrayal endured by a man of fine sensibilities who becomes a circus clown.

The bitter comedy *Love of One's Neighbor* reveals Andreyev's disenchantment with modern society. Constructing his play around a single episode—a man is about to fall from a high, dangerous position—he introduces a host of characters to satirize many aspects of the contemporary world and the fundamental baseness of human beings. With irony and humor he exposes the false piety of religion; the mercenary character of tradesmen; the falsehoods, sentimentality, and sensationalism of modern journalism and advertising; the supposed educational benefits of travel. As a relief from the boredom of their existence, his characters find enjoyment in a spectacle of violence. By stripping them of their pretenses of love and affection, he reveals the hypocrisy and innate cruelty in people of all nationalities.

Like Ben Jonson, Jonathan Swift, and Mark Twain, the Russian satirist seems misanthropic in his blanket denunciation of mankind. But his cynical diatribe is the natural reaction of a frustrated idealist. Believing in rationality, truth, and the good life, he becomes indignant at seeing people embracing folly, falsehood, and evil. Only by honestly exposing the hypocrisy and the baser drives of humanity in comic terms can he cure them of their vicious self-deceptions. Satire can thus serve a therapeutic function in society.

When we consider the popular appeal of gory details in our newspapers, violence in our movies and on television, and the morbid interest in murders in our cities and in killings on far-flung battlefields, perhaps Andreyev's mordant satire possesses more truth than we are willing to admit.

CHARACTERS

FIRST POLICEMAN

SECOND POLICEMAN

LADY

LITTLE GIRL

BOY

FIRST ENGLISH TOURIST

SECOND ENGLISH TOURIST

UNKNOWN MAN

TOURIST

MILITARY WOMAN

FIRST TOURIST

SECOND TOURIST

THIRD TOURIST,
    PHOTOGRAPHER

COMB VENDOR

VOICES

LITTLE LADY

FIRST STUDENT

SECOND STUDENT

FIRST GIRL

SECOND GIRL

FIRST PHOTOGRAPHER

SECOND PHOTOGRAPHER

JAMES

MARY

ALECK

TALL TOURIST

THE CURIOUS

KATE

FIRST DRUNKEN MAN

SECOND DRUNKEN MAN

CORRESPONDENT

PASTOR

SALVATION ARMY MAN

SALVATION ARMY WOMAN

THE MAN IN THE
    WHITE VEST

THE MAN CARRYING
    THE POLE

SCENE: *A wild place in the mountains. A man in an attitude of despair is standing on a tiny projection of a rock that rises almost sheer from the ground. How he got there it is not easy to say, but he cannot be reached either from above or below. Short ladders, ropes, and sticks show that attempts have been made to save the unknown person, but without success.*

It seems that the unhappy man has been in that desperate position a long time. A considerable crowd has already collected, extremely varied in composition. There are vendors of cold drinks; there is a whole little bar behind which the bartender skips about out of breath and perspiring—he has more on his hands than he can attend to; there are peddlers selling picture postal cards, coral beads, souvenirs, and all sorts of trash. One fellow is stubbornly trying to dispose of a tortoiseshell comb, which is really not tortoiseshell. Tourists keep pouring in from all sides, attracted by the report that a catastrophe is impending—Englishmen, Americans, Germans, Russians, Frenchmen, Italians, etc., with all their peculiar national traits of character, manner, and dress. Nearly all carry alpenstocks, fieldglasses, and cameras. The conversation is in different

233

> *languages, all of which, for the convenience of the reader, we shall translate into English.*
>
> *At the foot of the rock where the U*N-
> KNOWN MAN *is to fall, two policemen are chasing the children away and partitioning off a space, drawing a rope around short stakes stuck in the ground. It is noisy and jolly.*

POLICEMAN: Get away, you loafer! The man'll fall on your head and then your mother and father will be making a hullabaloo about it.

BOY: Will he fall here?

POLICEMAN: Yes, here.

BOY: Suppose he drops farther?

SECOND POLICEMAN: The boy is right. He may get desperate and jump, land beyond the rope and hit some people in the crowd. I guess he weighs at least about two hundred pounds.

FIRST POLICEMAN: Move on, move on, you! Where are you going? Is that your daughter, lady? Please take her away! The young man will soon fall.

LADY: Soon? Did you say he is going to fall soon? Oh, heavens, and my husband's not here!

LITTLE GIRL: He's in the café, Mamma.

LADY (*desperately*): Yes, of course. He's always in the café. Go call him, Nellie. Tell him the man will soon drop. Hurry! Hurry!

VOICES: Waiter!—Garçon—Kellner—Three beers out here!— No beer?—What?—Say, that's a fine bar—We'll have some in a moment—Hurry up—Waiter!—Waiter!—Garçon!

FIRST POLICEMAN: Say, boy, you're here again?

BOY: I wanted to take the stone away.

POLICEMAN: What for?

BOY: So he shouldn't get hurt so badly when he falls.

SECOND POLICEMAN: The boy is right. We ought to remove the stone. We ought to clear the place altogether. Isn't there any sawdust or sand about?

(*Two* ENGLISH TOURISTS *enter. They look at the* UN-

KNOWN MAN *through fieldglasses and exchange remarks.)*

FIRST TOURIST: He's young.

SECOND TOURIST: How old?

FIRST TOURIST: Twenty-eight.

SECOND TOURIST: Twenty-six. Fright has made him look older.

FIRST TOURIST: How much will you bet?

SECOND TOURIST: Ten to a hundred. Put it down.

FIRST TOURIST (*writing in his notebook. To the* POLICEMAN): How did he get up there? Why don't they take him off?

POLICEMAN: They tried, but they couldn't. Our ladders are too short.

SECOND TOURIST: Has he been here long?

POLICEMAN: Two days.

FIRST TOURIST: Aha! He'll drop at night.

SECOND TOURIST: In two hours. A hundred to a hundred.

FIRST TOURIST: Put it down. (*He shouts to the man on the rock.*) How are you feeling? What? I can't hear you.

UNKNOWN MAN (*in a scarcely audible voice*): Bad, very bad.

LADY: Oh, heavens, and my husband is not here!

LITTLE GIRL (*running in*). Papa said he'll get here in plenty of time. He's playing chess.

LADY: Oh, heavens! Nellie, tell him he must come. I insist. But perhaps I had rather—— Will he fall soon, Mr. Policeman? No? Nellie, you go. I'll stay here and keep the place for Papa.

(*A tall, lanky woman of unusually independent and military appearance and a* TOURIST *dispute for the same place. The* TOURIST, *a short, quiet, rather weak man, feebly defends his rights; the woman is resolute and aggressive.*)

TOURIST: But, lady, it is my place. I have been standing here for two hours.

MILITARY WOMAN: What do I care how long you have been standing here. I want this place. Do you understand? It offers a good view, and that's just what I want. Do you understand?

TOURIST (*weakly*): It's what I want, too.

MILITARY WOMAN: I beg your pardon, what do you know about these things anyway?

TOURIST: What knowledge is required? A man will fall. That's all.

MILITARY WOMAN (*mimicking*): "A man will fall. That's all." Won't you have the goodness to tell me whether you have ever seen a man fall? No? Well, I did. Not one, but three. Two acrobats, one ropewalker and three aeronauts.

TOURIST: That makes six.

MILITARY WOMAN (*mimicking*): "That makes six." Say, you are a mathematical prodigy. And did you ever see a tiger tear a woman to pieces in a zoo, right before your eyes? Eh? What? Yes, exactly. Now, I did—— Please! Please!

(*The* TOURIST *steps aside, shrugging his shoulders with an air of injury, and the tall woman triumphantly takes possession of the stone she has won by her prowess. She sits down, spreading out around her her bag, handkerchief, peppermints, and medicine bottle, takes off her gloves and wipes her fieldglass, glancing pleasantly on all around. Finally she turns to the* LADY *who is waiting for her husband in the café.*)

MILITARY WOMAN (*amiably*): You will tire yourself out, dear. Why don't you sit down?

LADY: Oh, my, don't talk about it. My legs are as stiff as that rock there.

MILITARY WOMAN: Men are so rude nowadays. They will never give their place to a woman. Have you brought peppermints with you?

LADY (*frightened*): No. Why? Is it necessary?

MILITARY WOMAN: When you keep looking up for a long time you are bound to get sick. Sure thing. Have you spirits of ammonia? No? Good gracious, how thoughtless! How will they bring you back to consciousness when he falls? You haven't any smelling salts either, I daresay. Of course not. Have you anybody to take care of you, seeing that you are so helpless yourself?

LADY (*frightened*): I will tell my husband. He is in the café.

MILITARY WOMAN: Your husband is a brute.

POLICEMAN: Whose coat is this? Who threw this rag here?

BOY: It's mine. I spread my coat there so that he doesn't hurt himself so badly when he falls.

POLICEMAN: Take it away.

(Two TOURISTS, *armed with cameras, contending for the same position.)*

FIRST TOURIST: I wanted this place.

SECOND TOURIST: You wanted it, but I got it.

FIRST TOURIST: You just came here. I have had this place for two days.

SECOND TOURIST: Then why did you go without even leaving your shadow?

FIRST TOURIST: I wasn't going to starve myself to death.

COMB VENDOR *(mysteriously)*: Tortoiseshell.

TOURIST *(savagely)*: Well?

VENDOR: Genuine tortoiseshell.

TOURIST: Go to the devil.

THIRD TOURIST, PHOTOGRAPHER: For heaven's sake, lady, you're sitting on my camera!

LITTLE LADY: Oh! Where is it?

TOURIST: Under you, under you, lady.

LITTLE LADY: I am so tired. What a wretched camera you have. I thought it felt uncomfortable and I was wondering why. Now I know; I am sitting on your camera.

TOURIST *(agonized)*: Lady!

LITTLE LADY: I thought it was a stone. I saw something lying there and I thought: A queer-looking stone; I wonder why it's so black. So that's what it was; it was your camera. I see.

TOURIST *(agonized)*: Lady, for heaven's sake!

LITTLE LADY: Why is it so large, tell me. Cameras are small, but this one is so large. I swear I never had the faintest suspicion it was a camera. Can you take my picture? I would so much like to have my picture taken with the mountains here for a background, in this wonderful setting.

TOURIST: How can I take your picture if you are sitting on my camera?

LITTLE LADY *(jumping up, frightened)*: Is it possible? You don't say so. Why didn't you tell me so? Does it take pictures?

VOICES: Waiter, one beer!—What did you bring wine for?—I gave you my order long ago.—What will you have, sir? One minute.—In a second. Waiter!—Waiter!—Toothpicks!—

(A fat tourist enters in haste, panting, surrounded by a numerous family.)

Tourist *(crying)*: Mary! Aleck! Jimmie!—Where is Mary? For God's sake! Where is Mary?

Student *(dismally)*: Here she is, Papa.

Tourist: Where is she? Mary!

Girl: Here I am, Papa.

Tourist: Where in the world are you? *(He turns around.)* Ah, there! What are you standing back of me for? Look, look! For goodness' sake, where are you looking?

Girl *(dismally)*: I don't know, Papa.

Tourist: No, that's impossible. Imagine! She never once saw a lightning flash. She always keeps her eyes open as wide as onions, but the instant it flashes she closes them. So she never saw lightning, not once. Mary, you are missing it again. There it is! You see!

Student: She sees, Papa.

Tourist: Keep an eye on her. *(Suddenly dropping into tone of profound pity.)* Ah, poor young man. Imagine! He'll fall from that high rock. Look, children, see how pale he is! That should be a lesson to you how dangerous climbing is.

Student *(dismally)*: He won't fall today, Papa!

Second Girl: Papa, Mary has closed her eyes again.

First Student: Let us sit down, Papa! Upon my word, he won't fall today. The porter told me so. I can't stand it anymore. You've been dragging us about every day from morning till night visiting art galleries.

Tourist: What's that? For whose benefit am I doing this? Do you think I enjoy spending my time with a dunce?

Second Girl: Papa, Mary is blinking her eyes.

Second Student: I can't stand it, either. I have terrible dreams. Yesterday I dreamed of garçons the whole night long.

Tourist: Jimmie.

First Student: I have gotten so thin I am nothing but skin and bones. I can't stand it anymore, Father. I'd rather be a farmer, or tend pigs.

Tourist: Aleck.

First Student: If he were really to fall—but it's a fake. You believe every lie told you! They all lie. Baedeker lies, too. Yes, your Baedeker lies!

MARY (*dismally*): Papa, children, he's beginning to fall.

(*The man on the rock shouts something down into the crowd. There is general commotion. Voices: "Look, he's falling." Fieldglasses are raised; the photographers, violently agitated, click their cameras; the policemen diligently clean the place where he is to fall.*)

PHOTOGRAPHER: Oh, hang it! What is the matter with me? The devil! When a man's in a hurry——

SECOND PHOTOGRAPHER: Brother, your camera is closed.

PHOTOGRAPHER: The devil take it.

VOICES: Hush! He's getting ready to fall.—No, he's saying something.—No, he's falling.—Hush!

UNKNOWN MAN ON THE ROCK (*faintly*): Save me! Save me!

TOURIST: Ah, poor young man. Mary, Jimmie, there's a tragedy for you. The sky is clear, the weather is beautiful, and has he to fall and be shattered to death? Can you realize how dreadful that is, Aleck?

STUDENT (*wearily*): Yes, I can realize it.

TOURIST: Mary, can you realize it? Imagine. There is the sky. There are people enjoying themselves and partaking of refreshments. Everything is so nice and pleasant, and he has to fall. What a tragedy! Do you remember *Hamlet?*

SECOND GIRL (*prompting*): Hamlet, Prince of Denmark, of Elsinore.

JAMES: Of Helsingfors, I know. Don't bother me, Father!

MARY (*dismally*): He dreamed about garçons all night long.

ALECK: Why don't you order sandwiches, Father.

COMB VENDOR (*mysteriously*): Tortoiseshell. Genuine tortoiseshell.

TOURIST (*credulously*): Stolen?

VENDOR: Why, sir, the idea!

TOURIST (*angrily*): Do you mean to tell me it's genuine if it isn't stolen? Go on. Not much.

MILITARY WOMAN (*amiably*): Are all these your children?

TOURIST: Yes, madam. A father's duty. You see, they are protesting. It is the eternal conflict between fathers and children. Here is such a tragedy going on, such a heartrending tragedy— Mary, you are blinking your eyes again.

MILITARY WOMAN: You are quite right. Children must be hardened to things. But why do you call this a terrible tragedy? Every roofer, when he falls, falls from a great height.

But this here—what is it? A hundred, two hundred feet. I saw a man fall plumb from the sky.

TOURIST (*overwhelmed*): You don't say?

ALECK: Children, listen. Plumb from the sky.

MILITARY WOMAN: Yes, yes. I saw an aeronaut drop from the clouds and go crash upon an iron roof.

TOURIST: How terrible!

MILITARY WOMAN: That's what I call a tragedy. It took two hours to bring me back to consciousness, and all that time they pumped water on me, the scoundrels. I was nearly drowned. From that day on I never step out of the door without taking spirits of ammonia with me.

> (*Enter a strolling troop of Italian singers and musicians: a short, fat tenor, with a reddish beard and large, watery, stupidly dreamy eyes, singing with extraordinary sweetness; a skinny humpback with a jockey cap, and a screeching baritone; a bass who is also a mandolinist, looking like a bandit; a girl with a violin, closing her eyes when she plays, so that only the whites are seen. They take their stand and begin to sing: "Sul mare lucica—Santa Lucia, Santa Lucia——")*

MARY (*dismally*): Papa, children, look. He is beginning to wave his hands.

TOURIST: Is that the effect the music has upon him?

MILITARY WOMAN: Quite possible. Music usually goes with such things. But that'll make him fall sooner than he should. Musicians, go away from here! Go!

> (*A* TALL TOURIST, *with up-curled mustache, violently gesticulating, enters, followed by a small group attracted by curiosity.*)

TALL TOURIST: It's scandalous. Why don't they save him? Ladies and gentlemen, you all heard him shout: "Save me." Didn't you?

THE CURIOUS (*in chorus*): Yes, yes, we heard him.

TALL TOURIST: There you are. I distinctly heard these words: "Save me! Why don't they save me?" It's scandalous. Policemen, policemen! Why don't you save him? What are you doing there?

POLICEMEN: We are cleaning up the place for him to fall.

TALL TOURIST: That's a sensible thing to do, too. But why

don't you save him? You ought to save him. If a man asks you to save him, it is absolutely essential to save him. Isn't it so, ladies and gentlemen?

THE CURIOUS (*in chorus*): True, absolutely true. It is essential to save him.

TALL TOURIST (*with heat*): We are not heathens, we are Christians. We should love our neighbors. When a man asks to be saved every measure which the government has at its command should be taken to save him. Policemen, have you taken every measure?

POLICEMAN: Every one!

TALL TOURIST: Every one without exception? Gentleman, every measure has been taken. Listen, young man, every measure has been taken to save you. Did you hear?

UNKNOWN MAN (*in a scarcely audible voice*): Save me!

TALL TOURIST (*excitedly*): Gentlemen, did you hear? He again asked to be saved. Policemen, did you hear?

ONE OF THE CURIOUS (*timidly*): It is my opinion that it is absolutely necessary to save him.

TALL TOURIST: That's right. Exactly. Why, that's what I have been saying for the last two hours. Policemen, do you hear? It is scandalous.

ONE OF THE CURIOUS (*a little bolder*): It is my opinion that an appeal should be made to the highest authority.

THE REST (*in chorus*): Yes, yes, a complaint should be made. It is scandalous. The government ought not to leave any of its citizens in danger. We all pay taxes. He must be saved.

TALL TOURIST: Didn't I say so? Of course we must put up a complaint. Young man! Listen, young man. Do you pay taxes? What? I can't hear.

TOURIST: Jimmie, Katie, listen! What a tragedy! Ah, the poor young man! He is soon to fall and they ask him to pay a domiciliary tax.

KATE (*the girl with glasses, pedantically*): That can hardly be called a domicile, Father. The meaning of domicile is——

JAMES (*pinching her*): Lickspittle.

MARY (*wearily*): Papa, children, look! He's again beginning to fall.

(*There is excitement in the crowd, and again a bustling and shouting among the photographers.*)

TALL TOURIST: We must hurry, ladies and gentlemen. He must be saved at any cost. Who's going with me?

THE CURIOUS *(in chorus)*: We are all going! We are all going!

TALL TOURIST: Policemen, did you hear? Come, ladies and gentlemen!

> *(They depart, fiercely gesticulating. The café grows more lively. The sound of clinking beer glasses and the clatter of steins is heard, and the beginning of a loud German song. The bartender, who has forgotten himself while talking to somebody, starts suddenly and runs off, looks up to the sky with a hopeless air and wipes the perspiration from his face with his napkin. Angry calls of Waiter! Waiter!)*

UNKNOWN MAN *(rather loudly)*: Can you let me have some soda water?

> *(The WAITER is startled, looks at the sky, glances at the man on the rock, and pretending not to have heard him, walks away.)*

MANY VOICES: Waiter! Beer!

WAITER: One moment, one moment!

> *(Two DRUNKEN MEN come out from the café.)*

LADY: Ah, there is my husband. Come here quick.

MILITARY WOMAN: A downright brute.

DRUNKEN MAN *(waving his hand to the UNKNOWN MAN)*: Say, is it very bad up there? Hey?

UNKNOWN MAN *(rather loudly)*: Yes, it's bad. I am sick and tired of it.

DRUNKEN MAN: Can't you get a drink?

UNKNOWN MAN: No, how can I?

SECOND DRUNKEN MAN: Say, what are you talking about? How can he get a drink? The man is about to die and you tempt him and try to get him excited. Listen, up there, we have been drinking your health right along. It won't hurt you, will it?

FIRST DRUNKEN MAN: Ah, go on! What are you talking about? How can it hurt him? Why, it will only do him good. It will encourage him. Listen, honest to God, we are very sorry for you, but don't mind us. We are going to the café to have another drink. Good-bye.

SECOND DRUNKEN MAN: Look, what a crowd.

FIRST DRUNKEN MAN: Come, or he'll fall and then they'll close the café.

(Enter a new crowd of tourists, a very elegant gentleman, the chief CORRESPONDENT *of European newspapers at their head. He is followed by an ecstatic whisper of respect and admiration. Many leave the café to look at him, and even the* WAITER *turns slightly around, glances at him quickly, smiles happily and continues on his way, spilling something from his tray.)*

VOICES: The correspondent! The correspondent! Look!

LADY: Oh, my, and my husband is gone again!

TOURIST: Jimmie, Mary, Aleck, Katie, Charlie, look! This is the chief correspondent. Do you realize it? The very highest of all. Whatever he writes goes.

KATE: Mary, dear, again you are not looking.

ALECK: I wish you would order some sandwiches for us. I can't stand it any longer. A human being has to eat.

TOURIST *(ecstatically)*: What a tragedy! Katie, dear, can you realize it? Consider how awful. The weather is so beautiful, and the chief correspondent. Take out your notebook, Jimmie.

JAMES: I lost it, Father.

CORRESPONDENT: Where is he?

VOICES *(obligingly)*: There, there he is. There! A little higher. Still higher! A little lower! No, higher!

CORRESPONDENT: If you please, if you please, ladies and gentlemen, I will find him myself. Oh, yes, there he is. Hm! What a situation!

TOURIST: Won't you have a chair?

CORRESPONDENT: Thank you. *(Sits down.)* Hm! What a situation! Very interesting. Very interesting, indeed! *(Whisks out his notebook; amiably to the* PHOTOGRAPHERS.*)* Have you taken any pictures yet, gentlemen?

FIRST PHOTOGRAPHER: Yes, sir, certainly, certainly. We have photographed the place showing the general character of the locality——

SECOND PHOTOGRAPHER: The tragic situation of the young man——

CORRESPONDENT: Ye-es, very, very interesting.

TOURIST: Did you hear, Aleck? This smart man, the chief correspondent, says it's interesting, and you keep bothering about sandwiches. Dunce!

ALECK: Maybe he has had his dinner already.

CORRESPONDENT: Ladies and gentlemen, I beg you to be quiet.

OBLIGING VOICES: It is quieter in the café.

CORRESPONDENT (*shouts to the* UNKNOWN MAN): Permit me to introduce myself. I am the chief correspondent of the European press. I have been sent here at the special request of the editors. I should like to ask you several questions concerning your situation. What is your name? What is your general position? How old are you? (*The* UNKNOWN MAN *mumbles something.*)

CORRESPONDENT (*a little puzzled*): I can't hear a thing. Has he been that way all the time?

VOICE: Yes, it's impossible to hear a word he says.

CORRESPONDENT (*jotting down something in his notebook*): Fine! Are you a bachelor? (*The* UNKNOWN MAN *mumbles.*)

CORRESPONDENT: I can't hear you. Are you married? Yes?

TOURIST: He said he was a bachelor.

SECOND TOURIST: No, he didn't. Of course, he's married.

CORRESPONDENT (*carelessly*): You think so? All right. We'll put down, married. How many children have you? Can't hear. It seems to me he said three. Hm! Anyway, we'll put down five.

TOURIST: Oh, my, what a tragedy. Five children! Imagine!

MILITARY WOMAN: He is lying.

CORRESPONDENT (*shouting*): How did you get into this position? What? I can't hear! Louder! Repeat. What did you say? (*Perplexed, to the crowd.*) What did he say? The fellow has a devilishly weak voice.

FIRST TOURIST: It seems to me he said that he lost his way.

SECOND TOURIST: No, he doesn't know himself how he got there.

VOICES: He was out hunting.—He was climbing up the rocks. —No, no! He is simply a lunatic!

CORRESPONDENT: I beg your pardon, I beg your pardon, ladies and gentlemen! Anyway, he didn't drop from the sky. However—— (*He quickly jots down in his notebook.*) Unhappy young man—suffering from childhood with attacks of lunacy.—The bright light of the full moon—the wild rocks.— Sleepy janitor—didn't notice——

FIRST TOURIST *(to the second, in a whisper)*: But it's a new moon now.

SECOND TOURIST: Go, what does a layman know about astronomy.

TOURIST *(ecstatically)*: Mary, pay attention to this! You have before you an ocular demonstration of the influence of the moon on living organisms. What a terrible tragedy to go out walking on a moonlit night and find suddenly that you have climbed to a place where it is impossible to climb down or be taken down.

CORRESPONDENT *(shouting)*: What feelings are you experiencing? I can't hear. Louder! Ah, so? Well, well! What a situation!

CROWD *(interested)*: Listen, listen! Let's hear what his feelings are. How terrible!

CORRESPONDENT *(writes in his notebook, tossing out detached remarks)*: Mortal terror, numbs his limbs.—A cold shiver goes down his spinal column.—No hope.—Before his mental vision rises a picture of family bliss. Wife making sandwiches; his five children innocently lisping their love.— Grandma in the armchair with a tube to her ear, that is, grandpa in the armchair, with a tube to *his* ear and grandma.—Deeply moved by the sympathy of the public.—His last wish before his death that the words he uttered with his last breath should be published in our newspapers——

MILITARY WOMAN *(indignantly)*: My! He lies like a salesman.

MARY *(wearily)*: Papa, children, look, he is starting to fall again.

TOURIST *(angrily)*: Don't bother me. Such a tragedy is unfolding itself right before your very eyes—and you—— What are you making such big eyes for again?

CORRESPONDENT *(shouting)*: Hold on fast. That's it! My last question: What message do you wish to leave for your fellow citizens before you depart for the better world?

UNKNOWN MAN: That they may all go to the devil.

CORRESPONDENT: What? Hm, yes— *(He writes quickly.)* Ardent love—is a staunch opponent of the law granting equal rights to Negroes. His last words: "Let the black——"

PASTOR *(out of breath, pushing through the crowd)*: Where is he? Ah, where is he? Ah, there! Poor young man. Has there been no clergyman here yet? No? Thank you. Am I the first?

CORRESPONDENT *(writes)*: A touching dramatic moment.—A minister has arrived.—All are trembling on the verge of suspense. Many are shedding tears——

PASTOR: Excuse me, excuse me! Ladies and gentlemen, a lost soul wishes to make its peace with God—— *(He shouts.)* My son, don't you wish to make your peace with God? Confess your sins to me. I will grant you remission at once! What? I cannot hear?

CORRESPONDENT *(writes)*: The air is shaken with the people's groans. The minister of the church exhorts the criminal, that is, the unfortunate man, in touching language.—The unfortunate creature with tears in his eyes thanks him in a faint voice——

UNKNOWN MAN *(faintly)*: If you won't go away I will jump on your head. I weigh three hundred pounds. *(All jump away, frightened, behind each other.)*

VOICES: He is falling! He is falling!

TOURIST *(agitatedly)*: Mary, Aleck, Jimmie.

POLICEMAN *(energetically)*: Clear the place, please! Move on!

LADY: Nellie, go quick and tell your father he is falling.

PHOTOGRAPHER *(in despair)*: Oh my, I am out of films. *(Tosses madly about, looking pitifully at the UNKNOWN MAN.)* One minute, I'll go and get them. I have some in my overcoat pocket over there. *(He walks a short distance, keeping his eyes fixed on the UNKNOWN MAN, and then returns.)* I can't, I am afraid I'll miss it. Good heavens! They are over there in my overcoat. Just one minute, please. I'll fetch them right away. What a fix.

PASTOR: Hurry, my friend. Pull yourself together and try to hold out long enough to tell me at least your principal sins. You needn't mention the lesser ones.

TOURIST: What a tragedy!

CORRESPONDENT *(writes)*: The criminal, that is, the unhappy man, makes a public confession and does penance. Terrible secrets revealed. He is a bank robber—blew up safes.

TOURIST *(credulously)*: The scoundrel.

PASTOR *(shouts)*: In the first place, have you killed? Secondly, have you stolen? Thirdly, have you committed adultery?

TOURIST: Mary, Jimmie, Katie, Aleck, Charlie, close your ears.

CORRESPONDENT *(writing)*: Tremendous excitement in the crowd.—Shouts of indignation.

PASTOR *(hurriedly)*: Fourthly, have you blasphemed? Fifthly, have you coveted your neighbor's ass, his ox, his slave, his wife? Sixthly——

PHOTOGRAPHER *(alarmed)*: Ladies and gentlemen, an ass!

SECOND PHOTOGRAPHER: Where? I can't see it!

PHOTOGRAPHER *(calmed)*: I thought I heard it.

PASTOR: I congratulate you, my son! I congratulate you! You have made your peace with God. Now you may rest easy.—— Oh, God, what do I see? The Salvation Army! Policeman, chase them away!

(Enter a Salvation Army band, men and women in uniforms. There are only three instruments, a drum, a violin and a piercingly shrill trumpet.)

SALVATION ARMY MAN *(frantically beating his drum and shouting in a nasal voice)*: Brethren and sisters——

PASTOR *(shouting even louder in a still more nasal voice in an effort to drown the other's)*: He has already confessed. Bear witness, ladies and gentlemen, that he has confessed and made his peace with heaven.

SALVATION ARMY WOMAN *(climbing on a rock and shrieking)*: I once wandered in the dark just as this sinner and I lived a bad life and was a drunkard, but when the light of truth——

A VOICE: Why, she is drunk now.

PASTOR: Policeman, didn't he confess and make his peace with heaven?

(The SALVATION ARMY MAN continues to beat his drum frantically; the rest begin to drawl a song. Shouts, laughter, whistling. Singing in the café, and calls of "Waiter!" in all languages. The bewildered POLICEMEN tear themselves away from the PASTOR, who is pulling them somewhere; the PHOTOGRAPHERS turn and twist about as if the seats were burning under them. An English lady comes riding in on a donkey, who, stopping suddenly, sprawls out his legs and refuses to go farther, adding his noise to the rest. Gradually the noise subsides. The Salvation Army band solemnly with-

> *draws, and the* PASTOR, *waving his hands, follows them.)*

FIRST ENGLISH TOURIST *(to the other)*: How impolite! This crowd doesn't know how to behave itself.

SECOND ENGLISH TOURIST: Come, let's go away from here.

FIRST ENGLISH TOURIST: One minute. *(He shouts.)* Listen, won't you hurry up and fall?

SECOND ENGLISH TOURIST: What are you saying, Sir William?

FIRST ENGLISH TOURIST *(shouting)*: Don't you see that's what they are waiting for? As a gentleman you should grant them this pleasure and so escape the humiliation of undergoing tortures before this mob.

SECOND ENGLISH TOURIST: Sir William.

TOURIST *(ecstatically)*: See? It's true. Aleck, Jimmie, it's true. What a tragedy!

SEVERAL TOURISTS *(going for the Englishman)*: How dare you?

FIRST ENGLISH TOURIST *(shoving them aside)*: Hurry up and fall! Do you hear? If you haven't the backbone I'll help you out with a pistol shot.

VOICES: That red-haired devil has gone clear out of his mind.

POLICEMAN *(seizing the Englishman's hand)*: You have no right to do it; it's against the law. I'll arrest you.

SOME TOURISTS: A barbarous nation!

> *(The* UNKNOWN MAN *shouts something. Excitement below.)*

VOICES: Hear, hear, hear!

UNKNOWN MAN *(aloud)*: Take that jackass away to the devil. He wants to shoot me. And tell the boss that I can't stand it any longer.

VOICES: What's that? What boss? He is losing his mind, the poor man.

TOURIST: Aleck! Mary! This is a mad scene. Jimmie, you remember *Hamlet?* Quick.

UNKNOWN MAN *(angrily)*: Tell him my spinal column is broken.

MARY *(wearily)*: Papa, children, he's beginning to kick with his legs.

KATE: Is that what is called convulsions, Papa?

TOURIST (*rapturously*): I don't know. I think it is. What a tragedy?

ALECK (*glumly*): You fool! You keep cramming and cramming and you don't know that the right name for that is agony. And you wear eyeglasses, too. I can't bear it any longer, Papa.

TOURIST: Think of it, children. A man is about to fall down to his death and he is bothering about his spinal column.

(*There is a noise. A* MAN IN A WHITE VEST, *very much frightened, enters, almost dragged by angry tourists. He smiles, bows on all sides, stretches out his arms, now running forward as he is pushed, now trying to escape in the crowd, but is seized and pulled again.*)

VOICES: A bare-faced deception! It is an outrage. Policeman, policeman, he must be taught a lesson!

OTHER VOICES: What is it? What deception? What is it all about? They have caught a thief!

THE MAN IN THE WHITE VEST (*bowing and smiling*): It's a joke, ladies and gentlemen, a joke, that's all. The people were bored, so I wanted to provide a little amusement for them.

UNKNOWN MAN (*angrily*): Boss!

THE MAN IN THE WHITE VEST: Wait awhile, wait awhile.

UNKNOWN MAN: Do you expect me to stay here until the Second Advent? The agreement was till twelve o'clock. What time is it now?

TALL TOURIST (*indignantly*): Do you hear, ladies and gentlemen? This scoundrel, this man here in the white vest hired that other scoundrel up there and just simply tied him to the rock.

VOICES: Is he tied?

TALL TOURIST: Yes, he is tied and he can't fall. We are excited and worrying, but he couldn't fall even if he tried.

UNKNOWN MAN: What else do you want? Do you think I am going to break my neck for your measly ten dollars? Boss, I can't stand it any more. One man wanted to shoot me. The pastor preached to me for two hours. This is not in the agreement.

ALECK: Father, I told you that Baedeker lies. You believe everything anybody tells you and drag us about without eating.

MAN IN THE WHITE VEST: The people were bored. My only desire was to amuse the people.

MILITARY WOMAN: What is the matter? I don't understand a thing. Why isn't he going to fall? Who, then, is going to fall?

TOURIST: I don't understand a thing either. Of course he's got to fall!

JAMES: You never understand anything, father. Weren't you told that he's tied to the rock?

ALECK: You can't convince him. He loves every Baedeker more than his own children.

JAMES: A nice father!

TOURIST: Silence!

MILITARY WOMAN: What is the matter? He must fall.

TALL TOURIST: The idea! What a deception. You'll have to explain this.

MAN IN THE WHITE VEST: The people were bored. Excuse me, ladies and gentlemen, but wishing to accommodate you —give you a few hours of pleasant excitement—elevate your spirits—inspire you with altruistic sentiments——

ENGLISHMAN: Is the café yours?

MAN IN THE WHITE VEST: Yes.

ENGLISHMAN: And is the hotel below also yours?

MAN IN THE WHITE VEST: Yes. The people were bored——

CORRESPONDENT (*writing*): The proprietor of the café, desiring to increase his profits from the sale of alcoholic beverages, exploits the best human sentiments.—The people's indignation——

UNKNOWN MAN (*angrily*): Boss, will you have me taken off at once or won't you?

HOTEL OWNER: What do you want up there? Aren't you satisfied? Didn't I have you taken off at night?

UNKNOWN MAN: Well, I should say so. You think I'd be hanging here nights, too!

HOTEL OWNER: Then you can stand it a few minutes longer. The people are bored——

TALL TOURIST: Say, have you any idea of what you have done? Do you realize the enormity of it? You are scoundrels, who for your own sordid personal ends have impiously exploited the finest human sentiment, love of one's neighbor. You have caused us to undergo fear and suffering. You have poisoned our hearts with pity. And now, what is the upshot of it all? The upshot is that this scamp, your vile accomplice, is bound to the rock and not only will he not fall as everybody expects, but he *can't*.

MILITARY WOMAN: What is the matter? He has got to fall.

TOURIST: Policeman! Policeman!

(The PASTOR enters, out of breath.)

PASTOR: What? Is he still living? Oh, there he is! What fakirs those Salvationists are.

VOICES: Don't you know that he is bound?

PASTOR: Bound! Bound to what? To life? Well, we are all bound to life until death snaps the cord. But whether he is bound or not bound, I reconciled him with heaven, and that's enough. But those fakirs——

TOURIST: Policeman! Policeman, you must draw up an official report. There is no way out of it.

MILITARY WOMAN *(going for the HOTEL OWNER)*: I will not allow myself to be fooled. I saw an aeronaut drop from the clouds and go crash upon a roof. I saw a tiger tear a woman to pieces——

PHOTOGRAPHER: I spoiled three films photographing that scamp. You will have to answer for this, sir. I will hold you responsible.

TOURIST: An official report! An official report! Such a barefaced deception. Mary, Jimmie, Aleck, Charlie, call a policeman.

HOTEL OWNER *(drawing back, in despair)*: But, I can't make him fall if he doesn't want to. I did everything in my power, ladies and gentlemen!

MILITARY WOMAN: I will not allow it.

HOTEL OWNER: Excuse me. I promise you on my word of honor that the next time he will fall. But he doesn't want to, today.

UNKNOWN MAN: What's that? What did you say about the next time?

HOTEL OWNER: You shut up there!

UNKNOWN MAN: For ten dollars?

PASTOR: Pray, what impudence! I just made his peace with heaven when he was in danger of his life. You have heard him threatening to fall on my head, haven't you? And still he is dissatisfied. Adulterer, thief, murderer, coveter of your neighbor's ass——

PHOTOGRAPHER: Ladies and gentlemen, an ass!

SECOND PHOTOGRAPHER: Where, where is an ass?

PHOTOGRAPHER *(calmed)*: I thought I heard one.

SECOND PHOTOGRAPHER: It is you who are an ass. I have become cross-eyed on account of your shouting: "An ass! An ass!"

MARY *(wearily)*: Papa, children, look! A policeman is coming.

> *(Excitement and noise. On one side a crowd pulling a* POLICEMAN, *on the other the* HOTEL OWNER; *both keep crying: "Excuse me! Excuse me!")*

TOURIST: Policeman, there he is, the fakir, the swindler.

PASTOR: Policeman, there he is, the adulterer, the murderer, the coveter of his neighbor's ass——

POLICEMAN: Excuse me, excuse me, ladies and gentlemen. We will bring him to his senses in short order and make him confess.

HOTEL OWNER: I can't make him fall if he doesn't want to.

POLICEMAN: Hey, you, young man out there! Can you fall or can't you? Confess!

UNKNOWN MAN *(sullenly)*: I don't want to fall!

VOICES: Aha, he has confessed. What a scoundrel!

TALL TOURIST: Write down what I dictate, policeman— "Desiring—for the sake of gain to exploit the sentiment of love of one's neighbor—the sacred feeling—a-a-a——"

TOURIST: Listen, children, they are drawing up an official report. What exquisite choice of language!

TALL TOURIST: The sacred feeling which——

POLICEMAN *(writing with painful effort, his tongue stuck out)*: Love of one's neighbor—the sacred feeling which——

MARY *(wearily)*: Papa, children, look! An advertisement is coming.

> *(Enter musicians with trumpets and drums, a man at their head carrying on a long pole a huge placard with the picture of an absolutely bald head, and printed underneath: "I was bald.")*

UNKNOWN MAN: Too late. They are drawing up a report here. You had better skidoo!

THE MAN CARRYING THE POLE *(stopping and speaking in a loud voice)*: I had been bald from the day of my birth and for a long time thereafter. That miserable growth, which in my tenth year covered my scalp, was more like wool than real hair. When I was married my skull was as bare as a pillow and my young bride——

TOURIST: What a tragedy! Newly married and with such a head! Can you realize how dreadful that is, children?

(All listen with interest; even the POLICEMAN *stopping in his arduous task and inclining his ear with his pen in his hand.)*

THE MAN CARRYING THE POLE *(solemnly)*: And the time came when my matrimonial happiness literally hung by a hair. All the medicines recommended by quacks to make my hair grow——

TOURIST: Your notebook, Jimmie.

MILITARY WOMAN: But when is he going to fall?

HOTEL OWNER *(amiably)*: The next time, lady, the next time. I won't tie him so hard—you understand?

CURTAIN

The Apollo
of Bellac

by JEAN GIRAUDOUX

*Translated from the French
by ALEX SZOGYI*

Jean Giraudoux (1882–1944)

In the last forty years France has enjoyed a theatrical renaissance that has had world-wide repercussions. Directors like Jacques Copeau, Louis Jouvet, and Jean-Louis Barrault and the playwrights Jean Anouilh, Jean-Paul Sartre, Henri Millon de Montherlant, Albert Camus, and Jean Genet have achieved a revitalization of French drama. One of the most important contributors to this renaissance was the diplomat-novelist Jean Giraudoux, who at the age of forty-six became a dramatist. Jouvet's production of Giraudoux's *Siegfried* in 1928 was the pioneer work in this spectacular dramatic revival.

Giraudoux was born in 1882 in the small provincial town of Bellac. A gifted, sensitive youth, he absorbed an excellent classical education. He continued his studies in Paris, specializing in German literature. After graduation a scholarship enabled him to study in Munich, where he combined the rebellious restlessness and mystical romanticism of Germany with his Gallic clarity and witty imagination. This strange duality is evident in all his plays. For a year he was a lecturer in French at Harvard; but determined to desert teaching for diplomacy, he attended the Consular School. For several years he satisfied his urge for traveling by wandering about Europe and North America. At the age of twenty-five he published three stories entitled *Provinciales*. Two years later he entered the French foreign service and served in many diplomatic posts all over the world. During this period he found time to develop his talents as a writer, producing novels, short stories, and essays.

He joined the infantry in World War I, was cited for bravery three times, and was decorated with the cross of the Légion d'Honneur. His war experiences made him a pacifist who abhorred chauvinistic nationalism. His dramatic career, which covered the last sixteen years of his life, was inaugurated with a successful dramatization of his novel *Siegfried et le limousin*. He developed a polished, poetic style in his "theater of language" in the plays that followed: *Amphitryon* (1929), *Judith* (1931), *Intermezzo* (1933, translated as *The Enchanted*), *The Trojan War Will Not Take Place* (1935, translated as *Tiger at the Gates*), *Electra* (1937), *Ondine* (1939) and *The Madwoman of Chaillot* (1943).

Giraudoux described the theater as a magical show, "a world of light, poetry, and imagination" which appealed to our senses and stirred our emotions, not by violent, physical action but by witty, sparkling dialogue of civilized people. Beneath the conversational conflicts of his urbane characters, there lurks an unobtrusive symbolism which is intellectually stimulating. His frequent use of archetypal characters drawn from biblical and classical sources reveals his interest in the universal problems of humanity, the eternal conflicts between reason and irrationality, war and peace, love and lust, the material and the spiritual worlds. His theatrical world—delicately touched by fantasy and the supernatural—is a reaction against the didactic realism of Ibsen and the shrill naturalism of Strindberg.

The *Apollo of Bellac*, written two years before Giraudoux's death, is, despite its levity and gaiety, as impressive a dramatic tribute to his birthplace as Sophocles' homage to Colonus in his last Oedipus play. In his short play Giraudoux has successfully combined satire, humor, fantasy, and philosophy —all expressed in brilliant dialogue that evokes the beauty, the heartbreak, and the mysteriousness of human existence.

In the opening scene Giraudoux satirizes the bureaucratic overorganization of modern business and the folly of searching for the Universal Vegetable to abolish the joy of good eating. He cleverly exploits the humorous situation of the naïve, charming Agnes practicing her magic formula: "How beautiful you are"—on a fly, a telephone, the chandelier, and then on people—with its surprising results. The reactions of the puppetlike directors are a clever theatrical illustration of Henri Bergson's theory of humor, the mechanical encrusted upon the living. The conflict of the President with his secretary Miss Goat Tooth and with Thérèse contributes to the humor of the play. The fantasy of the chandelier lighting up by itself and the shabby, nondescript Man who gives

Agnes a glimpse of transcendental beauty are further charming incongruities in the action. As in all Giraudoux plays, the conclusion satisfies our sense of rationality. Agnes realizes, like all of us, that she cannot live in the world of the Ideal, though it exists, but must accept the world of commonplace reality since she is human and not divine. By marrying the wealthy President, she will not live with a beautiful Greek god, but at least she will escape from the stale odors and the smell of gas in her slum dwelling. The President, too, by not returning to Thérèse, will be spared the sneers of her ugly porcelains—the East Indian dancing girl and the Dying Gaul—on the mantelpiece.

CHARACTERS

AGNES

RECEPTIONIST

MAN FROM BELLAC

VICE PRESIDENT

CLERK

MR. SPITTLE

MR. HARDHEAD

MR. RAZMUT

MR. SCHULTZ

THE PRESIDENT

MISS GOAT TOOTH

THÉRÈSE

SCENE: *The waiting room at the Inventors Bureau.*

SCENE ONE

AGNES: Is this the Inventors Bureau?

RECEPTIONIST: It is.

AGNES: I'd like to see the President.

RECEPTIONIST: What kind of invention? World-shaking, utilitarian, or household?

AGNES: I couldn't say.

RECEPTIONIST: If you're not sure, you'll have to see the Vice President. Come back Thursday.

MAN FROM BELLAC: Look here, my good man. What makes you think this young lady's invention is as unimportant as all that?

RECEPTIONIST: That's none of your business.

BELLAC: The chief trait of the inventor is his modesty. Pride was invented by noninventors. This young lady is not only modest about her creativity, she's also modest and charming looking, typical of her sex. But how do you know she isn't here to patent an invention that might cause a world upheaval?

AGNES: Sir . . .

RECEPTIONIST: For world upheavals, see the President. He's here on Mondays, from eleven to twelve.

BELLAC: But today is Tuesday.

RECEPTIONIST: If this young lady hasn't invented a way of making Tuesday precede Monday, I can't do a thing for her.

BELLAC: Can you imagine! The world is awaiting anxiously the invention which will make it possible to adapt the universal laws of gravity to the more efficient delivery of mail . . . perhaps this young lady. . . . Miss . . . ?

AGNES: Agnes.

BELLAC: Perhaps Miss Agnes has brought us what we've been waiting for . . . but no, she has to wait till Monday!

RECEPTIONIST: Will you please keep quiet . . .

BELLAC: I will not. I keep quiet on Mondays. And what about the Universal Vegetable! Five continents are withering while they wait for the Universal Vegetable, which will make the individual specialization of spinach, peas, and beans look ridiculous; the Universal Vegetable will take the place of bread, meat, wine, and chocolate, and will be transformable into cotton, wool, silk, and satin. Miss Agnes is bringing it to you herself. What the great alchemists and magicians of all time have not been able to accomplish, she has. The seeds of the Universal Vegetable are right there in that tiny little handbag she's carrying, sheltering in the creative warmth of her bosom, ready, once the patent has been initialled by your President, to break loose, germinate, and proliferate! Ah, but they'll have to wait till Monday!

AGNES: Sir . . .

RECEPTIONIST: The guest book is right here. Let her sign up for Monday.

BELLAC: I can see it now! Monday, bright and early, they'll all be lining up: the idiots who have invented the pointless tack and musical glue. They'll get to see the President at once, while the rest of humanity is plunged up to its buttocks in the mud of the rice fields, ruining its eyesight, separating seeds, not knowing that the Universal Vegetable is here . . . Miss Agnes will not sign up!

RECEPTIONIST: So what.

BELLAC: What did you say?

RECEPTIONIST: I said "So what" . . . is that clear?

BELLAC: It is. That's the answer the greats of all time have received when they tried to get help for their world-shaking inventions. All they got was "So what" . . .

RECEPTIONIST: You will excuse me. I have work to do. (*He goes out.*)

SCENE
TWO

AGNES: Thank you, Sir. But I'm not the inventor of the Universal Vegetable.

BELLAC: I know. I am.

AGNES: I'm looking for a job. That's all.

BELLAC: Oh. Are you a typist?

AGNES: Well . . .

BELLAC: Stenographer?

AGNES: Not really.

BELLAC: Linguist, editor, file clerk? Stop me when I get to your specialty.

AGNES: You could run the gamut. I wouldn't stop you.

BELLAC: Oh, I see. You're selling a quality. What's your specialty? Are you flirtatious, sweet, tender, voluptuous, naïve?

AGNES: That's more like it.

BELLAC: Good. These are the things that lead to a really successful career.

AGNES: I'm afraid not. You see, I'm afraid . . . of men . . .

BELLAC: Of which men?

AGNES: They make me weak all over. . . .

BELLAC: Are you afraid of that receptionist?

AGNES: I'm afraid of all of them. The receptionists, the presidents, the military men. Whenever I'm with a man, I feel like a shoplifter in a department store with a detective breathing down his neck.

BELLAC: A shoplifter?

AGNES: I feel like getting rid of the stolen object and shouting "Let me go!"

BELLAC: What object?

AGNES: I don't even let myself think about it. I'm afraid.

BELLAC: It must be their clothes that impress you. Their trousers? Their neckties?

263

AGNES: It happens when I go swimming. Their trousers are off. I get the same feeling.

BELLAC: Maybe you just don't like them, that's all.

AGNES: I don't think so. I like their doglike eyes, their hair, and their big feet. The way their Adam's apples bob up and down when they eat makes me feel all tender toward them. But as soon as they look at me, or talk to me, I feel queasy all over.

BELLAC: Would you be interested in getting over it?

AGNES: Hm?

BELLAC: Would you be interested in leading them around, to get what you want from them, to make receptionists, presidents, and swimmers crawl?

AGNES: Is there a way?

BELLAC: Only one. Infallible.

AGNES: Why would you tell me? You're a man . . .

BELLAC: Ignore it and you'll live a sordid life! Use it and you'll be on top of the world.

AGNES: On top of the world! What is it? Tell me!

BELLAC: Anybody listening?

AGNES: No. . . .

BELLAC: Tell them they're beautiful!

AGNES: Tell them they're handsome, intelligent, sensitive?

BELLAC: No! Tell them they're beautiful! They can manage their intelligence and their sensitivity! They know all about it. They have to be told that they're beautiful . . .

AGNES: You can't tell a senator he's beautiful. . . . I'd never dare . . .

BELLAC: Try it and see! Tell them all! The cowards, the milquetoasts, the old codgers, the bloated, beery ones. Tell it to a philosophy professor and you'll get your diploma. To the butcher and he'll have a choice cut of filet mignon left over for you in the freezer. To the President here, and you'll get whatever job you want.

AGNES: But you have to be so intimate with them before you'd ever get the chance to tell them . . .

BELLAC: Tell them right away. Let your first glance say it. . . .

AGNES: But you have to wait till you're alone! Just the two of you . . .

BELLAC: Tell them they're beautiful right in the middle of the bus, the exam room, the butcher shop. Your witnesses will be your guarantee!

AGNES: And if they're not beautiful, what do I say to them? That's the way it is most of the time, unfortunately . . .

BELLAC: Agnes, are you narrowminded? Tell it to the bow-legged, the pimply ones, the ugly ones. . . . Tell them all they're beautiful!

AGNES: They won't believe me!

BELLAC: They'll all believe you. They believe it all along. Every man, even the ugliest, harbors a secret feeling inside himself that he's beauty personified. He'll be hearing said aloud what his own self-satisfaction has been repeating to him all along. And those who don't believe it are the most flattered of all. They think they're ugly, but if they meet a woman who finds them beautiful, they hang onto her for dear life. For them she's the enchanted spy-glass and barometer of a universe which is full of eyes that deform what they see. They don't ever leave her side again. When you see a woman being escorted everywhere by a host of suitors, it's not because they find her beautiful—it's because she has told them they are beautiful.

AGNES: Oh, are there women who are in on the secret?

BELLAC: Yes, but they mess it up. They evade the issue. They tell a hunchback he's generous and a pimply face that he's tender. That won't get you anywhere. I saw a woman lose millions, pearls and necklaces, because she told a man with a clubfoot that he walked perfectly. She should have said—one must say—that they're beautiful. . . . Now go ahead. The President has no special day on which to hear he's beautiful.

AGNES: No. I'll be back. I have to practice first. I have a cousin who's not bad looking. I'll practice on him.

BELLAC: You're going to practice this very minute. On the receptionist!

AGNES: On that monster?

BELLAC: The monster is perfect for practicing. Then on the Vice President. He's just as good. Even more hideous. Then on the President.

(The RECEPTIONIST *appears, sees they are still there, then goes out again.)*

AGNES: Begin with the receptionist, never!

BELLAC: All right, begin with this bust.

AGNES: Who is it?

BELLAC: That's not important. It's the bust of a man. He's all ears.

AGNES: He doesn't have a beard. Only beards give me confidence in men . . .

BELLAC: Well, talk to anybody, anything! To this chair, to this clock!

AGNES: They're inanimate!

BELLA: To this butterfly! There he is, on your shoulder. He's torn himself away from the jasmine and the roses to come and suck up his praises. Go ahead.

AGNES: How beautiful he is!

BELLAC: Tell him yourself.

AGNES: How beautiful you are!

BELLAC: You see! He's flapping his wings. Embroider a little. Exaggerate. What is a butterfly specially proud of?

AGNES: His wings. His feelers.

BELLAC: Go on! How beautiful your wings are!

AGNES: How beautiful your wings are, butterfly! You're all velvety. How beautiful you are—all black and yellow. And your feelers. So prim and pretty!

BELLAC: Not bad at all. There's the receptionist. Chase it away.

AGNES: It's clinging to me!

BELLAC: Tell it you prefer the color red. Now, you understand, the same for the receptionist as for the butterfly, and for receptionists, the equivalent of wings and feelers!

AGNES: Let me talk to him about the weather first. Look at him. Heavens!

BELLAC: No, let your first words be *the* words; no delays, no hesitations!

AGNES: How can I?

BELLAC: You can flounder afterwards. Then it doesn't matter. It will have been said!

AGNES: But what shall I say?

BELLAC: Must I repeat it a thousand times? . . . How beautiful you are!

SCENE
THREE

AGNES (*after a thousand hesitations*): How beautiful you are!

RECEPTIONIST: What did you say?

AGNES: I said "How beautiful you are!"

RECEPTIONIST: Do you often get this way?

AGNES: It's the first time in my life . . .

RECEPTIONIST: That you've told a gorilla that he's beautiful?

AGNES: Beautiful is perhaps not the word. I don't judge people by the slope of their noses or the space between their eyes. I don't judge any one feature. I judge the way they look together.

RECEPTIONIST: So that's what you're saying to me. all your features are ugly but they look good *together!*

AGNES: If that's the way you look at it, just leave me alone! You can be sure it's not because I want to flatter a nasty old man like you that I tell him I think he's beautiful . . .

RECEPTIONIST: Now, calm down! Calm down!

AGNES: It's the first time I've said it to a man. I'll never do it again.

RECEPTIONIST: I know that at your age one says what one thinks. But why do you express yourself so poorly?

(*The* MAN FROM BELLAC's *head appears and encourages* AGNES.)

AGNES: I do not express myself poorly. I find you beautiful. I tell you you're beautiful. I could be wrong. Not everybody has taste.

RECEPTIONIST: You don't find me beautiful. I know women. They don't see anything. They don't even notice my few good points at all. What is there about me that is beautiful? My silhouette? . . . *That* you haven't even noticed. . . .

AGNES: Your silhouette? How could you think that? When you picked up the wastepaper basket just then, didn't

267

your silhouette bend down with you? And did you put your silhouette in your pocket when you crossed the room and went out?

RECEPTIONIST: You see it now because I've called your attention to it . . .

AGNES: You're perfectly right. You're not beautiful. I thought I was looking at you and all the time it was your silhouette.

RECEPTIONIST: Then why don't you say "What a beautiful silhouette!" Don't say "What a beautiful receptionist!"

AGNES: I'll never say it again!

RECEPTIONIST: Don't get angry! I'm just trying to make you more observant. I'm within my rights: I have a daughter myself, my dear. I know what girls are like at your age. Just because the silhouette of a man is pleasing to them, all of a sudden they find *him* beautiful. Beautiful from head to toe. A beautiful silhouette is, in fact, very rare. And a silhouette endures. You have it to your dying day. And even after. Even skeletons have silhouettes. And not much else. But these silly girls confuse the silhouette with the body, and if all the silly men in the world listened to their flattery, there would be a good many more spoiled lives than there are now . . . you can't live with a silhouette, my child!

(The MAN FROM BELLAC'*s head appears.)*

AGNES: How beautiful you are when you get angry! You won't make me believe those beautiful teeth are part of your silhouette . . .

RECEPTIONIST: There you're right. When I get angry, I show off my only perfect trait, my teeth. I don't smoke. And have you noticed that I have perfect eyeteeth? Not that one, it has a filling in it. On the right. . . . Oh, the Vice President is ringing . . . I'll see to it you get in to see him . . . I'll tell him you're my niece.

AGNES: How beautiful it is when you stand up straight! You'd think it belonged to Rodin's Thinker . . .

RECEPTIONIST: Yes, yes. That's enough. If you were my daughter, I'd take you over my knee!

SCENE
FOUR

BELLAC: That was a beginning.

AGNES: A bad beginning. I did better with the butterfly than I did with the receptionist.

BELLAC: That was because you stubbornly insisted on joining the idea of a caress with the idea of beauty. You women are all alike. A woman who finds the sky beautiful is a woman who caresses the sky. It's not your hands that have to do your talking for you; not your lips, nor your cheeks: it's your brain.

AGNES: He almost didn't believe me.

BELLAC: That was because you hesitated. He had you there with his silhouette. You're not ready yet for a Vice President.

AGNES: How shall I practice! He's coming.

BELLAC: Try me . . .

AGNES: Shall I tell you you're beautiful?

BELLAC: Is it so difficult as all that?

AGNES: Not at all.

BELLAC: Think carefully of what you're going to say. . . .

AGNES: You're not bad at all when you make fun of me like that. . . .

BELLAC: Very poor. You hesitated! You hesitated! Why particularly when I make fun of you? Am I not beautiful otherwise?

AGNES: Oh, yes! Magnificent!

BELLAC: Good! You're getting there! . . . Now it's not your hands that are doing the talking.

AGNES: Near you they tremble a little all the same . . .

BELLAC: Perfect!

AGNES: You have a beautiful build. I don't care about the shape of your head. The shape of your body is beautiful.

BELLAC: You don't care about . . . my head? What does that mean?

AGNES: No more than I care about the head of Rodin's Thinker.

BELLAC: His feet, evidently, are more important. . . . Now listen, Agnes. These allusions to a famous statue are very ingenious, but is Rodin's Thinker the only one you know?

AGNES: The only one. And the Venus de Milo, of course. But I can't use her for men.

BELLAC: That remains to be seen. It's very important for you to add to your repertoire. Talk about Michelangelo's Slave. Talk about the Apollo of Bellac.

AGNES: The Apollo of Bellac?

BELLAC: Yes. He doesn't exist. I've invented him specially for you. Nobody will challenge you. . . .

AGNES: What is he like?

BELLAC: A little like me, of course. I was born in Bellac. It's a little town in the center of France.

AGNES: They say that people from Bellac are so ugly. How did you ever become so beautiful?

BELLAC: My father was very beautiful. . . . How stupid I am! Bravo, you fooled me. . . .

AGNES: I wasn't even trying. You taught me how. I was just being honest with you.

BELLAC: There you are! She's understood.

(RECEPTIONIST *enters.* BELLAC *hides in a corner.*)

RECEPTIONIST: The Vice President will be here in a moment to see you, Miss Agnes. Don't get too excited. To see a silhouette like that, you generally have to pay a visit to the Museum of Natural History.

(*He goes out.* AGNES *talks to the* MAN FROM BELLAC, *who juts his head out.*)

AGNES: Did you hear that? How awful . . .

BELLAC: Practice!

AGNES: On who? On what?

BELLAC: On everything around you. Objects don't resist those who tell them they're beautiful. . . . Try that telephone. . . .

(*She talks to the telephone and touches it.*)

AGNES: How beautiful you are, my little telephone. . . .

BELLAC: Not with your hands . . .

AGNES: But it helps me so much!

BELLAC: The chandelier! You won't be able to touch it. . . .

AGNES: How beautiful you are, my big brass chandelier! More beautiful when you're lit up? Oh, don't say that. . . . Other chandeliers, yes. But not you. Ordinary lamps, burners, but not you. Look: The sun is playing with you; you're the sun's little chandelier. The gasoline lamp has to be lit up, and so do the stars. But not you. That's what I meant. You're as beautiful as a constellation, as a constellation would be, if instead of being a false chandelier, suspended for eternity, with its lights unsymmetrically arranged, it was this monument of marvellous brass with splendid sockets of Baccarat crystal and symmetrical peaks that make you look like you have a face and a body!

(The chandelier lights up by itself.)

BELLAC: Bravo!

SCENE
FIVE

VICE PRESIDENT: One moment, young lady, I have one moment at my disposal. What is it you want?

AGNES: I? Nothing . . .

VICE PRESIDENT: What are you looking at me that way for? Did you happen to take my course in dream-inventions at the Conservatory? Do you know me?

AGNES: Oh, no! On the contrary . . .

VICE PRESIDENT: On the contrary? What do you mean by "On the contrary?"

AGNES: I was waiting for a Vice President just like all the others, hunched over with a potbelly, skinny, and clumsy . . . and there you are!

VICE PRESIDENT: I am the way I am.

(BELLAC's *head appears.*)

AGNES: Yes. You're beautiful.

VICE PRESIDENT: What did you say?

AGNES: Nothing. Nothing at all.

VICE PRESIDENT: Yes you did. You said that I was beautiful. I heard it clearly and I must say I am quite surprised. If I were, somebody would have told me so.

AGNES: The idiots!

VICE PRESIDENT: Who's an idiot? My sister, my mother, my niece?

AGNES: Mister Vice President, I heard it from a friend of yours on the board, Mister Hardhead . . .

VICE PRESIDENT: Leave Mister Hardhead out of this. We were talking about *my* beauty. I'm a specialist in dreams, young lady. I'm the one the inventors come to when they make their discoveries while dreaming; I've succeeded in extracting inventions from dreams which are as remarkable as the cigarette lighter in the shape of a fork and the book

272

that reads itself, which, without me, would have remained but fragments of a dream. If while you were dreaming you had told me that I was beautiful, I would have understood. But you are wide awake. At least I presuppose you are. Let me pinch myself to be quite sure. And allow me to pinch you.

(He takes her hand.)

AGNES: Oh!

VICE PRESIDENT *(holding onto her hand)*: We are not dreaming. Then why it is that you told me I was beautiful escapes me. To get into my good graces? That would be too vulgar. To make fun of me? You look like a courteous girl, at least your eyes and your lips seem so . . .

AGNES: I said it because I find you beautiful. If your dear mother thought you were hideous, that's her business.

VICE PRESIDENT: Hideous is an exaggeration. I would not permit you to have such an unfavorable opinion of my mother. My mother, even when I was five years old, considered that I had the hands of a bishop.

AGNES: If your niece prefers Valentino to you, that doesn't do her credit.

VICE PRESIDENT: My niece is not an idiot. She claimed only yesterday that the perfection in the arch of my brow must have been designed by a great architect.

AGNES: If your sister . . .

VICE PRESIDENT: You're mistaken about my sister. She knows I'm not beautiful, but she always found that I was a type. And one of my friends who has a doctorate degree in Italian history recently identified the type. It is very famous. I am the image of a Medici.

AGNES: A Medici? Never! The Apollo of Bellac, yes!

VICE PRESIDENT: The Apollo of Bellac?

AGNES: Don't you think so?

VICE PRESIDENT: If you insist, my dear. You know, the Medici type is very unusual. I have seen some etchings . . .

AGNES: The Apollo of Bellac, *dressed* of course! But I do have some reservations about the way you dress. You don't dress very well, Mister Vice President. You see, I'm frank. You'll never make me say something I don't believe. You have the defects of truly beautiful men. You could have been a Nijinsky. But you dress as if you bought your clothes at the Flea Market.

VICE PRESIDENT: The things one has to listen to! And from a young lady who tells the first person she meets that he is beautiful!

AGNES: I've said it to only two men in my life. You are the second.

VICE PRESIDENT: Nobody evidently resembles everybody else, and I, less than anyone. (*To* RECEPTIONIST, *who has just entered.*) What do you want? Don't you see we're busy!

RECEPTIONIST: The members of the board are coming up the stairs. Shall I announce them?

VICE PRESIDENT: The Board requires my presence, my dear. But will you give me the pleasure of coming by tomorrow to continue this interesting conversation? Especially since the typist who works in my office has been making too many typing errors and I am thinking of getting rid of her. I'm sure you're an artist, in typing?

AGNES: Alas, no. I only know how to play the piano.

VICE PRESIDENT: Perfect. That's much rarer. Do you take dictation?

AGNES: Slowly.

VICE PRESIDENT: So much the better. The other one goes too fast and her attitude is far too superior.

AGNES: I can't read my writing back very well.

VICE PRESIDENT: Perfect. The other one is the height of indiscretion. Till tomorrow, then, my dear. You accept?

AGNES: Gratefully, but on one condition.

VICE PRESIDENT: You pose conditions to your employer!

AGNES: On the condition that I won't see you anymore with this awful jacket on. I just can't bear to imagine those two glorious shoulders in that covering. . . .

VICE PRESIDENT: I have a suit of very fine silk. But it's a summer suit and I might catch cold if I wear it.

AGNES: Take it or leave it. I love fine silk.

VICE PRESIDENT: Till tomorrow, then. . . . My sister and my mother will clean it this very afternoon. I'll have it on.

(*He leaves. The* MAN FROM BELLAC's *head reappears.*)

AGNES: Well?

BELLAC: Not bad. But you're still hesitating.

AGNES: But my hands were out of the way. I have a time controlling them.

BELLAC: No time to lose. The scarecrows are coming up the stairs. Keep practicing.

AGNES: On which one?

BELLAC: On all of them.

SCENE
SIX

RECEPTIONIST (*announcing them as they pass through*): Mister Spittle.

AGNES: How beautiful *he* is, over there.

SPITTLE (*low voice*): Charming girl.

(*He enters the board room.*)

RECEPTIONIST: Mister Hardhead . . .

HARDHEAD (*approaching* AGNES): Hello, you pretty thing . . .

AGNES: How beautiful you are!

HARDHEAD: How would you know?

AGNES: From your wife's friend, the Baroness Bigpussy. She thinks you're magnificent.

HARDHEAD: Ah, the Baroness Bigpussy finds me magnificent, does she? Say hello to her for me, till I get the opportunity to do it myself. It's true she doesn't have an easy time with the Baron. Does she still live at the old address?

AGNES: I'll tell her you're still just as beautiful as you always were.

HARDHEAD: Don't exaggerate . . . (*In a low voice.*) She's delightful!

(*He exits into board room.*)

RECEPTIONIST: Messrs Razmut and Schultz.

AGNES: How beautiful he is!

RAZMUT: Which one of us were you talking to, young lady?

AGNES: Look at each other. You'll know.

(*They take a look at each other.*)

SCHULTZ and RAZMUT: She's charming!

(*They enter the board room. The* MAN FROM BELLAC'S *head appears.*)

AGNES: You look sad. Something wrong?

BELLAC: It's going too well. I've unchained the devil. I should have realized that the worst monsters were once naïve . . .

(RECEPTIONIST *announces, with a flourish.*)

RECEPTIONIST: The President!

SCENE
SEVEN

PRESIDENT: Are you the phenomenon?

AGNES: I'm Agnes.

PRESIDENT: What are you doing to them, Miss Agnes? This corporation over which I preside was, until this very morning, stagnating in idleness and wallowing in it. You've barely arrived and I can no longer recognize it. My receptionist has become polite to the point where he greets his shadow on the wall. My Vice President is going to a board meeting in his shirt sleeves. They're all taking out pocket mirrors and contemplating themselves and each other. Mister Hardhead is examining his Adam's apple with pride; Mister Razmut is giving just as much attention to his wart. What have you done to them? I'll buy your secret; quote me a price. It's invaluable. What have you said to them?

AGNES: How beautiful you are!

PRESIDENT: What did you say?

AGNES: I said to them, to every one of them: "How beautiful you are!"

PRESIDENT: With smiles, simpers, and promises?

AGNES: No, in a loud, clear voice . . . "How beautiful you are!"

PRESIDENT: I thank you on their behalf. That's how children wind up mechanical dolls. My little puppets have been wound up—they have *joie de vivre!* Listen to that applause. It's Mister Spittle—he's been taking the vote on whether or not to buy a new bathroom mirror with three faces. Miss Agnes, thank you!

AGNES: It's nothing, I assure you.

PRESIDENT: What about the President, Miss Agnes? How come you haven't said it to the President?

AGNES: That he's beautiful?

PRESIDENT: Because he doesn't appear to you to be worth it?

278

AGNES: Oh, it's not that!

PRESIDENT: Because you've played enough with the vanity of men for one day?

AGNES: Come now, Mr. President! You know perfectly well!

PRESIDENT: No. I do not know.

AGNES: It's not necessary to tell it to you. Because you *are* beautiful!

PRESIDENT: Repeat that please!

AGNES: Because you are beautiful.

PRESIDENT: Think on it, Miss Agnes. This is a serious moment. Are you quite sure you find me beautiful?

AGNES: I do not find you beautiful. You *are* beautiful.

PRESIDENT: Would you be ready to say that again before witnesses? Before the receptionist? Think on it. Today I have a series of decisions to make, which will lead me to the very opposite poles according to whether I'm beautiful or ugly.

AGNES: Say it again? Certainly, I will. Again and again.

PRESIDENT: Thank God. *(He calls.)* Miss Goat Tooth.

(Enter GOAT TOOTH.*)*

PRESIDENT: Goat Tooth, for three years now you have been fulfilling the important duties of a private secretary. For three years now, not a morning or an afternoon has flown by in which the perspective of finding you in my office has not given me nausea. It's not only that you have a nasty nature, you seem to thrive on meanness like fungus on the bark of a tree. Because you were ugly, I thought you were generous. You're the only one I know who gives charity to a blindman and takes back change from his bowl. Don't deny it. He told me so. Because you had a mustache, I thought you had a heart. You told me that when my fox terrier gave out with those heartrending barks in his sleep— that he was dreaming of being on a panther hunt: and all the time you were pinching him under the table! I have put up for an endless number of days with someone who detests, scorns, and abominates me—and finds me ugly. You do think I'm ugly, don't you?

GOAT TOOTH: Yes! You're a gorilla.

PRESIDENT: Perfect. Now you will please listen. This young lady's eyes seem at first view to be better qualified to see than yours. She is not bloodshot or bleary-eyed. Her eyes reflect the sun and spring water. What do you think of me, actually, Miss Agnes?

AGNES: You're beautiful! Very beautiful!

GOAT TOOTH: Cheat!

PRESIDENT: Shut up, Goat Tooth. Give me one last glance. Hasn't this disinterested appreciation of my masculine charms modified your own views?

GOAT TOOTH: You make me laugh!

PRESIDENT: I'll make a note of that. Here is the problem we face: I have the choice of spending my days with a horrid individual who finds me ugly and a ravishing young lady who finds me beautiful. Draw your conclusions. Choose for me . . .

GOAT TOOTH: Is this madwoman taking my place?

PRESIDENT: This very instant, if she so desires.

GOAT TOOTH: What shame! I'm going up to tell Madame.

PRESIDENT: Go right ahead. I stand my ground.

GOAT TOOTH: If you value your porcelain vases, you'd better come along.

PRESIDENT: I've written them off. You can see that quite clearly.

(*Exit* GOAT TOOTH.)

AGNES: I'm sorry, Mr. President.

PRESIDENT: Congratulate me. You have arrived like an archangel at the crucial moment of my existence. I was just about to deliver an engagement ring to the lady Goat Tooth threatened me with . . . it was this diamond . . . how do you like it?

AGNES: How beautiful it is!

PRESIDENT: Astonishing! I was watching you. You said: "How beautiful it is" to the diamond with the same conviction as you did to me! Could it be inferior or full of flaws?

AGNES: It's magnificent. You are, too.

(THÉRÈSE *can be heard coming.*)

PRESIDENT: I must be just a little bit less so: Thérèse is coming.

SCENE
EIGHT

PRESIDENT: May I introduce you!

THÉRÈSE: Totally unnecessary. . . . Get out!

PRESIDENT: Agnes replaces Goat Tooth. She's staying.

THÉRÈSE: Agnes? You already know her first name?

PRESIDENT: I know even more than that.

THÉRÈSE: And may we be told why Agnes is to replace Goat Tooth?

PRESIDENT: Because she finds me beautiful.

THÉRÈSE: Are you mad?

PRESIDENT: No. I'm beautiful.

THÉRÈSE: You know what you were like this morning, at least?

PRESIDENT: This morning I was a man with slightly bowed legs, a wan complexion, and poor teeth. I was as you saw me.

THÉRÈSE: I still see you.

PRESIDENT: Yes, but Agnes sees me, too. I prefer her view. At least I hope that despite your being here, she will continue to see me just as well . . . as beautiful.

AGNES: I must say that excitement makes you even more beautiful!

THÉRÈSE: Shameless creature!

PRESIDENT: You hear that! I didn't make her say it. Excitement makes me even more beautiful, according to Agnes. And one gets the feeling that if I were sleeping, raging, or perspiring, Agnes would find that unconsciousness, surliness, or sweat would make me even more beautiful. You're smiling, Agnes?

AGNES: Yes, how beautiful, an intelligent man with courage, too.

THÉRÈSE: You probably think he's a great hero. A Napoleon!

AGNES: Oh, no! The president is more classical: merely the Apollo of Bellac.

THÉRÈSE: What a woman! She is a fraud!

PRESIDENT: What a woman! The true woman! Listen to me, Thérèse, for the last time. Women are put into this terrible world to tell us what Agnes tells us. They weren't born from our ribs with forceps so they can buy nylons, complain about the quality of nail-polish removers, or gossip about other women. They are on earth to tell men they are beautiful. And those who do are usually the most beautiful women. This young lady tells me I'm beautiful. It's because she is beautiful. You keep telling me I'm ugly. I always suspected it: you're a horror!

(*The* MAN FROM BELLAC *comes out of his hiding place.*)

BELLAC: Bravo! Bravo!

THÉRÈSE: Who is this other madman?

BELLAC: Bravo, President, and excuse me for intervening. But when this debate touches the very core of human existence, how can I restrain myself! Since Adam and Eve, Samson and Delilah, Antony and Cleopatra, the problem of men and women has remained intact and dangling between the sexes. If we could settle it once and for all today, it would benefit humanity immensely.

THÉRÈSE: And you think we're on the right track? Well, let's put the solution off until tomorrow. I'm in a great hurry. They're waiting for me upstairs to try on my engagement fur.

BELLAC: We are on the right track. The President has just stated the problem superbly!

AGNES: Superbly!

THÉRÈSE: Copycat!

AGNES: I say what I think!

THÉRÈSE: Liar!

PRESIDENT: I forbid you to insult Agnes!

THÉRÈSE: She's insulting me!

PRESIDENT: They insult you when they find me beautiful! You've just revealed the depths of your soul!

BELLAC: Agnes didn't lie to the President. And Cleopatra told the truth to Caesar, just as Delilah did to Samson. And the truth about men is that they are all beautiful, and always beautiful, and the woman who tells it to them never lies.

THÉRÈSE: So I'm the liar!

BELLAC: You're the blind one. Because all you really need to do to find them beautiful is to look at men while they're breathing or exercising. Each one of them has his own kind of beauty, appropriate to the occasion: the hunchback of Notre Dame is a masterpiece of Gothic beauty. But only on condition that he is in his rightful place. There's such a thing also as occupational beauty: the furniture mover has his own special kind, just as the President does. The only mistake is to try to take on someone else's beauty: a furniture mover can never look beautiful as a President, and vice versa.

AGNES: Oh, I don't know about that.

THÉRÈSE: No, you wouldn't. Nobody's noticed that he has the beauty of a hobo.

PRESIDENT: Thérèse, you know that's not true! You know that I'm . . .

THÉRÈSE: You're ugly!

PRESIDENT: Shut up!

THÉRÈSE: You *are* ugly. Believe me. I'm sincere when I tell it to you. This woman may force her lips to utter her lies. But all of me: my heart, my arteries, my arms, are shouting the truth to you! Even my legs . . .

PRESIDENT: Agnes' lips are better than your . . .

BELLAC: She's confessed!

THÉRÈSE: What do they all have against me? What have I confessed?

BELLAC: Your fault! Your crime! How could you expect the President to be beautiful with everything around him constantly repeating to him that he's ugly!

PRESIDENT: Bravo! Now I understand!

THÉRÈSE: You understand what?

PRESIDENT: The uneasiness that comes over me not only when I'm with you but with everything that belongs to you, your clothes, your belongings. That petticoat you left on the back of a chair makes me hunch over. How can I look my natural height? Your stockings left on a table make me feel as if one of my legs were shorter than the other. Your nail file makes me feel as if I'd lost a finger. They all keep telling me I'm ugly. Your onyx clock ticks it off at me every second. And why do I shiver when I stand in front of the fireplace? It's because your Dying Gaul on the mantelpiece whispers to me with his dying breath that I'm ugly. I'm going to get rid of it tonight. From now on I want to know the truth about myself!

THÉRÈSE: You wouldn't dare lay hands on my Dying Gaul . . .

PRESIDENT: Out it goes tonight with all the rest of the conspirators! Your Florentine page, your East Indian dancing girl with the voluptuous navel that ridicules my own little navel. Even your Directoire chairs with horsehair upholstery that makes my behind feel ugly by scratching at it. To the auction block with them all!

THÉRÈSE: You won't sell my Directoire chairs!

PRESIDENT: All right, I'll give them away! Tell me about the place where you live, Agnes.

AGNES: My chairs are upholstered in velvet.

PRESIDENT: Velvet? How beautiful! And what is there on the table?

AGNES: Flowers. Today there are roses.

PRESIDENT: Roses? How beautiful! And on the mantelpiece?

AGNES: A mirror.

PRESIDENT: A mirror? How beautiful! A way to get back to my real image!

THÉRÈSE: I thought I was talking to Oscar. It's really Narcissus!

BELLAC: Narcissus is only guilty when he finds others to be ugly. How could the President find the inspiration to dictate even a memo surrounded by such hostility?

PRESIDENT: When I was alone, with only my dog for companionship, I had the inspiration. That was when I wrote my best memos.

BELLAC: Because the eye of the dog is faithful and sees you as you really are. And a lion would have inspired more eloquent memos yet, because lions see everything three times larger than life and double the relief.

THÉRÈSE: Don't go on. He'll put lions in our apartment!

PRESIDENT: I will not put lions in the apartment! But the Dying Gaul and the East Indian dancing girl are going out the window with the rest of your porcelain.

THÉRÈSE: If you touch any one of them, I'll be the one to go.

PRESIDENT: That's up to you!

THÉRÈSE: What right have they to do this to us! I've given you my life and my talents without stinting. Have you ever been served a well-done roast or weak coffee? Thanks to me, you're one of the few men that can be sure he has a fresh handkerchief in his lapel every day and that his toes don't stick out of his socks—they don't stick out, do they? And in wintertime, the moths don't stand a chance with your suits. Why are you putting me through this trial? Haven't I always treated you as a woman should? Don't you like your home?

PRESIDENT: One question, please. Do you tell me that I'm ugly because you find me ugly or because it amuses you and revenges you to tell me?

THÉRÈSE: But you are ugly.

PRESIDENT: Go right ahead . . .

THÉRÈSE: All of a sudden this woman arrives. I can see at first glance what the man will have to put up with who lives with her. Slippers with warped insoles. Reading at night in bed with only one night-light on the other side of the room. Clothes that are frayed and moth-eaten. Constipation without Di Lax. Mosquitoes without citronella . . . Indigestion without Alka-Seltzer . . .

PRESIDENT: Agnes, do you tell me I'm beautiful because you find me beautiful or to laugh at me?

AGNES: Because you're beautiful.

THÉRÈSE: Marry him, then, if you find him so beautiful! You know he's rich!

AGNES: Even if he had millions, I'd still think he was beautiful!

THÉRÈSE: Well, what are you waiting for? Why don't you propose?

PRESIDENT: I don't intend to wait any longer. I shall propose. I have no regrets.

THÉRÈSE: Go right ahead. I've had enough. Take him, if you enjoy snoring at night.

AGNES: You snore? What luck! When I can't sleep, I'm so afraid of the silence.

THÉRÈSE: If you enjoy protruding kneecaps.

AGNES: I never liked legs that were too symmetrical. Who likes ninepins?

THÉRÈSE: And a sunken in chest.

AGNES: That's a lie! I'm very hard to please when it comes to chests.

THÉRÈSE: Well, doesn't he have a sunken in chest?

AGNES: No, he doesn't. He has the proud chest of a Crusader.

THÉRÈSE: A feudal lord!

AGNES: No, a king!

THÉRÈSE: That's too much! Farewell. I'm going to take refuge in a world where ugliness exists.

PRESIDENT: You don't need to go far. You carry it with you. You have it engraved on your soul and in your eyes . . . *(THÉRÈSE exits.)* And now, Agnes, accept this diamond as a token of a happy future. Since you compare its beauty to mine, I'll try to find the way to sparkle and shine under your gaze. Just one moment, please. I'm going to announce our engagement to the Board. *(To the* RECEPTIONIST.*)* And will you please buy up all the carnations you can find at the neighborhood florist's and . . . *(To the* MAN FROM BELLAC.*)* you, Sir, to whom I owe so much today, I hope that you will be kind enough to share a dinner with us. . . . Embrace me, my sweet Agnes. . . . You hesitate?

AGNES: I also hesitate to look at my diamond.

PRESIDENT: I'll be back in a moment. . . . Agnes. . . . I'm the happiest of men!

AGNES: The most beautiful . . .

(PRESIDENT exits.)

SCENE
NINE

BELLAC: A job, a husband, a diamond! I can say good-bye to you now, Agnes. You have everything.

AGNES: Yes, I do.

BELLAC: You're insatiable . . .

AGNES: Look at me. Haven't I changed since this morning?

BELLAC: Just a bit . . . gentler and tenderer . . .

AGNES: It's your fault. By repeating your slogan, I've gotten to like it. Why did you make me tell all those ugly men that they're beautiful? Now I feel ready to tell it to somebody who's truly beautiful. I need that reward and that punishment. Find him for me.

BELLAC: It's a beautiful day. The autumn is beautiful.

AGNES: That's too far away. You can't touch the day. You can't put your arms around the autumn. I'd like to tell the most beautiful human shape that he's beautiful.

BELLAC: And caress him a little bit?

AGNES: Yes. Caress him.

BELLAC: You always have the Apollo of Bellac . . .

AGNES: But he doesn't exist!

BELLAC: You're asking for too much. Whether he exists or not, he's the supreme beauty.

AGNES: You're right. I only really see what I touch. I have no imagination.

BELLAC: Teach your thoughts to touch. Suppose that what happens sometimes in the theater, in traditional plays, would happen to someone who led a decent life . . .

AGNES: And suddenly *became* beautiful?

BELLAC: Yes, that's it, thank you. That's almost it. . . . The truth is that the god of beauty visited you this morning, Agnes. That's perhaps why you had such good luck and were so moved and changed. . . . Suppose he were to reveal himself to you suddenly. Suppose I were he. Suppose

287

I appeared to you as I truly am, in my glory. Look at me, Agnes. Look at the Apollo of Bellac.

AGNES: I have to shut my eyes to see you, don't I?

BELLAC: You understand everything. Alas, yes!

AGNES: Speak. What are you like?

BELLAC: You want details, naturally. Well, here they are: my height is half again as high as human height. My head is small and measures one seventh of my body. The idea of the square came to geometers from my shoulders, and the rainbow from the curve of my brow. I am nude, and the idea of a breastplate occurred to goldsmiths from the sight of this nudity . . .

AGNES: Wings on your feet?

BELLAC: No. That's Mercury. Don't compare me to anyone.

AGNES: I don't really see you. Neither your eyes nor your feet . . .

BELLAC: Be glad you cannot see my eyes. The eyes of beauty are implacable. They are made of white gold and the pupils of graphite. The idea of death came to men from the eyes of beauty. And beauty's feet are ravishing. They never walk; they barely skim the ground and remain unstained. Never prisoner. Beauty's fingers are ringed and tapering. Its big toes jut out extraordinarily from the others and form an arc from which poets derive the idea of dignity. Now do you see me?

AGNES: Not well enough. My poor eyes are made of agate and sponge. You've played a cruel trick on them. They weren't made to see supreme beauty. It hurts them too much.

BELLAC: But your heart feels all the better for it.

AGNES: I doubt it. Don't expect too much of me, supreme beauty. You know, my life is a little thing. My days are mediocre and every time I come back again to my room, I have five flights to climb in the half-light among the stale smells. These five flights are the preliminary to all my work and rest . . . and how lonely I am! Sometimes I'm lucky enough to see a cat at a doorway. I caress it. A bottle of milk is spilled. I stand it up again. If there's a smell of gas, I tell the janitor. Between the third and the fourth floor, there's a bend where the steps are worn away with age. At this bend, all hope abandons you. At this bend, I sway and lose my balance and try to catch my halting breath. There's my life! It consists of shadows and oppressed flesh, just a little bruised. My conscience is reflected on a stairwell. I hesitate to imagine you as you really are because that's my only defense. Don't be angry with me . . .

BELLAC: Henceforth, you'll be among the happy few on earth, Agnes.

AGNES: Oh, yes. On the stairwell there, the doormats are new and brightly colored. The transoms are stained-glass windows with designs of flowers and birds, ibises with bellies that open for ventilation. None of the steps are worn away at all. The building never sways beneath one's feet and the pitching of the evening and the city. But climbing stairs here with you would be harder yet for me. Don't make the task too difficult for me. Please go away . . . forever! Oh, if you were only a beautiful man, substantial, solid, with body and soul . . . how I would take you in my arms! I see you now the way you probably are, distended with beauty, with slender hips that once gave women the idea of bearing boys, and the wavy hair above your cheeks which inspired the idea of girls . . . and that halo around you that makes one think of tears too brilliant for my stairwell. If I can't hold you tight against me there, I don't want you. I'll look at my diamond instead. A diamond can even travel in an elevator. Go away, Apollo! Disappear by the time my eyes are opened.

BELLAC: If I disappear, you'll find again a human being as lowly as you, with bags under his eyes and sagging skin.

AGNES: That's my lot. I prefer it. Let me embrace you. And then disappear.

(They kiss.)

BELLAC: There now. Apollo has gone, and I am going . . .

AGNES: How beautiful you are!

BELLAC: Dear Agnes.

AGNES: How beautiful life is in a man when you've just seen the beauty of a colored print. . . . And now that you're leaving me, do you think I'll marry the President?

BELLAC: He's good. He's rich. Farewell.

AGNES: I'll make you rich, too. I'll make him buy the invention of the Universal Vegetable at whatever price you say. Stay!

BELLAC: It's not ready yet. Its seeds are invisible; its stem grows to the height of a fir tree. It tastes like alum. I'll come back when I've perfected it.

(*He disappears at the moment the* PRESIDENT *re-enters, a carnation in his buttonhole.*)

AGNES: You swear it?

BELLAC: The very moment. We'll harvest it together. I assure you.

AGNES: I'll buy the garden.

PRESIDENT: Agnes dear, good news! The Board is delighted to know that the battle of the sexes has finally been resolved. They've voted to change the striped carpeting on the staircase for a broadloom with a beautiful design in the center and a Persian border. That's their engagement gift! What? You're alone! Isn't our friend still here?

AGNES: He just left.

PRESIDENT: Call him back. He's having dinner with us. . . . Do you know his name?

AGNES: IIis first name only . . . Apollo.

PRESIDENT (*at the door*): Apollo! Apollo! (*The members of the Board and the* RECEPTIONIST, *all wearing carnations in their buttonholes, arrive.*) Help me call! He must come back!

RECEPTIONIST (*down the stairwell, calling*) ⎫
RAZMUT and SCHULTZ (*at the windows, calling*) ⎬ Apollo! Apollo!
SPITTLE (*at the door, calling*) ⎭

HARDHEAD (*entering, to* AGNES): Is Apollo here?

AGNES: No . . . He's passed away. . . .

CURTAIN

The Long Christmas Dinner

Dinner

by THORNTON WILDER

Thornton Wilder (1897–   )

Thornton Wilder's literary career of over half a century has been a resolving of contradictions. Unlike Henry James, he has been successful both as a novelist and as a playwright. Known as an interpreter of typical American scenes and characters, he is at the same time a sophisticated cosmopolite. His simple, realistic dialogue evokes symbolic and universal meanings. Stripping the cluttered stage of modern realism to return to the simplicity of the Greek, Elizabethan, and Molièresque theater, he utilizes the revolutionary theatricalism of the twentieth century to stimulate the imagination of the audience. His ethical views, derived from his Judeo-Christian religious background, are modified by the Platonism of his classical education. His literary reputation has fluctuated widely; denigrated in the thirties and forties, he has won three Pulitzer Prizes, the Gold Medal from the Academy of Arts and Letters, and the 1968 National Book Award. The final paradox is that with only two full-length, indigenous American plays—*Our Town* and *The Skin of Our Teeth*—he has won an international reputation.

Thornton Wilder was born in Madison, Wisconsin, on April 17, 1897. His father, the owner and editor of a newspaper, was a devout Congregationalist and his mother was the daughter of a minister. During the second administration of Theodore Roosevelt, the elder Wilder was appointed Consul General to Shanghai and Hong Kong. Thornton Wilder attended a missionary school in China for four years, until the age of thirteen, but finished his early education in California. He continued his undergraduate studies at Oberlin and Yale, receiving his A.B. from the latter in 1920. He studied archaeology at the American Academy in Rome and did graduate work at Princeton. For two six-year periods of his life he was a teacher, first at the Lawrenceville School and later at the University of Chicago.

From 1915 to 1927 he served his dramatic apprenticeship by writing forty short dramatic sketches, most of them consisting of three-minute, nonrealistic plays on religious and aesthetic themes, utilizing classical and biblical material drawn from his wide cultural background. Sixteen of these he published in 1928 in a volume called *The Angel That Troubled the Waters.* Experimental in nature, these unsentimental and humanistic mini-dramas were a revolt against the realistic and naturalistic plays of the twenties. Lacking characterization and psychological motivation, they stressed ethical concepts and evoked universal ideas and emotions. The characters are not sharply individualized, but in their conflicts are seen testing eternal human values in a mysterious universe. Three years later he published another volume of six one-act plays, *The Long Christmas Dinner and Other Plays.*

In three of the plays—*The Long Christmas Dinner, Pullman Car Hiawatha,* and *The Happy Journey to Trenton and Camden*—he again demonstrates his theory of theatricalism by presenting the notion on the stage as a play, not as a realistic imitation of actual life. The settings are simple or are devoid of any scenery. The last two plays introduce the theatrical device of a Stage Manager as an objective commentator (as in *Our Town*). In these three plays the realistic homespun dialogue and the humdrum events of everyday life strive to achieve "the illuminated commonplace" of Zen. The concrete incidents—joyous, comic, and tragic—are elevated to cosmic significance and given symbolic truth and meaning as typical of the human family. By universalizing the factual, Wilder reveals the importance of the ordinary and raises the plays to a philosophic level.

Meanwhile, Thornton Wilder was pursuing his other career as a novelist by publishing *The Cabala* (1926), *The Bridge of San Luis Rey* (1927), and *The Woman of Andros* (1930). Like his plays, these romantic novels, for the most part, eschewed the realistic and naturalistic trends of much of twentieth-century fiction and were strongly influenced by the symbolic, humanistic, and classical works of Proust, Merimée, and Gide. His other three novels are *Heaven's My Destination* (1935), *The Ides of March* (1948), and *The Eighth Day* (1968).

The reputation of Wilder as an innovator, however, was not in the field of the novel but in the drama. With the production of *Our Town* (1938) and *The Skin of Our Teeth* (1942), he established himself as a successful and influential creator of nonillusionistic plays. In *Our Town* he relates typical events in the lives of ordinary people, but places them in a metaphysical framework of the flow of time. Skirting sentimentality and leavened by humor, the play reveals our failure to realize the full potentiality of life in the face of inevitable death. Like Wordsworth's "spots of time," Wilder extracts from the cycle of human existence moments of joy and pain and, by setting them against eternity, sharpens our awareness of the beauty and banality of the human condition.

Inspired by Joyce's *Finnegans Wake*, Wilder in *The Skin of Our Teeth* writes a dramatic paean to man's unconquerable will to survive in a hostile world. Living in a precarious universe and faced with the dangers of glacial invasion, flood, and war, the Antrobus family of Excelsior, New Jersey, struggles against the forces of nature, social disasters, and human weakness. Wilder again uses the pattern of the cyclical repetition of life found in *The Long Christmas Dinner*, except instead of using a ninety-year period he carries the embattled human family through geologic and biblical time as well as recorded history to record his humanistic faith in the eventual triumph of man's spirit.

Thornton Wilder's other dramatic works are the comedy *The Matchmaker* (1954), made into the successful musical comedy *Hello, Dolly!*, *A Life in the Sun (The Alcestiad)*, and, in progress, a cycle of one-act plays on the seven ages of man and one on the Seven Deadly Sins.

When Thornton Wilder declared, "I began writing one-act plays that tried to capture not verisimilitude but reality," he was expressing his dislike for the "slice-of-life" or realistic play that dominated the European and English stage at the end of the nineteenth and early twentieth century. *The Long Christmas Dinner* was his first successful play to illustrate his dramatic credo that drama is "based upon a pretense," not upon actual life. Universal emotions and ethical concepts can be evolved, not by a stage cluttered with realistic Belasco props, which stifle the imagination of the audience, but by simplified scenery, and by typical events in the lives of everyday characters raised to a symbolic level by the interpretative skill of the dramatist.

The Long Christmas Dinner is cyclical in its structure. In this short play we live through, in accelerated motion, ninety Christmas dinners in the Bayard household. As the pageant of the successive generations unfolds before us in repetitive dialogue, we sense the changing patterns of American life from the time Mother Bayard remembers when she had to cross the Mississippi on a new-made raft, when St. Louis and Kansas City were full of Indians, to Genevieve's complaint that now the old homestead is surrounded by polluting factories. Yet in the passing generations, there is an unchanging sequence, a continuity of essential happenings—births, marriages, illnesses, quarrels, and deaths. As the characters enter through the portal of birth "trimmed with garlands of fruits and flowers" and partake of the feast of life by eating their Christmas dinner "with imaginary forks and knives" and then stumble out or walk serenely through the portal of death "hung with black velvet," we are presented with a ritualistic demonstration of the changeless pattern of human existence.

CHARACTERS

LUCIA

MOTHER BAYARD

RODERICK

COUSIN BRANDON

CHARLES
GENEVIEVE $\Big\}$ children of RODERICK and LUCIA

THE NURSE

LEONORA,
 wife of CHARLES

ERMENGARDE

SAM
LUCIA II $\Big\}$ children of CHARLES and LEONORA
RODERICK II

SCENE: *The dining room of the Bayard home. Close to the footlights a long dining table is handsomely spread for Christmas dinner. The carver's place with a great turkey before it is at the spectator's right.*

A door, left back, leads into the hall.

At the extreme left, by the proscenium pillar, is a strange portal trimmed with garlands of fruits and flowers. Directly opposite is another edged and hung with black velvet. The portals denote birth and death.

Ninety years are to be traversed in this play which represents in accelerated motion ninety Christmas dinners in the Bayard household. The actors are dressed in inconspicuous clothes and must indicate their gradual increase in years through their acting. Most of them carry wigs of white hair which they adjust upon their heads at the indicated moment, simply and without comment. The ladies may have shawls concealed beneath the table that they gradually draw up about their shoulders as they grow older.

Throughout the play the characters continue eating imaginary food with imaginary knives and forks.

There is no curtain. The audience arriving at the theatre sees the stage set and the table laid, though still in partial

297

darkness. Gradually the lights in the auditorium become dim and the stage brightens until sparkling winter sunlight streams through the dining room windows.

Enter LUCIA *from the hall. She inspects the table, touching here a knife and there a fork. She talks to a servant girl who is invisible to us.*

LUCIA: I reckon we're ready now, Gertrude. We won't ring the chimes today. I'll just call them myself. *(She goes into the hall and calls.)* Roderick. Mother Bayard. We're all ready. Come to dinner.

(Enter RODERICK *pushing* MOTHER BAYARD *in a wheel chair.)*

MOTHER BAYARD: . . . and a new horse too, Roderick. I used to think that only the wicked owned two horses. A new horse and a new house and a new wife!

RODERICK: Well, Mother, how do you like it? Our first Christmas dinner in the new house, hey?

MOTHER BAYARD: Tz-Tz-Tz! I don't know what your dear father would say!

LUCIA: Here, Mother Bayard, you sit between us.

*(RODERICK *says grace.)*

My dear Lucia, I can remember when there were still Indians on this very ground, and I wasn't a young girl either. I can remember when we had to cross the Mississippi on a new-made raft. I can remember when St. Louis and Kansas City were full of Indians.

LUCIA *(tying a napkin around* MOTHER BAYARD'S *neck)*: Imagine that! What a wonderful day for our first Christmas dinner: a beautiful sunny morning, snow, a splendid sermon. Dr. McCarthy preaches a splendid sermon. I cried and cried.

RODERICK *(extending an imaginary carving fork)*: Come now, what'll you have, Mother? A little sliver of white?

LUCIA: Every least twig is wrapped around with ice. You almost never see that. Can I cut it up for you, dear? *(Over her shoulder.)* Gertrude, I forgot the jelly. You know—on the top shelf.—Mother Bayard, I found your mother's gravy-boat while we were moving. What was her name, dear? What were all your names? You were . . . a . . . Genevieve Wainright. Now your mother——

MOTHER BAYARD: Yes, you must write it down somewhere. I was Genevieve Wainright. My mother was Faith Morrison. She was the daughter of a farmer in New Hampshire who was something of a blacksmith too. And she married young John Wainright——

LUCIA (*memorizing on her fingers*): Genevieve Wainright. Faith Morrison.

RODERICK: It's all down in a book somewhere upstairs. We have it all. All that kind of thing is very interesting. Come, Lucia, just a little wine. Mother, a little red wine for Christmas day. Full of iron. "Take a little wine for thy stomach's sake."

LUCIA: Really, I can't get used to wine! What would my father say? But I suppose it's all right.

(*Enter* COUSIN BRANDON *from the hall. He takes his place by* LUCIA.)

COUSIN BRANDON (*rubbing his hands*): Well, well, I smell turkey. My dear cousins, I can't tell you how pleasant it is to be having Christmas dinner with you all. I've lived out there in Alaska so long without relatives. Let me see, how long have you had this new house, Roderick?

RODERICK: Why, it must be——

MOTHER BAYARD: Five years. It's five years, children. You should keep a diary. This is your sixth Christmas dinner here.

LUCIA: Think of that, Roderick. We feel as though we had lived here twenty years.

COUSIN BRANDON: At all events it still looks as good as new.

RODERICK (*over his carving*): What'll you have, Brandon, light or dark?—Frieda, fill up Cousin Brandon's glass.

LUCIA: Oh, dear, I can't get used to these wines. I don't know what my father'd say, I'm sure. What'll you have, Mother Bayard?

(*During the following speeches* MOTHER BAYARD's *chair, without any visible propulsion, starts to draw away from the table, turns toward the right, and slowly goes toward the dark portal.*)

MOTHER BAYARD: Yes, I can remember when there were Indians on this very land.

LUCIA *(softly)*: Mother Bayard hasn't been very well lately, Roderick.

MOTHER BAYARD: My mother was a Faith Morrison. And in New Hampshire she married a young John Wainright, who was a Congregational minister. He saw her in his congregation one day . . .

LUCIA: Mother Bayard, hadn't you better lie down, dear?

MOTHER BAYARD: . . . and right in the middle of his sermon he said to himself: "I'll marry that girl." And he did, and I'm their daughter.

LUCIA *(half rising and looking after her with anxiety)*: Just a little nap, dear?

MOTHER BAYARD: I'm all right. Just go on with your dinner. I was ten, and I said to my brother——

(She goes out. A very slight pause.)

COUSIN BRANDON: It's too bad it's such a cold dark day today. We almost need the lamps. I spoke to Major Lewis for a moment after church. His sciatica troubles him, but he does pretty well.

LUCIA *(dabbing her eyes)*: I know Mother Bayard wouldn't want us to grieve for her on Christmas day, but I can't forget her sitting in her wheel chair right beside us, only a year ago. And she would be so glad to know our good news.

RODERICK *(patting her hand)*: Now, now. It's Christmas. *(Formally.)* Cousin Brandon, a glass of wine with you, sir.

COUSIN BRANDON *(half rising, lifting his glass gallantly)*: A glass of wine with you, sir.

LUCIA: Does the Major's sciatica cause him much pain?

COUSIN BRANDON: Some, perhaps. But you know his way. He says it'll be all the same in a hundred years.

LUCIA: Yes, he's a great philosopher.

RODERICK: His wife sends you a thousand thanks for her Christmas present.

LUCIA: I forget what I gave her—Oh, yes, the workbasket!

(Through the entrance of birth comes a NURSE wheeling a perambulator trimmed with blue ribbons. LUCIA rushes toward it, the men following.)

O my wonderful new baby, my darling baby! Who ever saw such a child! Quick, Nurse, a boy or a girl? A boy! Roderick, what shall we call him? Really, Nurse, you've never seen such a child!

RODERICK: We'll call him Charles after your father and grandfather.

LUCIA: But there are no Charleses in the Bible, Roderick.

RODERICK: Of course, there are. Surely there are.

LUCIA: Roderick!—Very well, but he will always be Samuel to me. What miraculous hands he has! Really, they are the most beautiful hands in the world. All right, Nurse. Have a good nap, my darling child.

RODERICK: Don't drop him, Nurse. Brandon and I need him in our firm.

(*Exit* NURSE *and perambulator into the hall. The others return to their chairs,* LUCIA *taking the place left vacant by* MOTHER BAYARD *and* COUSIN BRANDON *moving up beside her.* COUSIN BRANDON *puts on his white hair.*)

Lucia, a little white meat? Some stuffing? Cranberry sauce, anybody?

LUCIA (*over her shoulder*): Margaret, the stuffing is very good today.—Just a little, thank you.

RODERICK: Now something to wash it down. (*Half rising.*) Cousin Brandon, a glass of wine with you, sir. To the ladies, God bless them.

LUCIA: Thank you, kind sirs.

COUSIN BRANDON: Pity it's such an overcast day today. And no snow.

LUCIA: But the sermon was lovely. I cried and cried. Dr. Spaulding does preach such a splendid sermon.

RODERICK: I saw Major Lewis for a moment after church. He says his rheumatism comes and goes. His wife says she has something for Charles and will bring it over this afternoon.

(*Enter* NURSE *again with perambulator. Pink ribbons. Same rush toward the left.*)

LUCIA: O my lovely new baby! Really, it never occurred to me that it might be a girl. Why, Nurse, she's perfect.

RODERICK: Now call her what you choose. It's your turn.

LUCIA: Loolooloolooloo. Aië. Aië. Yes, this time I shall have my way. She shall be called Genevieve after your mother. Have a good nap, my treasure.

(*She looks after it as the* NURSE *wheels the perambulator into the hall.*)

Imagine! Sometime she'll be grown up and say, "Good morning, Mother. Good morning, Father."—Really, Cousin Brandon, you don't find a baby like that every day.

COUSIN BRANDON: *And* the new factory.

LUCIA: A new factory? Really? Roderick, I shall be very uncomfortable if we're going to turn out to be rich. I've been afraid of that for years.—However, we mustn't talk about such things on Christmas day. I'll just take a little piece of white meat, thank you. Roderick, Charles is destined for the ministry. I'm sure of it.

RODERICK: Woman, he's only twelve. Let him have a free mind. *We* want him in the firm, I don't mind saying. Anyway, no time passes as slowly as this when you're waiting for your urchins to grow up and settle down to business.

LUCIA: I don't want time to go any faster, thank you. I love the children just as they are.—Really, Roderick, you know what the doctor said: One glass a meal. (*Putting her hand over his glass.*) No, Margaret, that will be all.

RODERICK (*rises, glass in hand. With a look of dismay on his face he takes a few steps toward the dark portal.*): Now I wonder what's the matter with me.

LUCIA: Roderick, do be reasonable.

RODERICK (*tottering, but with gallant irony*): But, my dear, statistics show that we steady, moderate drinkers . . .

LUCIA (*rises, gazing at him in anguish*): Roderick! My dear! What . . . ?

RODERICK (*returns to his seat with a frightened look of relief*): Well, it's fine to be back at table with you again. How many good Christmas dinners have I had to miss upstairs? And to be back at a fine bright one, too.

LUCIA: O my dear, you gave us a very alarming time! Here's your glass of milk.—Josephine, bring Mr. Bayard his medicine from the cupboard in the library.

RODERICK: At all events, now that I'm better I'm going to start doing something about the house.

LUCIA: Roderick! You're not going to change the house?

RODERICK: Only touch it up here and there. It looks a hundred years old.

(CHARLES *enters casually from the hall. He kisses his mother's hair and sits down.*)

LUCIA: Charles, you carve the turkey, dear. Your father's not well.—You always said you hated carving, though you are so good at it.

(*Father and son exchange places.*)

CHARLES: It's a great blowy morning, Mother. The wind comes over the hill like a lot of cannon.

LUCIA: And such a good sermon. I cried and cried. Mother Bayard loved a good sermon so. And she used to sing the Christmas hymns all around the year. Oh, dear, oh, dear, I've been thinking of her all morning!

CHARLES: Sh, Mother. It's Christmas day. You mustn't think of such things.—You mustn't be depressed.

LUCIA: But sad things aren't the same as depressing things. I must be getting old: I like them.

CHARLES: Uncle Brandon, you haven't anything to eat. Pass his plate, Hilda . . . and some cranberry sauce . . .

(*Enter* GENEVIEVE. *She kisses her father's temple and sits down.*)

GENEVIEVE: It's glorious. Every least twig is wrapped around with ice. You almost never see that.

LUCIA: Did you have time to deliver those presents after church, Genevieve?

GENEVIEVE: Yes, Mama. Old Mrs. Lewis sends you a thousand thanks for hers. It was just what she wanted, she said. Give me lots, Charles, lots.

RODERICK (*rising and starting toward the dark portal*): Statistics, ladies and gentlemen, show we steady, moderate . . .

CHARLES: How about a little skating this afternoon, Father?

RODERICK: I'll live till I'm ninety.

LUCIA: I really don't think he ought to go skating.

RODERICK (*at the very portal, suddenly astonished*): Yes, but . . . but . . . not yet! (*He goes out.*)

LUCIA (*dabbing her eyes*): He was so young and so clever, Cousin Brandon. (*Raising her voice for* COUSIN BRANDON'S *deafness.*) I say he was so young and so clever.—Never for-

get your father, children. He was a good man.—Well, he
wouldn't want us to grieve for him today.

CHARLES: White or dark, Genevieve? Just another sliver,
Mother?

LUCIA (*putting on her white hair*): I can remember our first
Christmas dinner in this house, Genevieve. Twenty-five
years ago today. Mother Bayard was sitting here in her
wheel chair. She could remember when Indians lived on this
very spot and when she had to cross the river on a new-
made raft.

CHARLES and GENEVIEVE: She couldn't have, Mother. That
can't be true.

LUCIA: It certainly was true—even I can remember when
there was only one paved street. We were very happy to
walk on boards. (*Louder, to* COUSIN BRANDON) We can remember when there were no sidewalks, can't we, Cousin
Brandon?

COUSIN BRANDON (*delighted*): Oh, yes! And those were the
days.

CHARLES and GENEVIEVE (*sotto voce. This is a family refrain.*):
Those were the days.

LUCIA: . . . and the ball last night, Genevieve? Did you have
a nice time? I hope you didn't *waltz*, dear. I think a girl
in our position ought to set an example. Did Charles keep
an eye on you?

GENEVIEVE: He had none left. They were all on Leonora Banning. He can't conceal it any longer, Mother. I think he's
engaged to marry Leonora Banning.

CHARLES: I'm not engaged to marry anyone.

LUCIA: Well, she's very pretty.

GENEVIEVE: I shall never marry, Mother—I shall sit in this
house beside you forever, as though life were one long,
happy Christmas dinner.

LUCIA: O my child, you mustn't say such things!

GENEVIEVE (*playfully*): You don't want me? You don't want
me?

(LUCIA *bursts into tears.*)

Why, Mother, how silly you are! There's nothing sad about
that—what could possibly be sad about that?

LUCIA (*drying her eyes*): Forgive me. I'm just unpredictable,
that's all.

*(CHARLES goes to the door and leads in LEONORA BAN-
NING.)*

LEONORA *(kissing LUCIA's temple)*: Good morning, Mother
Bayard. Good morning, everybody. It's really a splendid
Christmas day today.

CHARLES: Little white meat? Genevieve, Mother, Leonora?

LEONORA: Every least twig is encircled with ice.—You never
see that.

CHARLES *(shouting)*: Uncle Brandon, another?—Rogers, fill
my uncle's glass.

LUCIA *(to CHARLES)*: Do what your father used to do. It
would please Cousin Brandon so. You know— *(Pretending
to raise a glass.)* "Uncle Brandon, a glass of wine——"

CHARLES *(rising)*: Uncle Brandon, a glass of wine with you,
sir.

COUSIN BRANDON *(not rising)*: A glass of wine with you, sir.
To the ladies, God bless them every one.

THE LADIES: Thank you, kind sirs.

GENEVIEVE: And if I go to Germany for my music I promise
to be back for Christmas. I wouldn't miss that.

LUCIA: I hate to think of you over there all alone in those
strange pensions.

GENEVIEVE: But, darling, the time will pass so fast that you'll
hardly know I'm gone. I'll be back in the twinkling of
an eye.

(Enter, left, the NURSE and perambulator. Green ribbons.)

LEONORA: Oh, what an angel! The darlingest baby in the
world. Do let me hold it, Nurse.

*(But the NURSE resolutely wheels the perambulator across
the stage and out the dark door.)*

Oh, I did love it so!

*(LUCIA goes to her, puts her arm around LEONORA's
shoulders, and they encircle the room whispering—
LUCIA then hands her over to CHARLES who conducts
her on the same circuit.)*

GENEVIEVE *(as her mother sits down,—softly)*: Isn't there anything I can do?

LUCIA (*raises her eyebrows, ruefully*): No, dear. Only time, only the passing of time can help in these things.

(CHARLES *and* LEONORA *return to the table.*)

Don't you think we could ask Cousin Ermengarde to come and live with us here? There's plenty for everyone and there's no reason why she should go on teaching the First Grade for ever and ever. She wouldn't be in the way, would she, Charles?

CHARLES: No, I think it would be fine.—A little more potato and gravy, anybody? A little more turkey, Mother?

(COUSIN BRANDON *rises and starts slowly toward the dark portal.* LUCIA *rises and stands for a moment with her face in her hands.*)

COUSIN BRANDON (*muttering*): It was great to be in Alaska in those days . . .

GENEVIEVE (*half rising, and gazing at her mother in fear*): Mother, what is . . . ?

LUCIA (*hurriedly*): Hush, my dear. It will pass.—Hold fast to your music, you know. (*As* GENEVIEVE *starts toward her.*) No, no. I want to be alone for a few minutes. (*She turns and starts after* COUSIN BRANDON *toward the right.*)

CHARLES: If the Republicans collected all their votes instead of going off into cliques among themselves, they might prevent his getting a second term.

GENEVIEVE: Charles, Mother doesn't tell us, but she hasn't been very well these days.

CHARLES: Come, Mother, we'll go to Florida for a few weeks.

(*Exit* COUSIN BRANDON.)

LUCIA (*smiling at* GENEVIEVE *and waving her hand*): Don't be foolish. Don't grieve. (*She clasps her hands under her chin; her lips move, whispering; she walks serenely through the portal.*)

(GENEVIEVE *stares after her, frozen. At the same moment the* NURSE *and perambulator enter from the left. Pale yellow ribbons.* LEONORA *rushes to it.*)

LEONORA: O my darlings . . . twins . . . Charles, aren't they glorious! Look at them. Look at them.

(CHARLES *crosses to down left.*)

GENEVIEVE (*sinks down on the table, her face buried in her arms*): But what will I do? What's left for me to do?

CHARLES (*bending over the basket*): Which is which?

LEONORA: I feel as though I were the first mother who ever had twins.—Look at them now!—But why wasn't Mother Bayard allowed to stay and see them!

GENEVIEVE (*rising suddenly distraught, loudly*): I don't want to go on. I can't bear it.

CHARLES (*goes to her quickly. They sit down. He whispers to her earnestly taking both her hands*): But, Genevieve, Genevieve! How frightfully Mother would feel to think that . . . Genevieve!

GENEVIEVE (*wildly*): I never told her how wonderful she was. We all treated her as though she were just a friend in the house. I thought she'd be here forever.

LEONORA (*timidly*): Genevieve darling, do come one minute and hold my babies' hands. We shall call the girl Lucia after her grandmother—will that please you? Do just see what adorable little hands they have.

(GENEVIEVE *collects herself and goes over to the perambulator. She smiles brokenly into the basket.*)

GENEVIEVE: They are wonderful, Leonora.

LEONORA: Give him your finger, darling. Just let him hold it.

CHARLES: And we'll call the boy Samuel.—Well, now everybody come and finish your dinners. Don't drop them, Nurse; at least don't drop the boy. We need him in the firm.

LEONORA (*stands looking after them as the* NURSE *wheels them into the hall*): Some day they'll be big. Imagine! They'll come in and say, "Hello, Mother!" (*She makes clucking noises of rapturous consternation.*)

CHARLES: Come, a little wine, Leonora, Genevieve? Full of iron. Eduardo, fill the ladies' glasses. It certainly is a keen, cold morning. I used to go skating with Father on mornings like this and Mother would come back from church saying——

GENEVIEVE (*dreamily*): I know—saying, "Such a splendid sermon. I cried and cried."

LEONORA: Why did she cry, dear?

GENEVIEVE: That generation all cried at sermons. It was their way.

LEONORA: Really, Genevieve?

GENEVIEVE: They had had to go since they were children and I suppose sermons reminded them of their fathers and mothers, just as Christmas dinners do us. Especially in an old house like this.

LEONORA: It really is pretty old, Charles. And so ugly, with all that ironwork filigree and that dread cupola.

GENEVIEVE: Charles! You aren't going to change the house!

CHARLES: No, no. I won't give up the house, but great heavens! it's fifty years old. This spring we'll remove the cupola and build a new wing toward the tennis courts.

(From now on GENEVIEVE is seen to change. She sits up more straightly. The corners of her mouth become fixed. She becomes a forthright and slightly disillusioned spinster. CHARLES becomes the plain business man and a little pompous.)

LEONORA: And then couldn't we ask your dear old Cousin Ermengarde to come and live with us? She's really the self-effacing kind.

CHARLES: Ask her now. Take her out of the First Grade.

GENEVIEVE: We only seem to think of it on Christmas day with her Christmas card staring us in the face.

(Enter left, NURSE and perambulator. Blue ribbons.)

LEONORA: Another boy! Another boy! Here's a Roderick for you at last.

CHARLES: Roderick Brandon Bayard. A regular little fighter.

LEONORA: Good-by, darling. Don't grow up too fast. Yes, yes. Aië, aië, aië—stay just as you are.—Thank you, Nurse.

GENEVIEVE *(who has not left the table, repeats drily)*: Stay just as you are.

(Exit NURSE and perambulator. The others return to their places.)

LEONORA: Now I have three children. One, two, three. Two boys and a girl. I'm collecting them. It's very exciting. *(Over her shoulder.)* What, Hilda? Oh, Cousin Ermengarde's come! Come in, Cousin.

(She goes to the hall and welcomes COUSIN ERMENGARDE *who already wears her white hair.)*

ERMENGARDE *(shyly)*: It's such a pleasure to be with you all.

CHARLES *(pulling out her chair for her)*: The twins have taken a great fancy to you already, Cousin.

LEONORA: The baby went to her at once.

CHARLES: Exactly how are we related, Cousin Ermengarde?— There, Genevieve, that's your specialty.—First a little more turkey and stuffing, Mother? Cranberry sauce, anybody?

GENEVIEVE: I can work it out: Grandmother Bayard was your . . .

ERMENGARDE: Your Grandmother Bayard was a second cousin of my Grandmother Haskins through the Wainrights.

CHARLES: Well, it's all in a book somewhere upstairs. All that kind of thing is awfully interesting.

GENEVIEVE: Nonsense. There are no such books. I collect my notes off gravestones, and you have to scrape a good deal of moss—let me tell you—to find one great-grandparent.

CHARLES: There's a story that my Grandmother Bayard crossed the Mississippi on a raft before there were any bridges or ferry-boats. She died before Genevieve or I were born. Time certainly goes very fast in a great new country like this. Have some more cranberry sauce, Cousin Ermengarde.

ERMENGARDE *(timidly)*: Well, time must be passing very slowly in Europe with this dreadful, dreadful war going on.

CHARLES: Perhaps an occasional war isn't so bad after all. It clears up a lot of poisons that collect in nations. It's like a boil.

ERMENGARDE: Oh, dear, oh, dear!

CHARLES *(with relish)*: Yes, it's like a boil.—Ho! ho! Here are your twins.

(The twins appear at the door into the hall. SAM *is wearing the uniform of an ensign.* LUCIA *is fussing over some detail on it.)*

LUCIA: Isn't he wonderful in it, Mother?

CHARLES: Let's get a look at you.

SAM: Mother, don't let Roderick fool with my stamp album while I'm gone.

LEONORA: Now, Sam, do write a letter once in a while. Do be a good boy about that, mind.

SAM: You might send some of those cakes of yours once in a while, Cousin Ermengarde.

ERMENGARDE *(in a flutter)*: I certainly will, my dear boy.

CHARLES: If you need any money, we have agents in Paris and London, remember.

SAM: Well, good-by . . .

> *(SAM goes briskly out through the dark portal, tossing his unneeded white hair through the door before him. LUCIA sits down at the table with lowered eyes.)*

ERMENGARDE *(after a slight pause, in a low, constrained voice, making conversation)*: I spoke to Mrs. Fairchild for a moment coming out of church. Her rheumatism's a little better, she says. She sends you her warmest thanks for the Christmas present. The workbasket, wasn't it?—It was an admirable sermon. And our stained-glass window looked so beautiful, Leonora, so beautiful. Everybody spoke of it and so affectionately of Sammy. *(LEONORA's hand goes to her mouth.)* Forgive me, Leonora, but it's better to speak of him than not to speak of him when we're all thinking of him so hard.

LEONORA *(rising, in anguish)*: He was a mere boy. He was a mere boy, Charles.

CHARLES: My dear, my dear.

LEONORA: I want to tell him how wonderful he was. We let him go so casually. I want to tell him how we all feel about him.—Forgive me, let me walk about a minute.—Yes, of course, Ermengarde—it's best to speak of him.

LUCIA *(in a low voice, to GENEVIEVE)*: Isn't there anything I can do?

GENEVIEVE: No, no. Only time, only the passing of time can help in these things.

> *(LEONORA, straying about the room, finds herself near the door to the hall at the moment that her son RODERICK enters. He links his arm with hers and leads her back to the table.)*

RODERICK: What's the matter, anyway? What are you all so glum about? The skating was fine today.

CHARLES: Sit down, young man. I have something to say to you.

RODERICK: Everybody was there. Lucia skated in the corners with Dan Creighton the whole time. When'll it be, Lucia, when'll it be?

LUCIA: I don't know what you mean.

RODERICK: Lucia's leaving us soon, Mother. Dan Creighton, of all people.

CHARLES (*ominously*): Roderick, I have something to say to you.

RODERICK: Yes, Father.

CHARLES: Is it true, Roderick, that you made yourself conspicuous last night at the Country Club—at a Christmas Eve dance, too?

LEONORA: Not now, Charles, I beg of you. This is Christmas dinner.

RODERICK (*loudly*): No, I didn't.

LUCIA: Really, Father, he didn't. It was that dreadful Johnny Lewis.

CHARLES: I don't want to hear about Johnny Lewis. I want to know whether a son of mine——

LEONORA: Charles, I beg of you——

CHARLES: The first family of this city!

RODERICK (*rising*): I hate this town and everything about it. I always did.

CHARLES: You behaved like a spoiled puppy, sir, an ill-bred spoiled puppy.

RODERICK: What did I do? What did I do that was wrong?

CHARLES: You were drunk and you were rude to the daughters of my best friends.

GENEVIEVE (*striking the table*): Nothing in the world deserves an ugly scene like this. Charles, I'm ashamed of you.

RODERICK: Great God, you gotta get drunk in this town to forget how dull it is. Time passes so slowly here that it stands still, that's what's the trouble.

CHARLES: Well, young man, we can employ your time. You will leave the university and you will come into the Bayard factory on January second.

RODERICK (*at the door into the hall*): I have better things to do than to go into your old factory. I'm going somewhere where time passes, my God! (*He goes out into the hall.*)

LEONORA (*rising*): Roderick, Roderick, come here just a moment.—Charles, where can he go?

LUCIA (*rising*): Sh, Mother. He'll come back. Now I have to go upstairs and pack my trunk.

LEONORA: I won't have any children left!

LUCIA (*rising*): Sh, Mother. He'll come back. He's only gone to California or somewhere.—Cousin Ermengarde has done most of my packing—thanks a thousand times, Cousin Ermengarde. (*She kisses her mother.*) I won't be long. (*She runs out into the hall.*)

(GENEVIEVE *and* LEONORA *put on their white hair.*)

ERMENGARDE: It's a very beautiful day. On the way home from church I stopped and saw Mrs. Foster a moment. Her arthritis comes and goes.

LEONORA: Is she actually in pain, dear?

ERMENGARDE: Oh, she says it'll all be the same in a hundred years!

LEONORA: Yes, she's a brave little stoic.

CHARLES: Come now, a little white meat, Mother?—Mary, pass my cousin's plate.

LEONORA: What is it, Mary?—Oh, here's a telegram from them in Paris! "Love and Christmas greetings to all." I told them we'd be eating some of their wedding cake and thinking about them today. It seems to be all decided that they will settle down in the East, Ermengarde. I can't even have my daughter for a neighbor. They hope to build before long somewhere on the shore north of New York.

GENEVIEVE: There is no shore north of New York.

LEONORA: Well, east or west or whatever it is.

(*Pause.*)

CHARLES: My, what a dark day. (*He puts on his white hair. Pause.*) How slowly time passes without any young people in the house.

LEONORA: I have three children somewhere.

CHARLES (*blunderingly offering comfort*): Well, one of them gave his life for his country.

LEONORA (*sadly*): And one of them is selling aluminum in China.

GENEVIEVE (*slowly working herself up to a hysterical crisis*): I can stand everything but this terrible soot everywhere. We should have moved long ago. We're surrounded by factories. We have to change the window curtains every week.

LEONORA: Why, Genevieve!

GENEVIEVE: I can't stand it. I can't stand it any more. I'm going abroad. It's not only the soot that comes through the very walls of this house; it's the *thoughts,* it's the thought of what has been and what might have been here. And the feeling about this house of the years *grinding away.* My mother died yesterday—not twenty-five years ago. Oh, I'm going to live and die abroad! Yes, I'm going to be the American old maid living and dying in a pension in Munich or Florence.

ERMENGARDE: Genevieve, you're tired.

CHARLES: Come, Genevieve, take a good drink of cold water. Mary, open the window a minute.

GENEVIEVE: I'm sorry. I'm sorry. *(She hurries tearfully out into the hall.)*

ERMENGARDE: Dear Genevieve will come back to us, I think. *(She rises and starts toward the dark portal.)* You should have been out today, Leonora. It was one of those days when everything was encircled with ice. Very pretty, indeed.

(CHARLES rises and starts after her.)

CHARLES: Leonora, I used to go skating with Father on mornings like this.—I wish I felt a little better.

LEONORA: What! Have I got two invalids on my hands at once? Now, Cousin Ermengarde, you must get better and help me nurse Charles.

ERMENGARDE: I'll do my best. *(ERMENGARDE turns at the very portal and comes back to the table.)*

CHARLES: Well, Leonora, I'll do what you ask. I'll write the puppy a letter of forgiveness and apology. It's Christmas day. I'll cable it. That's what I'll do. *(He goes out the dark door.)*

LEONORA *(drying her eyes)*: Ermengarde, it's such a comfort having you here with me. Mary, I really can't eat anything. Well, perhaps, a sliver of white meat.

ERMENGARDE *(very old)*: I spoke to Mrs. Keene for a moment coming out of church. She asked after the young people.— At church I felt very proud sitting under our windows, Leonora, and our brass tablets. The Bayard aisle—it's a regular Bayard aisle and I love it.

LEONORA: Ermengarde, would you be very angry with me if I went and stayed with the young people a little this spring?

ERMENGARDE: Why, no. I know how badly they want you and need you. Especially now that they're about to build a new house.

LEONORA: You wouldn't be angry? This house is yours as long as you want it, remember.

ERMENGARDE: I don't see why the rest of you dislike it. I like it more than I can say.

LEONORA: I won't be long. I'll be back in no time and we can have some more of our readings-aloud in the evening.

(*She kisses her and goes into the hall.* ERMENGARDE, *left alone, eats slowly and talks to* MARY.)

ERMENGARDE: Really, Mary, I'll change my mind. If you'll ask Bertha to be good enough to make me a little eggnog. A dear little eggnog.—Such a nice letter this morning from Mrs. Bayard, Mary. Such a nice letter. They're having their first Christmas dinner in the new house. They must be very happy. They call her Mother Bayard, she says, as though she were an old lady. And she says she finds it more comfortable to come and go in a wheel chair.—Such a dear letter. . . . And, Mary, I can tell you a secret. It's still a great secret, mind! They're expecting a grandchild. Isn't that good news! Now I'll read a little. (*She props a book up before her, still dipping a spoon into a custard from time to time. She grows from very old to immensely old. She sighs. The book falls down. She finds a cane beside her, and totters into the dark portal, murmuring*) Dear little Roderick and little Lucia.

CURTAIN

The Love of Don Perlimplín and Belisa in the Garden

An Erotic Lace-Paper Valentine
in Four Scenes

Chamber Version

by FEDERICO GARCÍA LORCA

Translated from the Spanish
by JAMES GRAHAM-LUJAN
and RICHARD L. O'CONNELL

Federico García Lorca (1899–1936)

When a Fascist firing squad at dawn on August 19, 1936, murdered Federico García Lorca and buried him in an unknown grave, Spain lost her most popular twentieth-century poet, and the modern theater lost its greatest poetic dramatist. Adding to the shock of horror that swept over the literary world was the irony that Lorca was really an apolitical figure who had close friends on both sides of the Spanish Civil War, which had broken out a month earlier.

Lorca was born in a small village in the province of Granada. His father was a prosperous, well-read farmer, and his mother a former schoolteacher. In spite of a childhood illness that in early years affected his speech and walk, he developed into a gay, vivacious, sensitive youth adored by his parents and sisters. He read voraciously in the family library and early developed a precocious interest in music, which was later encouraged by the composer De Falla. An old peasant-servant Dolores taught him Spanish folk songs and legends. When the family moved to the city of Granada, he quickly absorbed many of the lingering traditions of the Romans, Moors, and Spanish Renaissance; and, gregarious by nature, he mingled with the intellectual elite and the aristocrats as well as with the Andalusian peasants and gypsies. At the University of Granada he studied law, but his interests were really in painting, literature, and research in folk music. Fernando de los Rios, a professor at the university, encouraged him in 1919 to go to Madrid.

In his eight years' residence in the capital, Lorca was strongly influenced by the cultural, cosmopolitan movements in poetry, painting, drama, and the film. His friends included the poet Gerardo Diego, the film director Luis Buñuel, and the painter Salvador Dalí. Lorca won acclaim as a painter, dramatist, musician, and particularly as a poet. His *Gypsy*

Ballads, published in 1928, a successful integration of traditional and modernistic techniques, made him famous in the Spanish-speaking world.

In 1929 he came to America and lived for a year at Columbia University. Although he took some courses, he spent most of his time wandering through Harlem absorbing Negro music, observing the skyscrapers, Wall Street, the bridges, and the wharves along the Hudson River. During a summer retreat in the Catskills, he wrote the poems included in his volume *Poet in New York.* Invited to lecture in Havana, he went to Cuba, where warmly received, he quickly identified himself with the Hispanic musical and dramatic traditions that survived there. When he returned to Spain in the summer of 1930, he had matured in self-knowledge and determined to devote all his energies to poetic drama.

In 1931, when the Spanish king fled and the Republic was proclaimed, Lorca was asked by de los Rios, now Minister of Public Education, to organize a traveling theatrical company of students to perform classical and modern plays in isolated villages. For this group, *La Barraca,* Lorca arranged traditional ballads and wrote original plays, such as *Blood Wedding* and *Yerma.* This successful experiment of bringing the theater to the people in the Spanish provinces spread Lorca's fame to Latin America. In 1933 he was invited to Buenos Aires to produce his own plays and the classics of the Spanish Golden Age. This theatrical tour was a resounding success, and Lorca became an international literary celebrity. In the last year of his life, he worked on another volume of poems and finished his last folk tragedy, *The House of Bernarda Alba.*

In July 1936 Lorca left Madrid to celebrate his saint's day, San Federico, with his family. When the revolt against the Republic began in that month, Lorca, rejecting the advice of friends and refusing invitations to come to Colombia and Mexico, stayed on in Granada. On August 18 he was arrested by one of the "Black Squads" of Franco's Civil Guard while he was visiting the Rosales family, whose house was a Falangist headquarters. The poet Luis Rosales was a good friend of Lorca's. The tragic death of Lorca brought to an end the Spanish dramatic renaissance of the 1930s.

The Love of Don Perlimplín and Belisa in the Garden, completed in 1931, although shorter and lighter in tone than

Lorca's three rural tragedies of sexual frustration—*Blood Wedding* (1933), *Yerma* (1934), and *The House of Bernarda Alba* (1936)—reveals his skillful integration of lyrical poetry, colorful stage design, music, and dramatic action. A romantic farce with tragic overtones, the play combines traditional elements with modern theatricalism in an artistic framework to communicate its love-death theme.

Lorca has declared his dramatic creed in the following statement, "The theatre is a school of weeping and of laughter, a rostrum where men are free to expose old and equivocal standards of conduct, and explain with living examples the eternal norms of the heart and feelings of man." Lorca handles an old story—the marriage of a naïve old man to a sensual young wife—with freshness and spontaneity, combining humor and pathos with a sinister quality. Chaucer, in "The Merchant's Tale" of January and May, handles a similar situation cynically, and Cervantes, in *The Jealous Old Man,* handles it realistically. Lorca, in his colorful extravaganza, shows Don Perlimplín initiated into the beauty and limitations of erotic love and Belisa, through her husband's ritual suicide, gaining

CHARACTERS

Don Perlimplín

Belisa

Marcolfa

Mother of Belisa

First Sprite

Second Sprite

PROLOGUE

House of DON PERLIMPLÍN. *Green
walls; chairs and furniture painted
black. At the rear, a deep window with
balcony through which* BELISA's *balcony
may be seen. A sonata is heard.* PER-
LIMPLÍN *wears a green cassock and a
white wig full of curls.* MARCOLFA, *the
servant, wears the classic striped dress.*

PERLIMPLÍN: Yes?

MARCOLFA: Yes

PERLIMPLÍN: But why "yes"?

MARCOLFA: Just because yes.

PERLIMPLÍN: And if I should say no?

MARCOLFA (*acidly*): No?

PERLIMPLÍN: No.

MARCOLFA: Tell me, Master, the reason for that "no."

PERLIMPLÍN: You tell me, you persevering domestic, the reasons for that "yes."

(*Pause.*)

MARCOLFA: Twenty and twenty are forty . . .

PERLIMPLÍN (*listening*): Proceed.

MARCOLFA: And ten, fifty.

PERLIMPLÍN: Go ahead.

MARCOLFA: At fifty years one is no longer a child.

PERLIMPLÍN: Of course!

MARCOLFA: I may die any minute.

PERLIMPLÍN: Good Lord!

MARCOLFA (*weeping*): And what will happen to you all alone
in the world?

PERLIMPLÍN: What will happen?

MARCOLFA: That's why you have to marry.

PERLIMPLÍN (*distracted*): Yes?

MARCOLFA (*sternly*): Yes.

PERLIMPLÍN (*miserably*): But Marcolfa . . . why "yes"? When I was a child a woman strangled her husband. He was a shoemaker. I can't forget it. I've always said I wouldn't marry. My books are enough for me. What good will marriage do me?

MARCOLFA: Marriage holds great charms, Master. It isn't what it appears on the outside. It's full of hidden things . . . things which it would not be becoming for a servant to mention. You see that . . .

PERLIMPLÍN: That what?

MARCOLFA: That I have blushed.

(*Pause. A piano is heard.*)

VOICE OF BELISA (*within, singing*):

> Ah love, ah love.
> Tight in my thighs imprisoned
> There swims like a fish the sun.
> Warm water in the rushes.
> Ah love.
> Morning cock, the night is going!
> Don't let it vanish, no!

MARCOLFA: My master will see the reason I have.

PERLIMPLÍN (*scratching his head*): She sings prettily.

MARCOLFA: She is the woman for my master. The fair Belisa.

PERLIMPLÍN: Belisa . . . but wouldn't it be better . . . ?

MARCOLFA: No. Now come. (*She takes him by the hand and goes toward the balcony.*) Say, "Belisa."

PERLIMPLÍN: Belisa . . .

MARCOLFA: Louder.

PERLIMPLÍN: Belisa!

(*The balcony of the house opposite opens and* BELISA *appears, resplendent in her loveliness. She is half naked.*)

BELISA: Who calls?

(MARCOLFA *hides behind the window curtains.*)

MARCOLFA: Answer!

PERLIMPLÍN (*trembling*): I was calling.

BELISA: Yes?

PERLIMPLÍN: Yes.

BELISA: But why, "yes"?

PERLIMPLÍN: Just because yes.

BELISA: And if I should say no?

PERLIMPLÍN: I would be sorry, because . . . we have decided that I want to marry.

BELISA (*laughs*): Marry whom?

PERLIMPLÍN: You.

BELISA (*serious*): But . . . (*Calling*) Mamá! Mamá-á-á!

MARCOLFA: This is going well.

> (*Enter the* MOTHER *wearing a great eighteenth-century wig full of birds, ribbons and glass beads.*)

BELISA: Don Perlimplín wants to marry me. What must I do?

MOTHER: The very best of afternoons to you, my charming little neighbor. I always said to my poor little girl that you have the grace and elegance of that great lady who was your mother, whom I did not have the pleasure of knowing.

PERLIMPLÍN: Thank you.

MARCOLFA (*furiously, from behind the curtain*): I have decided that we are going . . .

PERLIMPLÍN: We have decided that we are going . . .

MOTHER: To contract matrimony. Is that not so?

PERLIMPLÍN: That is so.

BELISA: But, Mamá, what about me?

MOTHER: You are agreeable, naturally. Don Perlimplín is a fascinating husband.

PERLIMPLÍN: I hope to be one, madam.

MARCOLFA (*calling to* DON PERLIMPLÍN): This is almost settled.

PERLIMPLÍN: Do you think so?

> (*They whisper together.*)

MOTHER (*to* BELISA): Don Perlimplín has many lands. On these are many geese and sheep. The sheep are taken to market. At the market they give money for them. Money produces beauty . . . and beauty is sought after by all men.

PERLIMPLÍN: Then . . .

MOTHER: Ever so thrilled . . . Belisa . . . go inside. It isn't well for a maiden to hear certain conversations.

BELISA: Until later. *(She leaves.)*

MOTHER: She is a lily. You've seen her face? *(Lowering her voice.)* But if you should see further! Just like sugar. But, pardon. I need not call these things to the attention of a person as modern and competent as you. . . .

PERLIMPLÍN: Yes?

MOTHER: Why, yes. I said it without irony.

PERLIMPLÍN: I don't know how to express our gratitude.

MOTHER: Oh, "our gratitude." What extraordinary delicacy! The gratitude of your heart and your self . . . I have sensed it. I have sensed it . . . in spite of the fact that it is twenty years since I have had relations with a man.

MARCOLFA *(aside)*: The wedding.

PERLIMPLÍN: The wedding . . .

MOTHER: Whenever you wish. Though . . . *(She brings out a handkerchief and weeps.)* . . . to every mother . . . until later! *(Leaves.)*

MARCOLFA: At last!

PERLIMPLÍN: Oh, Marcolfa, Marcolfa! Into what world are you going to thrust me?

MARCOLFA: Into the world of matrimony.

PERLIMPLÍN: And if I should be frank, I would say that I feel thirsty. Why don't you bring me some water? *(MARCOLFA approaches him and whispers in his ear.)* Who could believe it?

(The piano is heard. The stage is in darkness. BELISA opens the curtains of her balcony, almost naked, singing languidly.)

BELISA:

> Ah love, ah love.
> Tight in my warm thighs imprisoned,
> There swims like a fish the sun.

MARCOLFA: Beautiful maiden.

PERLIMPLÍN: Like sugar . . . white inside. Will she be capable of strangling me?

MARCOLFA: Woman is weak if frightened in time.

BELISA:

> Ah love, ah love.
> Morning cock, the night is going!
> Don't let it vanish, no!

PERLIMPLÍN: What does she mean, Marcolfa? What does she mean? *(MARCOLFA laughs.)* What is happening to me? What is it?

(The piano goes on playing. Past the balcony flies a band of black paper birds.)

CURTAIN

SCENE ONE

> DON PERLIMPLÍN's room. At the center
> there is a great bed topped by a canopy
> with plume ornaments. In the back wall
> there are six doors. The first one on the
> right serves as entrance and exit for
> DON PERLIMPLÍN. It is the wedding
> night. MARCOLFA, with a candelabrum
> in her hand, speaks at the first door on
> the left side.

MARCOLFA: Good night.
BELISA (offstage): Good night, Marcolfa.

> (DON PERLIMPLÍN enters, magnificently dressed.)

MARCOLFA: May my master have a good wedding night.
PERLIMPLÍN: Good night, Marcolfa. (MARCOLFA leaves. PER-
LIMPLÍN tiptoes toward the room in front and looks from
the door.) Belisa, in all that froth of lace you look like a
wave, and you give me the same fear of the sea that I had
as a child. Since you came from the church my house is
full of secret whispers, and the water grows warm by itself
in the glasses. Oh! Perlimplín . . . Where are you, Perlimplín?

> (Leaves on tiptoe. BELISA appears, dressed in a great
> sleeping garment adorned with lace. She wears an enor-
> mous headdress which launches cascades of needlework
> and lace down to her feet. Her hair is loose and her
> arms bare.)

BELISA: The maid perfumed this room with thyme and not
with mint as I ordered . . . (Goes toward the bed.) Nor did

she put on the fine linen which Marcolfa has. (*At this moment there is a soft music of guitars.* BELISA *crosses her hands over her breast.*) Ah! Whoever seeks me ardently will find me. My thirst is never quenched, just as the thirst of the gargoyles who spurt water in the fountains is never quenched. (*The music continues.*) Oh, what music! Heavens, what music! Like the soft warm downy feathers of a swan! Oh! Is it I? Or is it the music?

(*She throws a great cape of red velvet over her shoulders and walks about the room. The music is silent and five whistles are heard.*)

BELISA: Five of them!

(PERLIMPLÍN *appears.*)

PERLIMPLÍN: Do I disturb you?
BELISA: How could that be possible?
PERLIMPLÍN: Are you sleepy?
BELISA (*ironically*): Sleepy?
PERLIMPLÍN: The night has become a little chilly.

(*Rubs his hands. Pause.*)

BELISA (*with decision*): Perlimplín.
PERLIMPLÍN (*trembling*): What do you want?
BELISA (*vaguely*): It's a pretty name, "Perlimplín."
PERLIMPLÍN: Yours is prettier, Belisa.
BELISA (*laughing*): Oh! Thank you!

(*Short pause.*)

PERLIMPLÍN: I wanted to tell you something.
BELISA: And that is?
PERLIMPLÍN: I have been late in deciding . . . but . . .
BELISA: Say it.
PERLIMPLÍN: Belisa, I love you.
BELISA: Oh, you little gentleman! That's your duty.
PERLIMPLÍN: Yes?
BELISA: Yes.
PERLIMPLÍN: But why "yes"?
BELISA (*coyly*): Because.
PERLIMPLÍN: No.
BELISA: Perlimplín!

PERLIMPLÍN: No, Belisa, before I married you, I didn't love you.

BELISA *(jokingly)*: What are you saying?

PERLIMPLÍN: I married . . . for whatever reason, but I didn't love you. I couldn't have imagined your body until I saw it through the keyhole when you were putting on your wedding dress. And then it was that I felt love come to me. Then! Like the deep thrust of a lancet in my throat.

BELISA *(intrigued)*: But, the other women?

PERLIMPLÍN: What women?

BELISA: Those you knew before.

PERLIMPLÍN: But are there other women?

BELISA *(getting up)*: You astonish me!

PERLIMPLÍN: The first to be astonished was I. *(Pause. The five whistles are heard.)* What's that?

BELISA: The clock.

PERLIMPLÍN: Is it five?

BELISA: Bedtime.

PERLIMPLÍN: Do I have your permission to remove my coat?

BELISA: Of course *(yawning)* little husband. And put out the light, if that is your wish.

(PERLIMPLÍN puts out the light.)

PERLIMPLÍN *(in a low voice)*: Belisa.

BELISA *(loudly)*: What, child?

PERLIMPLÍN *(whispering)*: I've put the light out.

BELISA *(jokingly)*: I see that.

PERLIMPLÍN *(in a much lower voice)*: Belisa . . .

BELISA *(in a loud voice)*: What, enchanter?

PERLIMPLÍN: I adore you!

(The five whistles are heard much louder and the bed is uncovered. Two SPRITES, entering from opposite sides of the stage, run a curtain of misty gray. The theater is left in darkness. Flutes sound with a sweet, sleepy tone. The SPRITES should be two children. They sit on the prompt box facing the audience.)

FIRST SPRITE: And how goes it with you in this tiny darkness?

SECOND SPRITE: Neither well nor badly, little friend.

FIRST SPRITE: Here we are.

SECOND SPRITE: And how do you like it? It's always nice to cover other people's failings . . .

FIRST SPRITE: And then to let the audience take care of uncovering them.

SECOND SPRITE: Because if things are not covered up with all possible precautions . . .

FIRST SPRITE: They would never be discovered.

SECOND SPRITE: And without this covering and uncovering . . .

FIRST SPRITE: What would the poor people do?

SECOND SPRITE (*looking at the curtain*): There must not even be a slit.

FIRST SPRITE: For the slits of today are darkness tomorrow.

(*They laugh.*)

SECOND SPRITE: When things are quite evident . . .

FIRST SPRITE: Man figures that he has no need to discover them . . . in them secrets he already knew.

SECOND SPRITE: And he goes to dark things to discover them . . . in them secrets he already knew.

FIRST SPRITE: But that's what we're here for. We Sprites!

SECOND SPRITE: Did you know Perlimplín?

FIRST SPRITE: Since he was a child.

SECOND SPRITE: And Belisa?

FIRST SPRITE: Very well. Her room exhaled such intense perfume that I once fell asleep and awoke between her cat's claws.

(*They laugh.*)

SECOND SPRITE: This affair was . . .

FIRST SPRITE: Oh, of course!

SECOND SPRITE: All the world thought so.

FIRST SPRITE: And the gossip must have turned then to more mysterious things.

SECOND SPRITE: That's why our efficient and most sociable screen should not be opened yet.

FIRST SPRITE: No, don't let them find out.

SECOND SPRITE: The soul of Perlimplín, tiny and frightened like a newborn duckling, becomes enriched and sublime at these moments.

(*They laugh.*)

FIRST SPRITE: The audience is impatient.

SECOND SPRITE: And with reason. Shall we go?

FIRST SPRITE: Let's go. I feel a fresh breeze on my back already.

SECOND SPRITE: Five cool camellias of the dawn have opened in the walls of the bedroom.

FIRST SPRITE: Five balconies upon the city.

(They rise and throw on some great blue hoods.)

SECOND SPRITE: Don Perlimplín, do we help or hinder you?

FIRST SPRITE: Help: because it is not fair to place before the eyes of the audience the misfortune of a good man.

SECOND SPRITE: That's true, little friend, for it's not the same to say: "I have seen," as "It is said."

FIRST SPRITE: Tomorrow the whole world will know about it.

SECOND SPRITE: And that's what we wish.

FIRST SPRITE: One word of gossip and the whole world knows.

SECOND SPRITE: Sh . . .

(Flutes begin to sound.)

FIRST SPRITE: Shall we go through this tiny darkness?

SECOND SPRITE: Let us go now, little friend.

FIRST SPRITE: Now?

SECOND SPRITE: Now.

(They open the curtain. DON PERLIMPLÍN appears on the bed, with two enormous gilded horns. BELISA is at his side. The five balconies at the back of the stage are wide open, and through them the white light of dawn enters.)

PERLIMPLÍN *(awakening)*: Belisa! Belisa! Answer me!

BELISA *(pretending to awaken)*: Perlimplinpinito . . . what do you want?

PERLIMPLÍN: Tell me quickly.

BELISA: What do you want me to tell you? I fell asleep long before you did.

PERLIMPLÍN *(leaps from the bed. He has on his cassock)*: Why are the balconies open?

BELISA: Because this night the wind has blown as never before.

PERLIMPLÍN: Why do the balconies have five ladders that reach to the ground?

BELISA: Because that is the custom in my mother's country.

PERLIMPLÍN: And whose are those five hats which I see under the balconies?

BELISA: *(leaping from the bed)*: The little drunkards who come and go. Perlimplinillo! Love!

(PERLIMPLÍN *looks at her, staring stupefied.*)

PERLIMPLÍN: Belisa! Belisa! And why not? You explain everything so well. I am satisfied. Why couldn't it have been like that?

BELISA *(coyly)*: I'm not a little fibber.

PERLIMPLÍN: And I love you more every minute!

BELISA: That's the way I like it.

PERLIMPLÍN: For the first time in my life I am happy! *(He approaches and embraces her, but, in that instant, turns brusquely from her.)* Belisa, who has kissed you? Don't lie, for I know!

BELISA *(gathering her hair and throwing it over her shoulder)*: Of course you know! What a playful little husband I have! *(In a low voice.)* You! You have kissed me!

PERLIMPLÍN: Yes, I have kissed you . . . but . . . if someone else had kissed you . . . if someone else had kissed you . . . do you love me?

BELISA *(lifting a naked arm)*: Yes, little Perlimplín.

PERLIMPLÍN: Then, what do I care! *(He turns and embraces her.)* Are you Belisa?

BELISA *(coyly, and in a low voice)*: Yes! Yes! Yes!

PERLIMPLÍN: It almost seems like a dream!

BELISA *(recovering)*: Look, Perlimplín, close the balconies because before long people will be getting up.

PERLIMPLÍN: What for? Since we have both slept enough, we shall see the dawn. Don't you like that?

BELISA: Yes, but . . .

(She sits on the bed.)

PERLIMPLÍN: I have never seen the sunrise. (BELISA, *exhausted, falls on the pillows of the bed.)* It is a spectacle which . . . this may seem an untruth . . . thrills me! Don't you like it? *(Goes toward the bed.)* Belisa, are you asleep?

BELISA *(in her dreams)*: Yes.

(PERLIMPLÍN *tiptoes over and covers her with the red cape. An intense golden light enters through the balconies. Bands of paper birds cross them amidst the ringing of the morning bells.* PERLIMPLÍN *has seated himself on the edge of the bed.)*

PERLIMPLÍN:

> Love, love
> that here lies wounded.
> So wounded by love's going;
> so wounded,
> dying of love.
> Tell every one that it was just
> the nightingale.
> A surgeon's knife with four sharp edges;
> the bleeding throat—forgetfulness.
> Take me by the hands, my love,
> for I come quite badly wounded,
> so wounded by love's going.
> So wounded!
> Dying of love!

CURTAIN

SCENE
TWO

> PERLIMPLÍN's *dining room. The perspectives are deliciously wrong. All the objects on the table are painted as in a primitive Last Supper.*

PERLIMPLÍN: Then you will do as I say?

MARCOLFA *(crying)*: Don't worry, master.

PERLIMPLÍN: Marcolfa, why do you keep on crying?

MARCOLFA: Your Grace knows. On your wedding night five men entered your bedroom through the balconies. Five! Representatives of the five races of the earth. The European, with his beard—the Indian—the Negro—the Yellow Man—and the American. And you unaware of it all.

PERLIMPLÍN: That is of no importance.

MARCOLFA: Just imagine: yesterday I saw her with another one.

PERLIMPLÍN *(intrigued)*: Really?

MARCOLFA: And she didn't even hide from me.

PERLIMPLÍN: But I am happy, Marcolfa.

MARCOLFA: The master astonishes me.

PERLIMPLÍN: You have no idea how happy I am. I have learned many things and above all I can imagine many others.

MARCOLFA: My master loves her too much.

PERLIMPLÍN: Not as much as she deserves.

MARCOLFA: Here she comes.

PERLIMPLÍN: Please leave.

> *(MARCOLFA leaves and PERLIMPLÍN hides in a corner. Enter BELISA dressed in a red dress of eighteenth-century style. The skirt, at the back, is slit, allowing*

silk stockings to be seen. She wears huge earrings and a red hat trimmed with big ostrich plumes.)

BELISA: Again I have failed to see him. In my walk through the park they were all behind me except him. His skin must be dark, and his kisses must perfume and burn at the same time—like saffron and cloves. Sometimes he passes underneath my balconies and moves his hand slowly in a greeting that makes my breasts tremble.

PERLIMPLÍN: Ahem!

BELISA *(turning)*: Oh! What a fright you gave me.

PERLIMPLÍN *(approaching her affectionately)*: I observe you were speaking to yourself.

BELISA *(distastefully)*: Go away!

PERLIMPLÍN: Shall we take a walk?

BELISA: No.

PERLIMPLÍN: Shall we go to the confectioner's?

BELISA: I said No!

PERLIMPLÍN: Pardon.

(A letter rolled about a stone falls through the balcony. PERLIMPLÍN picks it up.)

BELISA: Give that to me.

PERLIMPLÍN: Why?

BELISA: Because it's for me.

PERLIMPLÍN *(jokingly)*: And who told you that?

BELISA: Perlimplín! Don't read it!

PERLIMPLÍN *(jokingly severe)*: What are you trying to say?

BELISA *(weeping)*: Give me that letter!

PERLIMPLÍN *(approaching her)*: Poor Belisa! Because I understand your feelings I give you this paper which means so much to you. *(BELISA takes the note and hides it in her bosom.)* I can see things. And even though it wounds me deeply, I understand you live in a drama.

BELISA *(tenderly)*: Perlimplín!

PERLIMPLÍN: I know that you are faithful to me, and that you will continue to be so.

BELISA *(fondly)*: I've never known any man other than my Perlimplinillo.

PERLIMPLÍN: That's why I want to help you as any good husband should when his wife is a model of virtue. . . . Look. *(He closes the door and adopts a mysterious air.)* I know everything! I realized immediately. You are young and I am old . . . What can we do about it! But I understand perfectly. *(Pause. In a low voice.)* Has he come by here today?

BELISA: Twice.

PERLIMPLÍN: And has he signaled to you?

BELISA: Yes . . . but in a manner that's a little disdainful . . . and that hurts me!

PERLIMPLÍN: Don't be afraid. Two weeks ago I saw that young man for the first time. I can tell you with all sincerity that his beauty dazzled me. I have never seen another man in whom manliness and delicacy meet in a more harmonious fashion. Without knowing why, I thought of you.

BELISA: I haven't seen his face . . . but . . .

PERLIMPLÍN: Don't be afraid to speak to me. I know you love him . . . and I love you now as if I were your father. I am far from that foolishness: therefore . . .

BELISA: He writes me letters.

PERLIMPLÍN: I know that.

BELISA: But he doesn't let me see him.

PERLIMPLÍN: That's strange.

BELISA: And it even seems . . . as though he scorns me.

PERLIMPLÍN: How innocent you are!

BELISA: But there's no doubt he loves me as I wish. . . .

PERLIMPLÍN *(intrigued)*: How is that?

BELISA: The letters I have received from other men . . . and which I didn't answer because I had my little husband, spoke to me of ideal lands—of dreams and wounded hearts. But these letters from him . . . they . . .

PERLIMPLÍN: Speak without fear.

BELISA: They speak about me . . . about my body . . .

PERLIMPLÍN *(stroking her hair)*: About your body!

BELISA: "What do I want your soul for?" he tells me. "The soul is the patrimony of the weak, of crippled heroes and sickly people. Beautiful souls are at death's door, leaning upon whitest hairs and lean hands. Belisa, it is not your soul that I desire, but your white and soft trembling body."

PERLIMPLÍN: Who could that beautiful youth be?

BELISA: No one knows.

PERLIMPLÍN *(inquisitive)*: No one?

BELISA: I have asked all my friends.

PERLIMPLÍN (*inscrutably and decisively*): And if I should tell you I know him?

BELISA: Is that possible?

PERLIMPLÍN: Wait. (*Goes to the balcony.*) Here he is.

BELISA (*running*): Yes?

PERLIMPLÍN: He has just turned the corner.

BELISA (*choked*): Oh!

PERLIMPLÍN: Since I am an old man, I want to sacrifice myself for you. This that I do no one ever did before. But I am already beyond the world and the ridiculous morals of its people. Good-by.

BELISA: Where are you going?

PERLIMPLÍN (*at the door, grandiosely*): Later you will know everything. Later.

CURTAIN

SCENE
THREE

A grove of cypresses and orange trees.
When the curtain rises, MARCOLFA *and*
PERLIMPLÍN *appear in the garden.*

MARCOLFA: Is it time yet?

PERLIMPLÍN: No, it isn't time yet.

MARCOLFA: But what has my master thought?

PERLIMPLÍN: Everything he hadn't thought before.

MARCOLFA *(weeping)*: It's my fault!

PERLIMPLÍN: Oh, if you only knew what gratitude there is in my heart for you!

MARCOLFA: Before this, everything went smoothly. In the morning, I would take my master his coffee and milk and grapes. . . .

PERLIMPLÍN: Yes . . . the grapes! The grapes! But . . . I? It seems to me that a hundred years have passed. Before, I could not think of the extraordinary things the world holds. I was merely on the threshold. On the other hand . . . today! Belisa's love has given me a precious wealth that I ignored before . . . don't you see? Now I can close my eyes and . . . I can see what I want. For example, my mother, when she was visited by the elves. Oh, you know how elves are . . . tiny. It's marvelous! They can dance upon my little finger.

MARCOLFA: Yes, yes, the elves, the elves, but . . . how about this other?

PERLIMPLÍN: The other? Ah! *(With satisfaction.)* What did you tell my wife?

MARCOLFA: Even though I'm not very good at these things, I told her what the master had instructed me to say . . . that that young man . . . would come tonight at ten o'clock sharp to the garden, wrapped, as usual, in his red cape.

337

PERLIMPLÍN: And she?

MARCOLFA: She became as red as a geranium, put her hands to her heart, and kissed her lovely braids passionately.

PERLIMPLÍN *(enthusiastic)*: So she got red as a geranium, eh? And, what did she say?

MARCOLFA: She just sighed; that's all. But, oh! such a sigh!

PERLIMPLÍN: Oh, yes! As no woman ever sighed before! Isn't that so?

MARCOLFA: Her love must border on madness.

PERLIMPLÍN *(vibrantly)*: That's it! What I need is for her to love that youth more than her own body. And there is no doubt that she loves him.

MARCOLFA *(weeping)*: It frightens me to hear you . . . but how is it possible? Don Perlimplín, how is it possible that you yourself should encourage your wife in the worst of sins?

PERLIMPLÍN: Because Perlimplín has no honor and wants to amuse himself! Now do you see? Tonight the new and unknown lover of my lady Belisa will come. What should I do but sing? *(Singing.)* Don Perlimplín has no honor! Has no honor!

MARCOLFA: Let my master know that from this moment on I consider myself dismissed from his service. We servants also have a sense of shame.

PERLIMPLÍN: Oh, innocent Marcolfa! Tomorrow you will be as free as a bird. Wait until tomorrow. Now go and perform your duty. You will do what I have told you?

MARCOLFA *(leaving, drying her tears)*: What else is there for me to do? What else?

PERLIMPLÍN: Good, that's how I like it.

(*A sweet serenade begins to sound.* DON PERLIMPLÍN *hides behind some rosebushes.*)

VOICES:

Upon the banks of the river
the passing night has paused to bathe.
The passing night has paused to bathe.
And on the breasts of Belisa
the flowers languish of their love.
The flowers languish of their love.

PERLIMPLÍN:

The flowers languish of their love.

VOICES:

> The naked night stands there singing,
> singing on the bridge of March.
> Singing on the bridge of March.
> Belisa, too, bathes her body
> with briny water and spikenard.
> With briny water and spikenard.

PERLIMPLÍN:

> The flowers languish of their love!

VOICES:

> The night of anise and silver
> on all the roofs glows and shines.
> On all the roofs glows and shines.
> The silver of streams and of mirrors
> and anise white of your thighs.
> And anise white of your thighs.

PERLIMPLÍN: The flowers languish of their love!

(BELISA *appears in the garden splendidly dressed. The moon lights the stage.*)

BELISA: What voices fill with sweet harmony the air of this fragment of the night? I have felt your warmth and your weight, delicious youth of my soul. Oh! The branches are moving . . .

(*A man dressed in a red cape appears and crosses the garden cautiously.*)

BELISA: Sh! Here! Here! (*The man signals with his hand that he will return immediately.*) Oh! Yes . . . come back my love! Like a jasmine floating and without roots, the sky will fall over my moistening shoulders. Night! My night of mint and lapis lazuli . . .

(PERLIMPLÍN *appears.*)

PERLIMPLÍN (*surprised*): What are you doing here?
BELISA: I was walking.
PERLIMPLÍN: Only that?
BELISA: In the clear night.
PERLIMPLÍN (*severely*): What were you doing here?
BELISA (*surprised*): Don't you know?
PERLIMPLÍN: I don't know anything.
BELISA: You sent me the message.

PERLIMPLÍN *(with ardent desire)*: Belisa . . . are you still waiting for him?

BELISA: With more ardor than ever.

PERLIMPLÍN *(severely)*: Why?

BELISA: Because I love him.

PERLIMPLÍN: Well, he will come.

BELISA: The perfume of his flesh passes beyond his clothes. I love him! Perlimplín, I love him! It seems to me that I am another woman!

PERLIMPLÍN: That is my triumph.

BELISA: What triumph?

PERLIMPLÍN: The triumph of my imagination.

BELISA: It's true that you helped me love him.

PERLIMPLÍN: As now I will help you mourn him.

BELISA *(puzzled)*: Perlimplín! What are you saying?

(The clock sounds ten. A nightingale sings.)

PERLIMPLÍN: It is the hour.

BELISA: He should be here this instant.

PERLIMPLÍN: He's leaping the walls of my garden.

BELISA: Wrapped in his red cape.

PERLIMPLÍN *(drawing a dagger)*: Red as his blood.

BELISA *(holding him)*: What are you going to do?

PERLIMPLÍN *(embracing her)*: Belisa, do you love him?

BELISA *(forcefully)*: Yes!

PERLIMPLÍN: Well, since you love him so much, I don't want him ever to leave you. And in order that he should be completely yours, it has come to me that the best thing would be to stick this dagger in his gallant heart. Would you like that?

BELISA: For God's sake, Perlimplín!

PERLIMPLÍN: Then, dead, you will be able to caress him in your bed—so handsome and well groomed—without the fear that he should cease to love you. He will love you with the infinite love of the dead, and I will be free of this dark little nightmare of your magnificent body. *(Embracing her.)* Your body . . . that I will never decipher! *(Looking into the garden.)* Look where he comes. Let go, Belisa. Let go! *(He exits running.)*

BELISA *(desperately)*: Marcolfa! Bring me the sword from the dining room; I am going to run my husband's throat through. *(Calling.)*

Don Perlimplín
Evil husband!
If you kill him,
I'll kill you!

(*A man wrapped in a large red cape appears among the branches. He is wounded and stumbling.*)

BELISA: My love! . . . Who has wounded you in the breast? (*The man hides his face in his cape. The cape must be enormous and cover him to the feet. She embraces him.*) Who opened your veins so that you fill my garden with blood? Love, let me look at your face for an instant. Oh! Who has killed you . . . Who?

PERLIMPLÍN (*uncovering himself*): Your husband has just killed me with this emerald dagger. (*He shows the dagger stuck in his chest.*)

BELISA (*frightened*): Perlimplín!

PERLIMPLÍN: He ran away through the fields and you will never see him again. He killed me because he knew I loved you as no one else. . . . While he wounded me he shouted: "Belisa has a soul now!" Come near. (*He has stretched out on the bench.*)

BELISA: Why is this? And you are truly wounded.

PERLIMPLÍN: Perlimplín killed me. . . . Ah, Don Perlimplín! Youngish old man, manikin without strength, you couldn't enjoy the body of Belisa . . . the body of Belisa was for younger muscles and warm lips. . . . I, on the other hand, loved your body only . . . your body! But he has killed me . . . with this glowing branch of precious stones.

BELISA: What have you done?

PERLIMPLÍN (*near death*): Don't you understand? I am my soul and you are your body. Allow me this last moment, since you have loved me so much, to die embracing it.

(BELISA, *half naked, draws near and embraces him.*)

BELISA: Yes . . . but the young man? Why have you deceived me?

PERLIMPLÍN: The young man?

(*Closes his eyes. The stage is left in magical light.* MARCOLFA *enters.*)

MARCOLFA: Madam . . .

BELISA *(weeping)*: Don Perlimplín is dead!

MARCOLFA: I knew it! Now his shroud will be the youthful red suit in which he used to walk under his own balconies.

BELISA *(weeping)*: I never thought he was so devious.

MARCOLFA: You have found out too late. I shall make him a crown of flowers like the noonday sun.

BELISA *(confused, as if in another world)*: Perlimplín, what have you done, Perlimplín?

MARCOLFA: Belisa, now you are another woman. You are dressed in the most glorious blood of my master.

BELISA: But who was this man? Who was he?

MARCOLFA: The beautiful adolescent whose face you never will see.

BELISA: Yes, yes, Marcolfa—I love him—I love him with all the strength of my flesh and my soul—but where is the young man in the red cape? Dear God, where is he?

MARCOLFA: Don Perlimplín, sleep peacefully. . . . Do you hear? Don Perlimplín. . . . Do you hear her?

(The bells sound.)

CURTAIN

The Man with the Heart in the Highlands

A One-Act Play

by WILLIAM SAROYAN

William Saroyan (1908–   )

William Saroyan, like Thornton Wilder, has pursued a dual career as an American author; he has been a prolific writer of prose fiction of a semiautobiographical nature and has enjoyed intermittent success as a playwright. He first won fame with his short stories *The Daring Young Man on the Flying Trapeze* (1934) and *My Name is Aram* (1940). His success in prose fiction was enhanced by the publication of his charming novel of boyhood, *The Human Comedy* (1942). His career as a dramatist began with two Broadway successes in 1939: *My Heart's in the Highlands* and *The Time of Your Life*.

Saroyan was born in 1908 in Fresno, California, of Armenian parentage. His father, a Presbyterian minister and a grape-grower, died when Saroyan was two years old. For five years the children in the family lived in an orphanage. When his mother obtained work in a cannery, the family was reunited. While young Saroyan attended grammar and junior high school, he worked at odd jobs: he did neighborhood chores; he worked as a newsboy, as a telegraph messenger boy, and in his uncle's vineyard. Although he was an erratic student, he read omnivorously books from the public library. At the age of thirteen, determined to become an author, he began to write short sketches. Next to reading and writing, his great passion was attending all kinds of theatrical entertainments: vaudeville shows, circuses, fairs, and summer stock performances. When he was seventeen, he left Fresno and wandered restlessly from one job to another, from farm labor to reporting. For a time he was the local manager of the Postal Telegraph office in San Francisco. Confident of his self-proclaimed "genius," he wrote many short stories.

In 1934 he won literary recognition by the publication of

The Daring Young Man on the Flying Trapeze in *Story* magazine. With this encouragement he proceeded to write at great speed many stories full of the zest for life, and he also wrote about the exotic characters he had encountered in his wanderings. He served in the U.S. Army in World War II and drew on his own military experiences to write his satiric novel *The Adventures of Wesley Jackson*.

The crisp, realistic dialogue, the appeal to simple emotions, and the improvisatory construction of Saroyan's prose fiction were carried over into his plays. His two surprising Broadway hits in 1939 dealt with the goodness of the common people, who, defeated in the battle for material gains, are by their courage and endurance spiritually triumphant. *My Heart's in the Highlands*, under the poetic direction of Robert Lewis, was given a superb production by the Group Theatre, and *The Time of Your Life*, written in six days and produced by the Theatre Guild, won both the Drama Critics Circle Award and the Pulitzer Prize. Some hard-boiled critics denounced the plays as sentimental, but Broadway theatergoers were delighted with Saroyan's depiction of the kindliness of the gentle, "beautiful" people in Fresno or in Nick's Bar in San Francisco. Brooks Atkinson characterized Saroyan as "the ebullient Armenian" and as "the imp of modern drama." Emotional rather than intellectual in their appeal, these two unconventional plays exemplified the truth of Pascal's saying, "The heart has its reasons, which reason knows nothing of."

Although Saroyan continued to be a prolific dramatist, turning out plays with seeming effortlessness, his later works did not achieve the theatrical success of his earlier ones, despite his Norman Mailer-like self-advertisements. Spicing his impressionistic and optimistic realism with fantasy, mysticism, and surrealism, he wrote *The Beautiful People, Jim Dandy,* and *Sweeney in the Trees.* The temporary triumph of Nazi totalitarianism, the outbreak of World War II, and its attendant pessimistic devaluation of human beings militated against Saroyan's cheerful bonhomie of average humanity. An additional factor was the careless, slapdash construction of these dramatic experiments. Saroyan's answer to his hostile critics that he had neglected the evil lurking in human beings and in social institutions was his depiction of a frame-up and lynching in *Hello, Out There* and his depressing *Don't Go Away Mad*. The old Saroyan made a Broadway comeback with his amusing and poignant *The Cave Dwellers* and enhanced his reputation in Europe in 1960 with his own production of *Sam the Highest Jumper of Them All* at the Theatre Royal in Stratford, England, and with *Lily Dafon, or a Paris Comedy* produced in Vienna.

Written in a series of short scenes in a unified tone of compassion and understanding, *The Man with the Heart in the Highlands* (a shortened version of the Group Theatre production *My Heart's in the Highlands*), is a paean to the faith and loyalty of a six-year-old-boy to his father, the impecunious poet. With sensitiveness and unashamed innocence, Saroyan celebrates the innate love for beauty in the heart of the simple folk of Fresno, who weeping and singing present their food offerings to old MacGregor as a tribute to the music that issues from his "golden-throated bugle." Despite the burdens of poverty, rejection, old age, and homelessness, the "gentle people," bound together by the sacramental ties of life and fortitude, joyfully accept the gift of life.

CHARACTERS

JOHNNY

JOHNNY'S FATHER

MACGREGOR

MR. KOSAK

JOHNNY'S GRANDMOTHER

RUFE APLEY

A YOUNG MAN

SCENE
ONE

An old white broken-down frame house with a front porch on San Benito Avenue in Fresno, California. There are no other houses nearby, only a desolation of bleak land and red sky. It is late afternoon of a day in August 1914. The evening sun is going down.

JOHNNY, aged six, but essentially ageless, is sitting, dynamic and acrobatic, on the steps of the porch, dead to the world and deep in thought of a high and holy order. Far away a train whistle cries mournfully. He listens eagerly, cocking his head on one side like a chicken, trying to understand the meaning of the cry and at the same time to figure out everything. He doesn't quite make it and when the cry ends he stops being eager. A fourteen-year-old boy on a bicycle, eating an ice-cream cone and carrying newspaper bags, goes by on the sidewalk in silence, oblivious of the weight on his shoulders and of the contraption on which he is seated because of the delight and glory of ice cream in the world. JOHNNY leaps to his feet and waves to the boy, smiling in a big humanitarian way, but is ignored. He sits down again and listens to a small overjoyed but angry bird. The bird flies away, after making a brief, forceful speech of no meaning.

349

> *From inside the house is heard the som-*
> *ber voice of* JOHNNY'S FATHER *reciting*
> *poetry of his own composition.*

JOHNNY'S FATHER: The long silent day journeys through the sore solemn heart, and—— (*Bitter pause.*) And—— (*Quickly.*) The long silent day journeys through the sore silent heart, and—— (*Pause.*) No. (*He roars and begins again.*) Crippled and weeping, time stumbles through the lone lorn heart.

> (*A table or chair is pushed over in anger. A groan. Si-*
> *lence. The boy listens. He gets up and tries to stand on*
> *his head, fails, tries again, fails, tries again, and suc-*
> *ceeds. While he is standing on his head he hears the*
> *loveliest and most amazing music in the world: a solo*
> *on a bugle. The music is so magnificent he doesn't*
> *dare get to his feet or move a muscle. The song is*
> *"My Heart's in the Highlands."*
> *The bugler, a very old man, finishes the solo in front*
> *of the house. The boy leaps to his feet and runs up to*
> *the old man, amazed, delighted, and bewildered.*)

JOHNNY: I sure would like to hear you play another song.

MACGREGOR: Young man, could you get a glass of water for an old man whose heart is not here, but in the highlands?

JOHNNY: What highlands?

MACGREGOR: The Scotch Highlands. Could you?

JOHNNY: What's your heart doing in the Scotch Highlands?

MACGREGOR: My heart's grieving there. Could you get me a glass of cool water?

JOHNNY: Where's your mother?

MACGREGOR: My mother's in Tulsa, Oklahoma, but her heart isn't.

JOHNNY: Where *is* her heart?

MACGREGOR: In the Scotch Highlands. I'm very thirsty, young man.

JOHNNY: How come the members of your family are always leaving their hearts in the highlands?

MACGREGOR: That's the way we are. Here today and gone tomorrow.

JOHNNY (*aside*): Here today and gone tomorrow? (*To* MACGREGOR.) How do you figure?

MacGregor: Alive one minute and dead the next.

Johnny: Where's your mother's mother?

MacGregor: She's up in Vermont, in a little town called White River, but her heart isn't.

Johnny: Is her poor old withered heart in the highlands, too?

MacGregor: Right smack in the highlands. Son, I'm dying of thirst.

(Johnny's Father *comes out of the house in a fury, as if he has just broken out of a cage, and roars at the boy like a tiger that has just awakened from evil dreams.*)

Johnny's Father: Johnny, get the hell away from that poor old man. Get him a pitcher of water before he falls down and dies. Where in hell are your manners?

Johnny: Can't a fellow try to find out something from a traveler once in a while?

Johnny's Father: Get the old man some water, damn it! Don't stand there like a dummy. Get him a drink before he falls down and dies.

Johnny: *You* get him a drink. You ain't doing nothing.

Johnny's Father: Ain't doing nothing? Why, Johnny, you know I'm getting a new poem arranged in my mind.

Johnny: How do you figure I know?

Johnny's Father (*unable to find an answer*): Well, you ought to know. You're my son. If you shouldn't know, who should?

MacGregor: Good afternoon. Your son has been telling me how clear and cool the climate is in these parts.

Johnny (*aside*): Jesus Christ, I didn't say anything about the climate. Where's he getting that stuff from?

Johnny's Father: How do you do? Won't you come in for a little rest? We should be honored to have you at our table for a bite of supper.

MacGregor: Sir, I am starving. I shall come right in.

(*He moves to enter the house.* Johnny *gets in his way, looking up at him.*)

Johnny: Can you play "Drink to Me Only with Thine Eyes"? I sure would like to hear you play that song on the bugle. That song is my favorite. I guess I like that song better than any song in the world.

MacGregor: Son, when you get to be my age you'll know songs aren't important, bread's the thing.

Johnny: Anyway, I sure would like to hear you play that song.

(MacGregor *goes up on the porch and shakes hands with* Johnny's Father.)

MacGregor: My name is Jasper MacGregor. I am an actor.

Johnny's Father: I'm mighty glad to make your acquaintance. Johnny, get Mr. MacGregor a pitcher of water.

(Johnny *runs around the house.*)

MacGregor: Charming boy.

Johnny's Father: Like myself, he's a genius.

MacGregor: I suppose you're very fond of him?

Johnny's Father: We are the same person—he is the heart of my youth. Have you noticed his eagerness?

MacGregor: I should say I have.

Johnny's Father: I am the same way myself, though older and less brilliant.

(Johnny, *running, returns with a pitcher of water, which he hands to the old man. The old man throws back his shoulders, lifts his head, his nostrils expand, he snorts, his eyes widen, he lifts the pitcher of water to his lips and drinks all the water in one long swig, while* Johnny *and his* Father *watch with amazement and admiration. The old man breathes deeply, looks around at the landscape and up at the sky and to the end of San Benito Avenue, where the evening sun is going down.*)

MacGregor: I reckon I'm five thousand miles from home. Do you think we could eat a little bread and cheese to keep my body and spirit together?

Johnny's Father: Johnny, run down to the grocer's and get a loaf of French bread and a pound of cheese.

Johnny: Give me the money.

Johnny's Father: You know I ain't got a penny, Johnny. Tell Mr. Kosak to give us credit.

Johnny: He won't do it. He's tired of giving us credit. He says we don't work and never pay our bills. We owe him forty cents.

JOHNNY'S FATHER: Go on down there and argue it out with him. You know that's your job.

JOHNNY: He says he doesn't know anything about anything, all he wants is the forty cents.

JOHNNY'S FATHER: Go on down there and make him give you a loaf of bread and a pound of cheese. You can do it, Johnny.

MACGREGOR: Go on down there and tell Mr. Kosak to give you a loaf of bread and a pound of cheese, son.

JOHNNY'S FATHER: Go ahead, Johnny. You haven't yet failed to leave that store with provender. You'll be back here in ten minutes with food fit for a king.

JOHNNY: I don't know. Mr. Kosak says we are trying to give him the merry run-around. He wants to know what kind of work you do.

JOHNNY'S FATHER (*furiously*): Well, go ahead and tell him. I have nothing to conceal. I write poetry, night and day.

JOHNNY: Well, all right, but I don't think he'll be impressed. He says you never go out and look for work. He says you're lazy and no good.

JOHNNY'S FATHER (*roaring*): You go on down there and tell him he's crazy, Johnny. You go on down there and tell that fellow your father is one of the greatest unknown poets living.

JOHNNY: He won't care, but I'll go. I'll do my best. Ain't we got nothing in the house?

JOHNNY'S FATHER: Only popcorn. We've been eating popcorn four days in a row now, Johnny. You got to get bread and cheese if you expect me to finish that long poem.

JOHNNY: I'll do my best.

MACGREGOR: Don't take too long, Johnny. I'm *five* thousand miles from home.

JOHNNY: I'll run all the way.

JOHNNY'S FATHER: If you find any money on the way, remember we go fifty-fifty.

JOHNNY: All right.

(JOHNNY *runs down the street.*)

SCENE
TWO

The inside of MR. KOSAK'S *grocery store.* MR. KOSAK *is sleeping on his folded arms when* JOHNNY *runs into the store.* MR. KOSAK *lifts his head. He is a fine, gentle, serious man with a big blond old-fashioned mustache. He shakes his head, trying to waken.*

JOHNNY: Mr. Kosak, if you were in China and didn't have a friend in the world and no money, you'd expect some Christian over there to give you a pound of rice, wouldn't you?

MR. KOSAK: What do you want?

JOHNNY: I just want to talk a little. You'd expect someone to help you out a little, wouldn't you, Mr. Kosak?

MR. KOSAK: How much money you got?

JOHNNY: It ain't a question of money, Mr. Kosak. I'm talking about being in China.

MR. KOSAK: I don't know nothing about nothing.

JOHNNY: How would you feel in China that way?

MR. KOSAK: I don't know. What would I be doing in China?

JOHNNY: Well, you'd be visiting there, and you'd be hungry and five thousand miles from home and not a friend in the world. You wouldn't expect a good Christian to turn you away without even a pound of rice, would you, Mr. Kosak?

MR. KOSAK: I guess not, but you ain't in China, Johnny, and neither is your Pa. You or your Pa's got to go out and work sometime in your lives, so you might as well start now. I ain't going to give you no more groceries on credit because I know you won't pay me.

JOHNNY: Mr. Kosak, you misunderstand me. I'm not talking

354

about a few groceries. I'm talking about all them heathen people around you in China, and you hungry and dying.

MR. KOSAK: This ain't China. You got to go out and make your living in this country. Everybody's got to work in America.

JOHNNY: Mr. Kosak, suppose it was a loaf of bread and a pound of cheese you needed to keep you alive in the world, would you hesitate to ask a Christian missionary for those things?

MR. KOSAK: Yes, I would. I would be ashamed to ask.

JOHNNY: Even if you knew you would give him back *two* loaves of bread and *two* pounds of cheese instead of one loaf and one pound? Even then, Mr. Kosak?

MR. KOSAK: Even then.

JOHNNY: Don't be that way, Mr. Kosak. That's defeatist talk, and you know it. Why, the only thing that would happen to you would be death. You would die out there in China, Mr. Kosak.

MR. KOSAK: I wouldn't care if I would. You and your Pa have got to pay for bread and cheese. Why don't your Pa go out and get a job?

JOHNNY: Mr. Kosak, how are you anyway?

MR. KOSAK: I'm fine, Johnny. How are you?

JOHNNY: Couldn't be better, Mr. Kosak. How are the children?

MR. KOSAK: They're all fine, Johnny. Stepan is beginning to walk now.

JOHNNY: That's great. How's Angela?

MR. KOSAK: Angela's beginning to sing. How's your grandmother?

JOHNNY: She's fine. She's beginning to sing too. She says she'd rather be an opera singer than Queen of England. How's your wife, Martha, Mr. Kosak?

MR. KOSAK: Oh, swell.

JOHNNY: I can't tell you how glad I am to hear that everything is well at your house. I know Stepan is going to be a great man someday.

MR. KOSAK: I hope so. I'm going to send him to high school and see that he gets every chance I didn't get. I don't want him to open a grocery store.

JOHNNY: I have great faith in Stepan, Mr. Kosak.

MR. KOSAK: What do you want, Johnny, and how much money you got?

JOHNNY: Mr. Kosak, you know I didn't come here to buy anything. You know I enjoy a quiet philosophical chat with you every now and then. (*Quickly.*) Let me have a loaf of French bread and a pound of cheese.

MR. KOSAK: You got to pay cash, Johnny.

JOHNNY: And Esther? How is your beautiful daughter Esther?

MR. KOSAK: She's all right, Johnny, but you got to pay cash. You and your Pa are the worst citizens in this county.

JOHNNY: I'm glad Esther's all right, Mr. Kosak. Jasper MacGregor is visiting our house. He's a great actor.

MR. KOSAK: Never heard of him.

JOHNNY: And a bottle of beer for Mr. MacGregor.

MR. KOSAK: I can't give you a bottle of beer.

JOHNNY: Sure, you can.

MR. KOSAK: I can't. I'll let you have one loaf of French bread and a pound of cheese, but that's all. What kind of work does your Pa do when he works, Johnny?

JOHNNY: My father writes poetry, Mr. Kosak. That's the only work my father does. He's one of the greatest writers of poetry in the world.

MR. KOSAK: When does he get any money?

JOHNNY: He never gets any money. You can't have your cake and eat it too.

MR. KOSAK: I don't like that kind of work. Why doesn't your Pa work like everybody else, Johnny?

JOHNNY: He works harder than everybody else. My father works twice as hard as the average man.

(MR. KOSAK *hands* JOHNNY *a loaf of French bread and a pound of cheese.*)

MR. KOSAK: Well, that's fifty-five cents you owe me, Johnny. I'll let you have some stuff this time, but never again.

JOHNNY (*at the door*): Tell Esther I love her.

MR. KOSAK: All right.

JOHNNY: Good-by, Mr. Kosak.

MR. KOSAK: Good-by, Johnny.

(JOHNNY *runs out of the store.* MR. KOSAK *swings at a fly, misses, swings again, misses, and, objecting to the world in this manner, he chases the fly all around the store, swinging with all his might.*)

SCENE
THREE

> *The same as Scene One.* JOHNNY'S FA-
> THER *and the old man are looking down
> the street to see if* JOHNNY *is coming
> back with food. His* GRANDMOTHER *is
> standing on the porch, also eager to
> know if there is to be food.*

MACGREGOR: I think he's got some food with him.
JOHNNY'S FATHER *(with pride)*: Of course he has.

> *(He waves at the old lady on the porch, who runs into
> the house to set the table.* JOHNNY *runs to his* FATHER
> *and* MACGREGOR.*)*

JOHNNY'S FATHER: I knew you'd do it.
MACGREGOR: So did I.
JOHNNY: He says we got to pay him fifty-five cents. He says
he ain't going to give us no more stuff on credit.
JOHNNY'S FATHER: That's his opinion. What did you talk
about?
JOHNNY: First I talked about being hungry and at death's door
in China. Then I inquired about the family.
JOHNNY'S FATHER: How is everyone?
JOHNNY: Fine. I didn't find any money, though, not even a
penny.
JOHNNY'S FATHER: That's all right.

> *(They go into the house.)*

SCENE
FOUR

*The living room. They are all at the
table after supper.* MACGREGOR *finds
crumbs here and there, which he places
delicately in his mouth. He looks around
the room to see if there isn't something
more to eat.*

MACGREGOR: That green can up there, Johnny. What's in
there?

JOHNNY: Marbles.

MACGREGOR: That cupboard. Anything edible in there, Johnny?

JOHNNY: Crickets.

MACGREGOR: That big jar in the corner there, Johnny. What's
good in there?

JOHNNY: I got a gopher snake in that jar.

MACGREGOR: Well, I could go for a bit of boiled gopher
snake in a big way, Johnny.

JOHNNY: You can't have that snake.

MACGREGOR: Why not, Johnny? Why the hell not, son? I hear
of fine Borneo natives eating snakes and grasshoppers. You
ain't got a half dozen fat grasshoppers around, too, have
you, Johnny?

JOHNNY: Only four.

MACGREGOR: Well, trot them out, son, and after we've had
our fill, I'll play "Drink to Me Only with Thine Eyes" for
you. I'm mighty hungry, Johnny.

JOHNNY: So am I, but I don't want anybody killing them poor
things.

JOHNNY'S FATHER (*to* MACGREGOR): How about a little music?
I think the boy would be delighted.

JOHNNY: I sure would, Mr. MacGregor.

MacGregor: All right, Johnny.

(MacGregor *gets up and begins to blow into the bugle. He blows louder and more beautifully and mournfully than anybody ever blew into a bugle. Eighteen neighbors gather in front of the house and cheer when he finishes the solo.*)

Johnny's Father: I want you to meet your public.

(*They go out on the porch.*)

SCENE
FIVE

The same as Scene One. The crowd is looking up at JOHNNY'S FATHER, MAC-GREGOR, *and* JOHNNY.

JOHNNY'S FATHER: Good neighbors and friends, I want you to meet Jasper MacGregor, the greatest Shakespearean actor of our day.

MACGREGOR: I remember my first appearance in London in 1867 as if it was yesterday. I was a boy of fourteen from the slums of Glasgow. My first part was a courier in a play, the title of which I have unfortunately forgotten. I had no lines to speak but moved about a good deal, running from officer to officer, and from lover to his beloved, and back again, over and over again.

RUFE APLEY (*a carpenter*): How about another song, Mr. MacGregor?

MACGREGOR: Have you got an egg at your house?

RUFE APLEY: I sure have. I got a dozen eggs at my house.

MACGREGOR: Would it be convenient for you to go and get one of them dozen eggs? When you return I'll play a song that will make your heart leap with joy and grief.

RUFE APLEY: I'm on my way already.

(*He goes.*)

MACGREGOR (*to the crowd*): My friends, I should be delighted to play another song for you on this golden-throated bugle, but time and distance from home find me weary. If you will be so good as to go, each of you to his home, and return in a moment with some morsel of food, I shall be delighted to gather my spirit together and play a song I know will change the course of each of your lives, and change it, mind you, for the better.

360

(The people go. MACGREGOR, JOHNNY'S FATHER, *and* JOHNNY *sit on the steps and remain in silence, and one by one the people return, bringing food to* MAC-GREGOR: *an egg, a sausage, a dozen green onions, two kinds of cheese, butter, two kinds of bread, boiled potatoes, fresh tomatoes, a melon, tea, and many other good things to eat.)*

MACGREGOR: Thank you, my friends, thank you.

(He stands solemnly, waiting for absolute silence, straightens himself, looks about him furiously, lifts the bugle to his lips, and plays "My Heart's in the Highlands, My Heart Is Not Here." The people weep and go away. MACGREGOR *turns to the father and son.)*

MACGREGOR: Sir, if it is all the same to you I should like to dwell in your house for some time to come.
JOHNNY'S FATHER: Sir, my house is your house.

(They go into the house.)

SCENE SIX

> The same as Scene Four. Eighteen days later. MACGREGOR is lying on the floor, face up, asleep. JOHNNY is walking about quietly in the room, looking at everybody. His FATHER is at the table, writing poetry. His GRANDMOTHER is sitting in the rocking chair, rocking. There is a knock on the door. Everybody but MACGREGOR jumps up and runs to it.

JOHNNY'S FATHER *(at the door)*: Yes?

A YOUNG MAN: I am looking for Jasper MacGregor, the actor.

JOHNNY'S FATHER: What do you want?

JOHNNY: Well, ask him in anyway, Pa.

JOHNNY'S FATHER: Yes, of course. Excuse me. Won't you please come in?

(The YOUNG MAN *enters.)*

YOUNG MAN: My name is Philip Carmichael. I am from the Old People's Home. I have been sent to bring Mr. Mac-Gregor home.

MACGREGOR *(wakening and sitting up)*: Home? Did someone mention home? I'm five thousand miles from home, always have been, and always will be. Who is this young man?

YOUNG MAN: Mr. MacGregor, I'm Philip Carmichael, from the Old People's Home. They've sent me to bring you back. We are putting on our annual show in two weeks and need you for the leading role.

MACGREGOR *(getting up with the help of* JOHNNY'S FATHER *and* JOHNNY*)*: What kind of a part is it? I can't be playing young adventurers any longer.

362

YOUNG MAN: The part is King Lear, Mr. MacGregor. It is perfect for you.

MACGREGOR (*to* JOHNNY'S FATHER, JOHNNY *and the* GRANDMOTHER): Good-by, my beloved friends. Good-by. In all the hours of my life, in all the places I have visited, never and nowhere have I had the honor and pleasure to commune with souls loftier, purer, or more delightful than yours. Good-by.

> (*They say good-by, and the old man and the young man leave the house.*
> *There is a long silence, full of melancholy and loneliness.*)

JOHNNY'S FATHER: Johnny, go on down to Mr. Kosak's store and get a little something to eat. I know you can do it, Johnny. Get *anything*.

JOHNNY: Mr. Kosak wants eighty-five cents. He won't give us anything more without money.

JOHNNY'S FATHER: Go on down there, Johnny. You know you can get that fine Slovak gentleman to give you a bit of something to eat.

JOHNNY (*with despair*): Aw, Pa.

JOHNNY'S FATHER (*amused*): What? You, my son, in a mood like that? Come on. I've fought the world this way before you were born, and after you were born we've fought it together, and we're going to keep on fighting it. The people love poetry but don't know it. Nothing is going to stop us, Johnny. Go on down there now and get something to eat. You didn't do so well last time. Remember? I can't write great poetry on the bird seed and maple syrup you brought back. Go on now.

JOHNNY: All right, Pa. I'll do my best. (*He runs to the door.*)

JOHNNY'S FATHER: Remember, if you find any money on the way, we go fifty-fifty.

CURTAIN

Sunday Costs
Five Pesos

A Comedy of Mexican Village Life

by JOSEPHINA NIGGLI

Josephina Niggli (1911–   )

The creator of Mexican folk drama, Josephina Niggli, was born in Monterrey, in northern Mexico, of well-to-do parents. Her mother, a former concert violinist, taught her daughter (with the exception of four months spent in the American school in Mexico City) until she entered a high school in San Antonio, Texas. After graduation Miss Niggli went to the Incarnate Word College, where she was encouraged in her writing by the head of the English department.

In the summer of 1935 she came to the University of North Carolina to study playwriting. In her first year she wrote *Sunday Costs Five Pesos* and four other one-act plays, which were successfully performed by the Carolina Playmakers. During the next two years, she wrote two full-length plays, *Singing Valley*, depicting the conflict between the old and new order in Mexico, and *The Fair-God*, dealing with the ill-fated attempt of Maximilian and Carlotta to establish a Mexican empire.

In addition to studying at the University of North Carolina, Josephina Niggli attended Stanford University. In 1938 she received a playwriting fellowship from the New York Theatre Guild.

Although known primarily as a skillful writer of Mexican folk comedies such as *Tooth or Shave*, *The Red Velvet Goat*, and *The Bull Ate Nutmeg*, she has also written some historical plays: *Azteca*, a tragedy of Pre-Conquest Mexico, and *This Is Villa* and *Soldier-Woman*, both dealing with the Mexican Revolution of 1914. In addition to her dramatic work, she has written poetry, short stories, and a novel, *West from Saddle Mountain*.

Sunday Costs Five Pesos is a charming folk comedy in its realistic and poetic rendition of the customs, beliefs, and feelings of the common people in the village of Four Cornstalks in northern Mexico. The plot revolves around an old Mexican law stating, "A woman who starts a fight on Sunday must pay a fine of five pesos." The reluctance of the antagonists to precipitate a quarrel on the Lord's day is understandable when we realize that this amount of money would support a village family for a month.

The importance of religion in the life of the simple village folk is stressed not only in the prohibition of Sunday fighting but in many other details. Don Nimfo gives the church a large contribution when his rooster wins the cockfight, a gift which gives Fidel the opportunity to carve the wooden doors of the church in Topo Grande. Fidel goes to light a candle to Our Blessed Lady and ask for forgiveness. When rejected by the tempestuous Berta, he threatens to enter a monastery. Berta is fearful of telling a lie, for which she may get ten days' penance from the priest.

The Mexicans' love of bright colors is evident in the houses of the villagers and by their dress. Tonia's house is pink, Salomé's is blue, and Berta's is a "disappointed" yellow. Fidel's bandanna is purple with orange spots, and Berta wears blue tennis shoes.

The five characters are shrewdly differentiated, and the action, centering around the village well in the housed-in square, is lively and amusing, culminating in the physical battle between Salomé and Celestina and the threat of the latter against Berta. The dialogue, with its homely similes and poetic invectives, accurately reflects the temperaments of the villagers. The reunion of the lovers, manipulated with gentle irony by the clever Berta, brings the comedy to a happy ending. Unlike some writers of folk plays, Josephina Niggli does not take a patronizing attitude toward the villagers. As a Mexican critic, Rodolfe Usigli, has commented, "There is a tender touch of smiling maternity in her treatment which gives a peculiar grace to her characters."

CHARACTERS

FIDEL,
  who is in love with BERTA

BERTA

SALOMÉ }
TONIA   } friends of BERTA

CELESTINA

THE SCENE: *A housed-in square in the town of the Four Cornstalks* (Las Cuatro Milpas) *in Northern Mexico.*

THE TIME: *The present. Early one Sunday afternoon.*

A housed-in square in the town called the Four Cornstalks in the northern part of Mexico. On the left of the square is the house of TONIA *with a door and a stoop. At the back is a wall cut neatly in half. The left side is the house of* BERTA, *and boasts not only a door but a barred window. On the right is a square arch from which dangles an iron lantern. This is the only exit to the rest of the town, for on the right side proper is the house of* SALOMÉ. TONIA'S *house is pink, and* SALOMÉ'S *is blue, while* BERTA'S *is content with being a sort of disappointed yellow. All three houses get their water from the well that is down center left.*

It is early afternoon on Sunday, and all sensible people are sleeping, but through the arch comes FIDEL DURÁN, *His straw hat in his hand, his hair plastered to his head with water, he thinks he is a very handsome sight indeed as he pauses, takes a small mirror from his pocket, fixes his neck bandanna . . . a beautiful purple one · with orange spots, and shyly knocks, then turns around with a broad grin on his face.*

BERTA *opens the door.* BERTA *is very pretty, but unfortunately she has a very high temper, possibly the result of her*

> *red hair. She wears a neat cotton dress
> and tennis shoes, blue ones. Her hands
> fastened on her hips, she stands and
> glares at* FIDEL.

BERTA: Oh, so it is you!

FIDEL (*beaming on her*): A good afternoon to you, Berta.

BERTA (*sniffing*): A good afternoon indeed, and I bothered by
fools at this hour of the day.

FIDEL (*in amazement*): Why, Berta, are you angry with me?

BERTA (*questioning Heaven*): He asks me if I am angry with
him. Saints in Heaven has he no memory?

FIDEL (*puzzled*): What have I done, Berta?

BERTA (*sarcastically*): Nothing, Fidel, nothing. That is the
trouble. But if you come to this house again I will show
you the palm of my hand, as I'm showing it to you now.
(*She slaps him, steps inside the door, and slams it shut.*)

FIDEL (*pounding on the door*): Open the door, Berta. Open the
door! I must speak to you!

> (*The door of* SALOMÉ's *house opens, and* SALOMÉ, *her-
> self, comes out with a small pitcher and begins drawing
> water from the well. She is twenty-eight, and so many
> years of hunting a husband have left her with an acid
> tongue.*)

SALOMÉ: And this is supposed to be a quiet street.

FIDEL (*who dislikes her*): You tend to your affairs, Salomé,
and I will tend to mine. (*He starts pounding again. He bleats
like a young goat hunting for its mother.*) Berta, Berta.

BERTA (*opens the door again*): I will not have such noises.
Do you not realize that this is Sunday afternoon? Have
you no thoughts for decent people who are trying to sleep?

FIDEL: Have you no thoughts for me?

BERTA: More than one. And none of them nice.

SALOMÉ: I would call this a lovers' quarrel.

BERTA: Would you indeed! (*Glares at* FIDEL) I would call it
the impertinence of a wicked man!

FIDEL (*helplessly*): But what have I done?

SALOMÉ: She loved him yesterday, and she will love him tomorrow.

BERTA (*runs down to* SALOMÉ): If I love him tomorrow, may I
lose the use of my tongue, yes, and my eyes and ears, too.

FIDEL (*swinging* BERTA *to one side*): Is it fair, I ask you, for a woman to smile at a man one day, and slap his face the next? Is this the manner in which a promised bride should treat her future husband?

SALOMÉ (*grins and winks at him*): You could find yourself another bride.

BERTA (*angrily*): We do not need your advice, Salomé Molina. You and your long nose . . . sticking it in everyone's business.

SALOMÉ (*her eyes flashing*): Is this an insult to me? To me?

BERTA: And who are you to be above insults?

SALOMÉ: I will not stay and listen to such words!

BERTA: Did I ask you to leave the safety of your home?

SALOMÉ (*to* FIDEL): She has not even common politeness. I am going!

BERTA: We shall adore your absence.

SALOMÉ: If this were not Sunday, I would slap your face for you.

BERTA (*taunting*): The great Salomé Molina, afraid of a Sunday fine.

FIDEL (*wanting to be helpful*): You can fight each other tomorrow. There is no fine for weekdays.

SALOMÉ: You stay out of this argument, Fidel Durán.

FIDEL: If you do not leave us I will never find out why Berta is angry with me. (*Jumps toward her*) Go away!

SALOMÉ (*jumps back, then tosses her head*): Very well. But the day will come when you will be glad of my company. (*She goes indignantly into her house.*)

FIDEL (*turns to* BERTA): Now, Berta.

BERTA (*interrupting*): As for you, my fine rooster, go and play the bear to Celestina García. She will appreciate you more than I.

FIDEL (*with a guilty hand to his mouth*): So that is what it is.

BERTA (*on the stoop of her own house*): That is all of it, and enough it is. Two times you walked around the plaza with the Celestina last night, and I sitting there on a bench having to watch you. (*Goes into the house*)

FIDEL (*speaking through the open door*): But it was a matter of business.

BERTA (*enters with a broom and begins to sweep off the stoop*): Hah! Give me no such phrases. And all of my friends thinking, "Poor Berta, with such a sweetheart." Do you think I have no pride?

FIDEL: But it is that you do not understand. . . .

BERTA: I understand enough to know that all is over between us.

FIDEL: Berta, do not say that. I love you.

BERTA: So you say. And yet you roll the eye at any passing chicken.

FIDEL: Celestina is the daughter of Don Nimfo García.

BERTA: She can be the daughter of the president for all of me. When you marry her she will bring you a fine dowry, and there will be no more need of Fidel Durán trying to carve wooden doors.

FIDEL (*his pride wounded*): Trying? But I have carved them. Did I not do a new pair for the saloon?

BERTA: Aye, little doors . . . doors that amount to no more than that. . . . (*She snaps her fingers.*) Not for you the great doors of a church.

FIDEL: Why else do you think I was speaking with the Celestina?

BERTA (*stops sweeping*): What new manner of excuse is this?

FIDEL: That is why I came to speak with you. Sit down here on the step with me for a moment.

BERTA (*scandalized*): And have Salomé and Tonia say that I am a wicked, improper girl?

FIDEL (*measuring a tiny space between his fingers*): Just for one little moment. They will see nothing.

BERTA (*sitting down*): Let the words tumble out of your mouth, one, two, three.

FIDEL: Perhaps you do not know that the town of Topo Grande, not thirty kilometers from here, is building a new church.

BERTA (*sniffs*): All the world knows that.

FIDEL: But did you know that Don Nimfo is secretly giving the money for the building of that church?

BERTA: Why?

FIDEL: He offered the money to the Blessed Virgin of Topo Grande if his rooster won in the cockfight. It did win, so now he is building the church.

BERTA (*not yet convinced*): How did you find out about this? Or has Don Nimfo suddenly looked upon you as a son, and revealed all his secrets to you?

FIDEL: Last night on the plaza the Celestina happened to mention it. With a bit of flattery I soon gained the whole story from her.

BERTA: So that is what you were talking about as you walked around the plaza? *(Stands)* It must have taken a great deal of flattery to gain so much knowledge from her.

FIDEL *(stands)*: Do you not realize what it means? They will need someone to carve the new doors.

(He strikes a pleased attitude, expecting her to say, "But how wonderful, Fidel.")

BERTA *(knowing very well what FIDEL expects, promptly turns away from him, her hand hiding a smile, as she says with innocent curiosity)*: I wonder whom Don Nimfo will get? *(With the delight of discovery)* Perhaps the Brothers Ochóa from Monterrey.

FIDEL *(crestfallen)*: He might choose me.

BERTA: You? Hah!

FIDEL: And why not? Am I not the best wood carver in the valley?

BERTA: So you say.

FIDEL: It would take three years to carve those doors, and he would pay me every week. There would be enough to buy you a trousseau and enough left over for a house.

BERTA: Did you tell all that to the Celestina?

FIDEL: Of course not! Does a girl help a man buy a trousseau for another girl? That was why it had to appear as though I were rolling the eye at her. *(He is very much pleased with his brilliance.)*

BERTA: Your success was more than perfect. Today all the world knows that the Celestina has won Berta's man.

FIDEL: But all the world does not know that Fidel Durán, who is I, myself, will carve those doors so as to buy a trousseau and house for Berta, my queen.

BERTA: Precisely. All the world does not know this great thing. . . . *(Flaring out at him)* And neither do I!

FIDEL: Do you doubt me, pearl of my life?

BERTA: Does the rabbit doubt the snake? Does the tree doubt the lightning? Do I doubt that you are a teller of tremendous lies? Speak not to me of cleverness. I know what my own eyes see, and I saw you flirting with the Celestina. Last night I saw you . . . and so did all the world!

FIDEL (*beginning to grow angry*): So that is how you trust me, your intended husband.

BERTA: I would rather trust a hungry fox.

FIDEL: Let me speak plainly my little dove. Because we are to be married is no reason for me to enter a monastery.

BERTA: And who says that we are to be married?

FIDEL (*taken aback*): Why . . . I said it.

BERTA: Am I a dog to your heel that I must obey your every wish?

FIDEL (*firmly*): You are my future wife.

BERTA (*laughs loudly*): Am I indeed?

FIDEL: Your mother has consented, and my father has spoken. The banns have been read in the church! (*Folds his arms with satisfaction*)

BERTA (*screaming*): Better to die without children than to be married to such as you.

FIDEL (*screaming above her*): We shall be married within the month.

BERTA: May this hand rot on my arm if I ever sign the marriage contract.

FIDEL: Are you saying that you will not marry me?

BERTA: With all my mouth I am saying it, and a good day to you. (*Steps inside the house and slams the door. Immediately opens it and sticks her head out*) Tell that good news to that four-nosed shrew of a Celestina. (*Slams the door again*)

(FIDEL *puts on his hat and starts toward the archway, then runs down and pounds on* TONIA's *door, then runs across and pounds on* SALOMÉ's. *In a moment both girls come out.* TONIA *is younger and smaller in size than either* SALOMÉ *or* BERTA *and has a distressing habit of whining.*)

SALOMÉ: What is the meaning of this noise?

TONIA: Is something wrong?

FIDEL: I call you both to witness what I say. May I drop dead if I am ever seen in this street again!

(*He settles his hat more firmly on his head, and with as much dignity as he can muster, he strides out through the arch. The girls stare after him, then at* BERTA's *door, then at each other. Both shrug, then with one accord they run up and begin knocking on the door.)*

SALOMÉ: Berta!

TONIA: Berta, come out!

(BERTA enters. She is obviously trying to keep from crying.)

SALOMÉ: Has that fool of a sweetheart of yours lost his mind?

TONIA: What happened?

BERTA *(crying in earnest)*: This day is blacker than a crow's wing. Oh, Salomé!

(She flings both arms about the girl's neck and begins to wail loudly. TONIA and SALOMÉ stare at each other, and then TONIA pats BERTA on the shoulder.)

TONIA: Did you quarrel with Fidel?

SALOMÉ: Of course she quarrelled with him. Any fool could see that.

BERTA: He will never come back to me. Never!

TONIA *(to SALOMÉ)*: Did she say anything about the Celestina him?

SALOMÉ *(to BERTA)*: You should have kept your mouth shut on the outside of your teeth.

BERTA: A girl has her pride, and no Celestina is going to take any man of mine.

TONIA: But did she take him?

BERTA *(angrily to TONIA)*: You take your face away from here!

SALOMÉ: The only thing you can do now is to ask him to come back to you.

TONIA *(starting toward the archway)*: I will go and get him.

BERTA *(clutches at her)*: I will wither on my legs before I ask him to come back. He would never let me forget that I had to beg him to marry me. *(Wails again)* And now he will marry the Celestina. *(TONIA begins to cry with her.)*

TONIA: There are other men.

BERTA: My heart is with Fidel. My life is ruined.

SALOMÉ *(thoughtfully)*: If we could bring him back without his knowing Berta had sent for him. . . . *(She sits on the edge of the well.)*

TONIA: Miracles only happen in the church.

SALOMÉ (*catches her knee and begins to rock back and forth*): What could we tell him? What could we tell him?

TONIA: You be careful, Salomé, or you will fall in the well. Then we will all have to go into mourning, and Berta can not get married at all if she is in mourning.

SALOMÉ (*snaps her fingers*): You could fall down the well, Berta! That would bring him back.

BERTA (*firmly*): I will not fall down the well and drown for any man, not even Fidel.

TONIA: What good would bringing him back do if Berta were dead?

SALOMÉ: Now that is a difficulty. (*Begins to pace up and down*) If you are dead, you cannot marry Fidel. If you are not dead, he will not come back. The only thing left for you is to die an old maid.

TONIA: That would be terrible.

BERTA (*wailing*): My life is ruined. Completely ruined.

SALOMÉ (*with sudden determination*): Why? Why should it be?

TONIA (*with awe*): Salomé has had a thought.

BERTA: You do not know what a terrible thing it is to lose the man you love.

SALOMÉ: I am fixing up your life, not mine. Suppose . . . suppose you did fall in the well.

BERTA: I tell you I will not do it.

SALOMÉ: Not really, but suppose he thought you did. What then?

BERTA: You mean . . . pretend? But that is a sin! The priest would give me ten days' penance at confessional.

SALOMÉ (*flinging out her hands*): Ten days' penance or a life without a husband. Which do you choose?

TONIA: I will tell you. She chooses the husband. What do we do, Salomé?

SALOMÉ: You run and find this carver of doors. Tell him that a great scandal has happened . . . that Berta has fallen in the well.

TONIA (*whose dramatic imagination has begun to work*): Because she could not live without him. . . .

BERTA: You tell him that and I will scratch out both your eyes!

TONIA: On Sunday?

BERTA (*sullenly*): On any day.

SALOMÉ: Tell him that Berta has fallen in the well, and that you think she is dying.

TONIA: Is that all?

BERTA: Is that not enough?

SALOMÉ *(entranced with the idea)*: Oh, it will be a great scene, with Berta so pale in her bed, and Fidel kneeling in tears beside it.

BERTA: I want you to know that I am a modest girl.

SALOMÉ *(irritated)*: You can lie down on the floor then. *(Glaring at TONIA)* What are you standing there for? Run!

TONIA *(starts toward the archway, then comes back)*: But . . . where will I go?

SALOMÉ: To the place where all men go with a broken heart . . . the saloon. Are you going to stand there all day?

(TONIA gives a little gasp and runs out through the arch.)

BERTA: I do not like this idea. If Fidel finds out it is a trick, he will be angrier than ever.

SALOMÉ: But if he does not find out the truth until after you are married . . . what difference will it make?

BERTA: He might beat me.

SALOMÉ: Leave that worry until after you are married. *(Inspecting BERTA)* Now how will we make you look pale? Have you any flour? Corn meal might do.

BERTA: No! No! I will not do it.

SALOMÉ: Now, Berta, be reasonable.

BERTA: If I had really fallen down the well, it would be different. But I did not fall down it.

SALOMÉ: Do you not want Fidel to come back to you? Are you in love with him?

BERTA: Yes, I do love him. And I will play no tricks on him. If he loves the Celestina better than he does me . . . *(with great generosity)* he can marry her.

SALOMÉ *(pleading with such idiocy)*: But Tonia has gone down to get him. If he comes back and finds you alive . . . he will be angrier than ever.

BERTA *(firmly)*: This is your idea. You can get out of it the best way you can. But Fidel will not see me lying down on a bed, nor on a floor, nor any place else.

SALOMÉ: Then there is only one thing to do.

BERTA: What is that?

SALOMÉ: You will go into the house, and I will tell him that you are too sick to see him.

BERTA: That will be just as bad as the other.

SALOMÉ: How can it be? Then if he finds out it is a trick, he will blame me, and you can pretend you knew nothing of it. I do not care how angry he is. I do not want to marry him.

BERTA (*with pleased excitement*): Then he could not be angry with me, could he? I mean if he thought I had nothing to do with it? And I would not have to do penance either, would I?

SALOMÉ: Not one day of penance. Tonia should have found him by now. (*Goes to the arch and peers through.*) Here they come . . . and Fidel is running half a block in front of her.

BERTA (*joyously*): Then he does love me!

SALOMÉ: Into the house with you. You can watch through the window.

BERTA (*on stoop*): Now, remember, if he get angry, this was your idea.

SALOMÉ (*claps her hands*): And what a beautiful idea it is!

> (BERTA *disappears into the house.* SALOMÉ *looks about her, then dashes over to her own stoop, sits down, flings her shawl over her face, and begins to moan loudly, rocking back and forth. In a moment* FIDEL *dashes through the arch, and stops, out of breath, at seeing* SALOMÉ.)

FIDEL (*gasping*): Berta!

SALOMÉ (*whose moaning grows louder*): Poor darling, poor darling. She was so young.

FIDEL (*desperately*): She is . . . she is dead?

SALOMÉ (*wailing*): She will make such a beautiful corpse. Poor darling. Poor darling.

> (TONIA, *exhausted and out of breath, has reached the arch.*)

TONIA (*looks about her in astonishment*): Why, where is Berta? Did she go into the house?

SALOMÉ (*in normal tones*): Of course she went into the house, you fool. Did she not jump down the well? (*Remembering* FIDEL) Poor darling.

TONIA *(blankly)*: Did she really jump down it? I thought she just fell in by accident.

SALOMÉ *(grimly)*: Are you telling this story . . . or am I? *(Wailing)* Now she can never go to the plaza again.

(FIDEL *looks helplessly from* TONIA, *who cannot quite get the details of the story straight, to* SALOMÉ *who is having a beautiful time mourning.*)

FIDEL: Where is she? I want to see her.

TONIA *(coming out of her trance)*: She is right in here. Did you say she was on the bed or on the floor, Salomé?

SALOMÉ *(getting between them and* BERTA'S *door)*: You don't want to see her, Fidel. You know how people look after they've been drowned.

TONIA: But he was supposed to see her. That was why you sen . . .

SALOMÉ *(glaring at her)*: Tonia, dear, suppose that you let me tell the story. After all, I was here and you were not.

FIDEL *(exploding)*: For the love of the saints, tell me! Is she dead?

SALOMÉ *(thinking this over)*: Well . . . not exactly.

FIDEL: You mean . . . you mean there is hope?

SALOMÉ: I would say there was great hope.

FIDEL *(takes off his hat and mops his face)*: What can I do? Oh, if I could only see her. . . .

SALOMÉ: If you would go to the church and light a candle to Our Blessed Lady and ask her to forgive you for getting angry with Berta . . . perhaps things will arrange themselves.

FIDEL: Do you think she will get well soon?

SALOMÉ: With a speed that will amaze you.

FIDEL: I will go down and light the candle right now.

(*As he turns to leave, who should come through the archway but* CELESTINA GARCÍA. *She can match temper for temper with* BERTA *any day, and right now she is on the warpath. Brushing past these three as though they did not exist, she goes up to* BERTA'S *door and pounds on it.*)

CELESTINA: I dare you to come out and call this Celestina García a four-nosed shrew to her face.

SALOMÉ (*trying to push* FIDEL *through the arch*): You had best run to the church.

FIDEL (*pushing past her and going up to* CELESTINA): How dare you speak like that to a poor drowned soul?

SALOMÉ (*to* CELESTINA): Why do you not go away? We never needed you so little.

CELESTINA: So she is pretending to be drowned, eh? Is that her coward's excuse?

BERTA (*through window*): Who dares to call Berta Cantú a coward?

CELESTINA: You know well enough who calls you, and I the daughter of Don Nimfo García.

TONIA: Ai, Salomé! And now Fidel will know that Berta was not drowned at all.

FIDEL (*who has been listening to this conversation with growing surprise and suspicion, now turns furiously toward* BERta's *house*): Not drowned, eh? So this was a trick to bring me back, eh? I am through with your tricks, you hear me? Through with them!

BERTA (*through window*): You stay right there until I come out. (*She disappears from view.*)

FIDEL (*turning to* SALOMÉ): I see your hand in this.

SALOMÉ: The more fool you to be taken in by a woman's tricks.

CELESTINA: What care I for tricks? No woman is going to call me names!

BERTA (*coming through the door*): You keep silence, Celestina García. I will deal with you in a minute. And as for you, Fidel Durán. . . .

FIDEL (*stormily*): As for me, I am finished with all women. The world will see me no more. I will enter a monastery and carve as many doors as I like. Do you hear me, Berta Cantú?

BERTA (*putting both hands over her ears*): What do I care for your quack, quack, quack!

FIDEL: Now she calls me a duck! Good afternoon to you! (*He stalks out with wounded dignity.*)

CELESTINA (*catching* BERTA *by the shoulder and swinging her around*): I ask you again; did you call me a four-nosed shrew?

BERTA: I did, and I will repeat it with the greatest of pleasure. You are a four-nosed shrew and a three-eyed frog!

CELESTINA: I have always looked on you as my friend . . . you pink-toed cat!

BERTA: And I have always trusted you . . . you sly robber of bridegrooms!

(She raises her hand to slap CELESTINA. SALOMÉ *catches it.)*

SALOMÉ: This is Sunday, Berta! And Sunday costs five pesos.

TONIA: If you had to pay a fine for starting a fight on top of losing Fidel. . . . Ay, that would be terrible.

*(*BERTA *and* CELESTINA *glare at each other, and then slowly begin to circle each other, spitting out their insults as they do so.)*

CELESTINA: It is my honor that is making me fight, or I would wait until tomorrow.

BERTA: If I had five pesos to throw away, I would pull out your dangling tongue . . . leaving only the flapping roots.

CELESTINA: Ha! I make a nose at your words.

BERTA: As for you . . . you eater of ugly smelling cheese. . . .

(They jump at each other, but remember the penalty just in time and pull back. Again they begin to circle around, contenting themselves with making faces at each other. SALOMÉ *suddenly clasps her hands.)*

SALOMÉ: You are both certain that you want to fight today?

CELESTINA: Why else do you think I came here?

BERTA: These insults have gone too far to stop now.

SALOMÉ: The only thing that stands in the way is the five pesos for the Sunday fine.

TONIA: And five pesos is a lot of money.

SALOMÉ: Then the only thing to do is to play the fingers.

CELESTINA: What?

BERTA: Eh?

SALOMÉ: Precisely. Whoever loses strikes the first blow and pays the fine. Then you can fight as much as you like.

TONIA *(with awed admiration)*: Ay, Salomé, you have so many brains.

CELESTINA *(doubtfully)*: It is a big risk.

BERTA *(shrugging)*: Perhaps you are afraid of taking a risk.

CELESTINA: I am not afraid of anything. But Tonia will have to be the judge. Salomé is too clever.

BERTA: Very well. But Salomé has to stand behind you to see that you do not cheat. I would not trust you any more than I would a mouse near a piece of fresh bacon.

CELESTINA (*pulls back her clenched fist, then thinks better of it, and speaks with poor grace*): Very well.

(CELESTINA *and* BERTA *stand facing each other.* TONIA *stands between them up on the stoop.* SALOMÉ *stands behind* CELESTINA.)

TONIA (*feeling a little nervous over this great honor of judging*): Both arms behind your backs. (*The girls link their arms behind them.*) Now, when I drop my hand, Berta will guess first as Celestina brings her fingers forward. The first girl to guess correctly twice wins. Are you ready? (*All nod.*) I am going to drop my arm.

SALOMÉ: Celestina, put out your fingers before Berta guesses. We will have no cheating.

CELESTINA (*sullenly*): Very well. (*She puts out two fingers behind her, and* SALOMÉ, *seeing this, raises up her arm with two fingers extended, opening and closing them scissors fashion.* BERTA *frowns a little as she looks up at the signal and* CELESTINA, *seeing this, swings around and looks at* SALOMÉ, *who promptly grins warmly and pretends to be waving at* BERTA. CELESTINA *then looks at* TONIA.)

BERTA: Very well.

CELESTINA (*guessing as* BERTA *swings her arm forward*): Three.

(BERTA *triumphantly holds up one finger. Biting her lip,* CELESTINA *starts to swing forward her own arm.* SALOMÉ, *intent on signalling* BERTA, *holds up her own five fingers spread wide, and does not notice until too late that* CELESTINA *has swung around to watch her.*)

CELESTINA (*screaming*): So I cheat, eh? (*With that she gives* SALOMÉ *a resounding slap on the cheek. The next moment the two women are mixed up in a beautiful howling, grunting fight, while* TONIA *and* BERTA, *wide-eyed, cling together and give the two women as much space as possible. Let it be understood that this is only a fight of kicking, hair-pulling and scratching. There is no man involved, nor a point of honor. Rather a matter of angry pride. So the two are not attempting to mutilate each other. They are simply gain-*

ing satisfaction. The grand finale comes when CELESTINA *knocks* SALOMÉ *to the ground and sits on her.)*

CELESTINA *(breathing hard)*: There! That was worth five pesos.

TONIA: You have to pay it. And Don Nimfo will be angry with you.

CELESTINA *(pulling herself to her feet)*: I am too tired to fight any more now, but I will be back next Tuesday, Berta, and then I will beat you up.

BERTA *(sniffing)*: If you can.

CELESTINA *(warningly)*: And there is no fine on Tuesday.

BERTA: Come any day you like. I will be ready for you.

TONIA *(to* CELESTINA*)*: You should be ashamed to fight.

CELESTINA: Who are you to talk to me? *(Stamps her foot at* TONIA *who jumps behind* BERTA.*)* Good afternoon my brave little rabbits!

(She staggers out as straight as she can, but as she reaches the archway she feels a twinge of agony and is forced to limp. By this time SALOMÉ *has gathered together what strength she has left, and she slowly stands up. Once erect, she looks at* BERTA *and* TONIA *as though she were considering boiling in oil too good for them.)*

SALOMÉ *(with repressed fury)*: My friends. My very good friends.

TONIA *(frightened)*: Now, Salomé. . . .

SALOMÉ *(screaming)*: Do not speak to me! Either of you! *(She manages to get to the door of her house.)* When I need help, do you give me aid? No! But just you wait . . . both of you!

TONIA: What are you going to do?

SALOMÉ: I am going to wait for a weekday, and then I am going to beat up both of you at once. One *(she takes a deep breath)* with each hand! *(She nearly falls through the door of her house.)*

BERTA *(with false bravado)*: Who is afraid of her?

TONIA: I am. Salomé is very strong. It is all your fault. If you had not gotten mad at Fidel, this would not have happened.

BERTA *(snapping at her)*: You leave Fidel out of this.

TONIA *(beginning to cry)*: When Salomé beats me up, that will be your fault too.

BERTA: Stop crying!

TONIA: I am not a good fighter, but I can tell Fidel the truth about how you would not jump down the well to win him back.

BERTA: You open your mouth to Fidel and I will push you in the well.

TONIA: You will not have strength enough to push a baby in the well when they get through with you.

BERTA: Get out! Get out of here! (*She stamps her foot at* TONIA *and the girl, frightened, gives a squeak and runs into her own house.* BERTA *looks after her, then, beginning to sniffle, she goes over and sits on the well. She acts like a child who has been told that it is not proper for little girls to cry, and she is very much in need of a handkerchief. Just then* FIDEL *sticks his head around the arch.*)

FIDEL (*once more the plaintive goat*): Berta.

(BERTA *half jumps, then pretends not to hear him.*)

FIDEL (*enters cautiously, not taking his eyes off of* BERTA'S *stiff back. He moves around at the back, skirts* TONIA'S *house, then works his way round to her*): Berta.

BERTA (*sniffing*): What is it?

FIDEL (*circling the back of the well*): Are you crying, Berta?

BERTA (*stubbornly*): No!

FIDEL (*sitting beside her*): Yes, you are. I can see you crying.

BERTA: If you can see, why do you ask, then?

FIDEL: I am sorry we quarrelled, Berta.

BERTA: Are you?

FIDEL: Are you sorry?

BERTA: No!

FIDEL: I was hoping you were, because . . . do you know whom I saw on the plaza?

BERTA: Grandfather Devil.

FIDEL: Don Nimfo himself.

BERTA: Perhaps you saw the Celestina, too.

FIDEL (*placatingly*): Now, Berta, you know I do not care if I never see the Celestina again. (*Pulls out a handkerchief and extends it to her.*) Here, wipe your face with this.

BERTA: I have a handkerchief of my own. (*Nevertheless she takes it, and wipes her eyes and then blows her nose.*)

FIDEL: Don Nimfo said I could carve the church doors for

him. But he said I would have to move to Topo Grande to work on them. He said I had to leave right away.

BERTA *(perking up her interest)*: You mean . . . move away from here?

FIDEL: And I was wondering if we could get married tomorrow. I know this is very sudden, Berta, but after all, think how long I have waited to carve a church door.

BERTA: Tomorrow. *(She looks toward* SALOMÉ's *house.)* They would both be too sore to do anything by tomorrow.

FIDEL *(too concerned with his own plans to hear what she is saying)*: Of course I know that you may not be able to forgive me. . . .

BERTA: Fidel, I want you to understand that if I do marry you tomorrow . . . that means we will leave here tomorrow, eh?

FIDEL: Ay, yes. I have to be in Topo Grande on Tuesday.

BERTA: I hope you will always understand what a great thing I have done for you. It is not every girl who would forgive so easily as I.

FIDEL *(humbly)*: Indeed, I know that, Berta.

BERTA: Are you quite sure that we will leave here tomorrow?

FIDEL: Quite sure.

BERTA: Very well. I will marry you.

FIDEL *(joyfully)*: Berta! *(Bends forward to kiss her. She jumps up.)*

BERTA: Just a moment. We are not married yet. Do you think that I am just any girl that you can kiss me . . . like that! *(She snaps her fingers.)*

FIDEL *(humbly)*: I thought . . . just this once. . . .

BERTA *(gravely thoughtful)*: Well, perhaps . . . just this once . . . you may kiss my hand.

   As he kisses it

THE CURTAINS CLOSE